PENGUIN BOOKS

KANDA...

Patrick Hennessey was born in 1982 and educated at Berkhamsted School and Balliol College, Oxford, where he read English. He joined the Army and served from 2004 to 2009 as an officer in The Grenadier Guards. In between guarding towers, castles and palaces he worked in the Balkans, Africa, South East Asia, the Falkland Islands and deployed on operational tours of Iraq and Afghanistan. On leaving the Army he wrote his first book, *The Junior Officers' Reading Club*. He is now a barrister.

Kandak

Fighting with Afghans

PATRICK HENNESSEY

PENGUIN BOOKS

PENGUIN BOOKS

Published by the Penguin Group
Penguin Books Ltd, 80 Strand, London WC2R ORL, England
Penguin Group (USA) Inc., 375 Hudson Street, New York, New York 10014, USA
Penguin Group (Canada), 90 Eglinton Avenue East, Suite 700, Toronto, Ontario, Canada M4P 2Y3
(a division of Pearson Penguin Canada Inc.)
Penguin Ireland, 25 St Stephen's Green, Dublin 2, Ireland (a division of Penguin Books Ltd)
Penguin Group (Australia), 707 Collins Street, Melbourne, Victoria 3008, Australia
(a division of Pearson Australia Group Pty Ltd)
Penguin Books India Pvt Ltd, 11 Community Centre,
Panchsheel Park, New Delhi – 110 017, India
Penguin Group (NZ), 67 Apollo Drive, Rosedale, Auckland 0632, New Zealand
(a division of Pearson New Zealand Ltd)
Penguin Books (South Africa) (Pty) Ltd, Block D, Rosebank Office Park,
181 Jan Smuts Avenue, Parktown North, Gauteng 2193, South Africa

Penguin Books Ltd, Registered Offices: 80 Strand, London WC2R ORL, England

condition being imposed on the subsequent purchaser

ISBN: 978-0-241-95127-9

www.greenpenguin.co.uk

ALWAYS LEARNING   **PEARSON**

For Qiam, Syed and Mujib

And for all the *askar* for whom there is no distinction
between wars of choice and necessity, no drawdown
plan and exit strategy, who are simply fighting
for their homes and their lives

Contents

A Note on Names and Interpreters

I wanted in this book to give a voice to ordinary Afghan soldiers, and all of those quoted and the majority mentioned were keen to be heard. In some places I have been unable precisely to verify the name of an individual soldier and in others places names and small details have been changed in order to spare some people from undue embarrassment, or because of fear of reprisal.

I have done the same, to a much greater extent, when depicting the various interpreters I have worked with in the course of writing this book. Their names have been changed in order to protect their identities, as they find themselves increasingly targeted. This book could not have been written without their help, and whatever good is being done in Afghanistan by ISAF is made possible only by these brave and unsung men and women who risk their lives every day patrolling unarmed alongside better-paid and better-protected soldiers.

What else would you do, but take up the sword?
You who were born of an Afghan mother.

                                                   Tajik poem, *c.* 1600.

For he today that sheds his blood with me
Shall be my brother;

                                             Henry V (Act IV, Scene iii)

Prologue

In a way, everything can be encapsulated in the story of the *kaman-e-rostam*.

For three nights over Christmas the whole of Nad-e Ali had been quiet, unnervingly and unexpectedly quiet. The enemy did not tend to reciprocate our observance of his religious festivals. Weary ISAF soldiers might have breathed the odd secret sigh of relief at the reduction in the frequency of patrolling and intensity of operations that invariably accompanied Eid and Ramadan, but Taliban propaganda invariably promised a bumper Christmas stocking of suicide attacks and ambushes and had gleefully proclaimed 2009 would be no exception – so much for peace on earth and goodwill to all mankind. Yet since the punchy little ambush north of Check Point Blue 17 there had been barely a whisper across the battlegroup area of operations. The ops officer's situation whiteboard, more usually a busy blur of scribbled red shot-reps and incident grid-references, hung uncluttered except by the incongruous tinsel dangling from its corners – *stille Nacht* in Helmand.

Now, suddenly and almost a relief, something was up. The intelligence brief for the day had warned of trouble brewing, and not long after dinner an urgent whisper came from the entrance to the ops tent: quick, come outside, you've got to see this. Huddled outside there were more than just the usual assorted smokers crowded round the flagpoles; bloated, Michelin-Man silhouettes in various puffa jackets against the multi-coloured fairy lights of the token but somehow no less comforting Christmas tree that stood defiant in the desert outside Battlegroup

HQ. My first thought was trouble, a casualty perhaps, but there was no worried muttering or urgent coming and going. Instead, everyone was just stood, craning backwards, looking up at the night sky.

A perfect ring around the gigantic moon: vast, refracted, presumably, through thin cloud otherwise invisible and seeming to encircle the very ground we stood on; pushed much further out than the papier-mâché rings of primary-school-project Saturns; a bright, crisp, wondrous halo above our heads. They that dwell in the land of the shadow of death, upon them hath a light shined. It was the sergeant major, inevitably with an eye on the job in hand, who broke up the Patrick Moore party. Sentries were reminded to stay alert and focus on their arcs, duty bods were ushered back to their desks to brace themselves for the promised busy night. Someone was sent to wake the battalion photographer to try and capture the phenomenon, but, beautiful or not, there was a war on, there was work to be done.

I wandered over to the Afghan side of camp to see what they made of this phenomenon and, in contrast to the gazing huddle of Guardsmen snapping away outside their tents, found the camp almost abandoned. I poked my head into the *chai** room and was surprised to find everyone crammed inside, the back of the windowless hut barely visible from the front through the swirling cigarette smoke. I pointed outside and upwards as they beckoned me in, and they all nodded sagely. I looked around to see if Taj or one of the other 'terps† was there, but it was just the ANA.

'*Tajiman?*' I asked hopefully, Syed shook his head. There

---

* Tea.

† Short for interpreters: in the heat and confusion of an operation the four syllables were too much of a mouthful. *Tajiman* was the Dari for 'translator', but was lost as quickly when shouted. Most 'terps wisely picked an easy, monosyllabic nickname and stuck with that.

was a pause; usually this would have been the cue for one of the junior soldiers to be sent scurrying off to the 'terps compound, but no one was moving. I shrugged and climbed back out of the room to go and grab someone myself, nearly walking smack into the Hesco as I craned my head up at the curious rings, but still noticing somehow subliminally that it was all very quiet.

By the time I had walked across camp and back again with Taj in tow I still hadn't seen or heard a single Afghan warrior.

'Where is everyone?' I asked, of no one in particular. Syed muttered something in English about being asleep, but Qiam let out a chuckle and said something I couldn't catch.

'They're scared,' translated Taj.

'Scared?' I asked.

Taj paused, looking for the word: 'superstitious', he ventured. I was confused. Surely they weren't worried about tonight's attack warning – all the threats were directed against the isolated patrol bases to the north; Shawqat itself was as safe as you could hope to be in the middle of Helmand.

'Because of the Taliban warning?' I asked, and the atmosphere in the room instantly relaxed, sly glances exchanged and low chuckles.

Qiam shook his head with calm authority. He didn't think there would be any enemy activity at all. Not tonight.

Now I was really confused. Syed motioned up towards the low ceiling, and presumably through it to the strange night sky above.

'What is it?' I asked.

'*Kaman-e-rostam*,' he said, and the whole room burst out laughing.

Possibly the most comprehensive academic study of the Afghan National Army, always just the ANA, to date concludes that 'Evidence of operational proficiency is largely anecdotal, although there are some quantitative indicators. Numerous anecdotes attest to the operational capability of the ANA units. Quantitative ratings present a more restrained endorsement.'[1] There is nothing quantitative about this story, and this entire book is anecdotal, but sometimes stories can tell you more than statistics. I still don't know what the *kaman-e-rostam* is or how frequently it occurs. I got Taj to repeat it and even write the words down in my notebook; it means 'rainbow', which sort of makes sense, but that's only half the story, because it's where it came from that was interesting. Every culture has ancient tales of gender confusion: the Afghans had the *kaman-e-rostam*, whatever it was. The old wives' tale said that the rings in the sky marked an invisible line on earth and that if a man unwittingly crossed it he would immediately turn into a woman. Of course, none of the cosmopolitan, relatively secular men of the ANA would believe such stories, I was instantly assured, but the Taliban – backward, God-fearing, uneducated peasants – they wouldn't move at all that night for fear of crossing the invisible line and suddenly finding themselves to be a woman (and presumably, in keeping with their prevailing ideology, immediately and wholeheartedly subjugating themselves – you could see why they would be reluctant to risk it). I didn't point out that there were no ANA anywhere to be seen outside either. The normal chatter in the room resumed as if I wasn't there and I quietly slipped out.

On the British side, the ops room was still buzzing, patchy kill-TV playing out on banks of flat screens, Blue Force Tracker icons blinking on monitors, Sky News rolling in the corner. There was no further intelligence on the threatened attacks, but the phenomenon in the night sky was causing consternation, and no one was quite sure how to respond to it. In the end it was thought that the heightened ambient light of what some nerd suggested was a perigee moon could play into the hands of the enemy, who lacked our night-vision capabilities. It was probably best to increase security for now. But there were no incidents on the night of the *kaman-e-rostam*, whatever it was. Qiam was right. Enough of the ANA and enough of the Taliban sufficiently believed the fairy-tale that they stayed put till Boxing Day.

I put it to Qiam that if he hated Helmand so much – if he looked down on the local Pashtun 'peasants' and their 'boring, backwards' desert home and longed for his wife and family in cosmopolitan Kabul so much – why not give up? Why not stop fighting and leave the lawless south to its fate, squabbled over by the warlords and the bigots and the Pakistanis? Bolstered by US dollars, why not pull back to build a peaceful and progressive north? No more foreigners, no more ISAF, no more dead civilians, no more long years away in this shithole province losing comrades and friends to an invisible, indefatigable enemy.

Qiam looked at me with an intense, dangerous gleam in his never less than fiery eyes and spoke very slowly and very softly. Taj glanced up from his *chai*, not grinning as usual, but deadly serious as he helped himself to another cigarette and translated the reply: 'But this is my country.' Pause. Drag. Exhale. 'This is my homeland.'

There was no comeback to that. I was used to Qiam's joking, his bullshit, bravado and occasional bursts of temper, but the atmosphere in the room had completely changed. I felt like we had crossed a line without realizing it and wasn't sure how to row back. Taj's smoking filled the increasingly awkward silence. I glanced at my watch; it was nearly midnight. Afghanistan is three and a half hours ahead of London, which meant that at home people would be out for one last night of Christmas partying before heading back with fuzzy heads to their families, to their presents and comfy beds. Somewhere in the distance the damp fizz of a schmoolie★ being fired triggered a chorus of barking dogs.

Qiam leaned forward, his eyes still gleaming but with a slight change, a little twinkle. He said something, still quietly but with less intensity this time, and then roared with laughter and leaned back. Taj stubbed out the cigarette, smiling, what tension there had been completely, suddenly gone.

'He says: "Make sure you put that at the start of your book!" '

★ Hand-held rocket flares which provide about thirty seconds of illumination over the immediate area, in the hands of nervous sentries often as much good for scaring local dogs as spotting the enemy on the perimeter.

Introduction

A far better soldier and story-teller than I once wrote that 'war is not a matter of maps with red and blue arrows and oblongs, but of weary, thirsty men with sore feet and aching shoulders wondering where they are'.[2] Recalling fighting through Burma at the end of the Second World War, George MacDonald Fraser contrasts his own vivid and jumbled recollections of burning tanks and long, slow advances with the brief notes in appendices of official histories; the bald numbers of casualties and passing allusions to 'minor' diversions which were life and death for the men who fought in them. Perhaps it is the nature of official histories not to lose themselves in detail, to focus on the strategic and not the tactical. Perhaps the very scale of the Second World War precludes comprehending the personal aspect. It is harrowing enough when MacDonald Fraser describes stumbling on and shooting a single Japanese soldier – 'His body was settling, twitching a little, then he was still'[3] – that maybe we just don't want to know about the other 1,100 that died in the battle for Pyawbwe. 1,100 in one relatively small battle, on one front, in one theatre, in a war of many theatres, hundreds of fronts, thousands of battles and millions of dead.

Despite the now familiar invocations of 'the fiercest fighting the Army has seen since . . .' things are somewhat different these days. Around 400 British servicemen and women have been killed in the ten years we have been fighting in Afghanistan. 400 grim-faced officers have knocked on 400 unhappy doors to break the very worst news. In some respects, war does not change: the dead were 400 weary, thirsty men and women with sore feet and aching shoulders wondering where they were. However, unlike the nameless 1,100 of the Battle of Pyawbwe or the forgotten scores of 'minor diversions' neglected by history's footnotes, there is, today, a raised consciousness of the casualties of war. We know, or can know if we wish, all of their names, all about the families they have left behind and often exactly where, when and how they died, even if not, deep down, why. The Ministry of Defence's own website charts a macabre but poignant history of mini-eulogies, a catalogue of heartbreaking tributes from colleagues to those among many who were 'gifted, considerate and popular', 'completely reliable as a soldier and a mate', a 'proud, happy father', a 'devoted husband', 'intelligent, determined, brave' and even 'a very good footballer'. For most of us the current war in Afghanistan is not a matter of maps with red and blue arrows and oblongs but of casualties, of amputees and the slow procession of coffins through Wootton Bassett.*

War has become highly personalized. To a certain extent this is a question of scale: it is far easier to report and mourn single deaths than hundreds; easier to comprehend the loss of three young men in a vehicle than the decimation of whole battalions. But it is surely also a reflection of a changed society, a society of individuals and self-interest counter-intuitively hungrier and hungrier for minute and trivial detail about the lives of everyone else. Irascible, brilliant old George MacDonald Fraser hated this 'nauseating' development. He railed against a society which grieves so publicly and indiscriminately and worried that such a nation lacked the will to endure conflicts as costly and painful as the one in which he himself had fought. He might have been right, he might have been wrong; in a way it doesn't matter.

* Now Royal Wootton Bassett, although the funeral processions have gone now too, and the streets of Brize Norton have taken up the dubious honour.

Fraser wondered, 'if mankind is lucky', whether he might have fought in the 'the last great land battle of the last great war'.[4] I'm not sure what great means in that context; surely we all hope that he did.

Yet MacDonald Fraser's war, with all its horrors, was seemingly also the last 'good' war. The last war of unambiguous right versus wrong, the last war which it was the unquestioned civic and moral duty of every person to support. There were minutes in the Second World War when 385 men died, mere seconds it took for terrible bombs to explode and kill more civilian women and children than we have lost fighting men, professional volunteers all, in a decade in Afghanistan. A less stoical society and more cynical media are insufficient explanation as to why the deaths in their hundreds of thousands of Fraser's comrades were mourned but not questioned, while each separate individual casualty in Helmand provokes another round of forensic introspection and doubt.

There is, of course, a crucial difference between MacDonald Fraser's war and that currently being fought: it is the difference, in the sanitized, strategy-speak of politicians and chiefs of staff, between 'wars of necessity' and 'wars of choice'. The existential threat Nazism posed to the very notions of civilization meant that the Second World War was the definition of a war of necessity, a fight for survival. There are precious few people who are convinced that the IED* operators, suicide bombers and sharpshooters of Sangin pose an existential threat to London, let alone civilized humanity. The enemy in Afghanistan may be a manifestation of a complex entity other elements of which seek to pose such a threat; there may even be a nexus between their activities and the activities of those who have sought in the past,

---

* Improvised explosive device, a wonderfully neutral and somewhat sanitized way of talking about a great big bomb.

and will seek again in the future, to threaten our homes, but that is all. Put simply, following every death in Afghanistan, each deeply personalized, highly publicized loss and ritual of tribute and subsequent reservation and soul-searching is because most of us don't know what the hell 'our boys' are doing out there. This is not for want of information nor for lack of trying.

Over the last few years there has been a surge in interest in, and a torrent of writing and reporting on, Afghanistan, the ISAF mission in general and the British deployment in Helmand specifically. Politicians and pop stars vie for the reflected glory of a Bastion photo-op. Documentaries full of shaky headcam footage and seriously narrated special reports fill our TV screens; no six-month brigade deployment is complete without a raft of accompanying literature, and bookshop shelves groan under the weight of contemporary military history and TiC* Lit. There have been books by brigadiers and colonels, by sergeants and corporals, heroic and ordinary soldiers and even junior officers; there have been books by journalists who were there and books by journalists who weren't; books about whole brigades and books about single men; books about pilots and their helicopters; about JTACs and their bombs; about Paras and Marines; about actors and princes; books that tell the 'true' story, the 'real' story and even, dangerously, the 'explosive' story. But in all these many soldiers' stories, each one striving in its own way to make sense of its subject, a voice is conspicuously missing — the voice of those for whom this is not a war of choice, the troops for whom there are no homecoming parades or *X-Factor* tribute songs: the Afghan soldiers themselves.

The soldiers, the *askar* or 'warriors' of the Afghan National Army, are no different from the British soldiers they have fought

---

* Troops in contact, an equally anodyne way of referring to being shot at.

alongside for a decade. They are weary, thirsty men with sore feet and aching shoulders wondering where they are. What is more, as our involvement in Afghanistan enters a second decade and our leaders cast around for excuses to extricate us sooner rather than later, it is on the Afghan National Army and Police that the burden to hold the country together will fall; it is in the hands of the young Afghan soldiers that the future of their troubled nation rests. As each British unit completes another six-month tour, marks its safe return with homecoming parades and royal visits for tea and medals and waits to tell its stories in inevitable documentaries and paintings and books, the media portrayal of the ANA is limited to chaotic caricature. The stories of the Afghan soldiers who were there when we arrived and who remain there when we come home – all just as real, true and explosive – go largely untold.

For what seemed like a never-ending summer I lived, worked, ate, slept and laughed alongside some of those very soldiers: the men of the 1st Battalion, or Kandak, of the 3rd Brigade of the 205 'Atal' ('Hero') Corps of the Afghan National Army (1/3/205, for short). British and Afghan, Guardsman and *askar*, first in neighbouring camps and then in shared bases and ultimately side by side in ditches and compounds we fought together: ferocious Qiam Udin, the alternately terrifying and inspiring life-force of the *kandak*; measured Lieutenant Mujib Ullah, with his wicked sense of humour and wry courage; the moustachioed, Flashman-esque Sharaf Udin and his vintage sniper rifle; Major Hazrat, the scourge of Sangin; and the seemingly effortless, immaculately professional Sergeant Syed Meraj; soldiers and men who defied and confounded all expectations. When the ANA were at their anarchic, pot-smoking, car-swimming, suicidal worst, they were terrible, but we all had our moments. When they were good, under-trained, under-resourced and fighting for something real in a way that none of us ISAF tourists were, they were awesome.

By a neat accident of fate Qiam, Syed and the rest were among the very first Afghan soldiers into Helmand, back in 2006 when we were all going to leave without a shot being fired. In the five years and counting and God knows how many shots that have followed, the warriors of 1/3/205 have fought alongside eight different British brigades,* each one larger and more heavily equipped than the previous, each one fighting harder and taking more casualties than the last.† Individual units returning home every six months to Aldershot and Colchester and Sennelager‡ and Catterick talk knowingly of towns like Gereshk and Sangin and Garmsir and Musa Qala, of the 'Green Zone' and the 'Fishhook', of ANP and JTAC hills, of dams and sluice-gates and every other feature they fought by, on or through. They are proud veterans of ops like Augustus, Silicon, Snakebite, Panther's Claw and Moshtarak. Qiam, Syed and the rest had fought on them all, and when each one was done and the code words forgotten, the patrol bases were renamed and the brigade commander had his DSO and we'd all gone home, the exhausted *kandak* remained behind; fighting in the middle of nowhere.

There is an inherent danger in generalizing about anything: 'the Afghans' this; 'Helmand' that; 'all soldiers . . .' Bold, sweeping assertions are bound to be wrong somewhere and catch in their net that and those to which they don't apply. Perhaps the Afghans I fought with and got to know were not typical. Perhaps 1st Kandak, 3/205 was not typical of the Afghan

---

* 16 Air Assault, 3 Commando, 12 Mechanized, 52 Infantry, 16 Air Assault (again), 3 Commando (again), 19 Light, 11 Light, 4 Mechanized, 16 Air Assault (getting bored now), 3 Commando (as I write), 20 Armoured (all to look forward to).

† Fortunately as of the end of 2011 the fatality rate at least was starting to creep down from the peaks of 2009 and 2010.

‡ In Paderborn, Germany. Home, for at least a little while longer, to 20 Armoured Brigade.

National Army. Perhaps all the experiences we shared were freak occurrences and the stories they later told me were grossly exaggerated or misrepresented. But I doubt it. Telling other people's stories is more difficult than telling your own: there are more gaps in the narrative, certain things don't quite add up, and dangerous assumptions are made: there is an extra layer of uncertainty in the telling, extra filters of time and space between what is being recalled and the moment of recollection. More subtly, there is an imbalance in the relationship between teller and subject: the heroes and villains of any legend are uncomfortably subjugated to the narrator; is it their story, or his? None of this means that the original stories are not worth telling.

Moreover, the ANA weren't victims. Qiam didn't need his story in print to validate it and certainly didn't need me to tell it like some expensive, weepy charity commercial taking up the whole advert break: neither did anyone else in the *kandak*. Perhaps it was something I needed to do more than anything else, was a way of dealing with the guilt of the incredulous and accusatory looks the Afghans had all given my civilian attire. After a two-and-a-half-year break, the first thing Qiam wanted to know was: why the hell wasn't I still a soldier? I couldn't answer. I couldn't sit in the middle of the bare-arse FOB, in the middle of the most godforsaken province of a pretty god-forsaken country, and palm him off with some excuse about wanting a change of direction; couldn't reel off the usual excuses about having had my adventures and the Army being a young man's game to these men, twice my age and who lived it all day every day and for whom it wasn't a game, hadn't ever been a game in the first place.

Partly out of guilt and partly out of gratitude, for memories of times both good and bad, and, most importantly, because Qiam told me to, what follows is an attempt to describe how we tried, failed and succeeded to fight together; to explain why Afghanistan is passing inexorably into the collective memory of the British Army; the Just So Stories of a *kandak*: of how Qiam got his wounds and tattoos; of why Mujib was so quiet when we first met him; of Hazrat's heroics and how Sergeant Kamal ended up in prison; the story of living and fighting with Afghans.

PART I
Fighting with Afghans

First Impressions

I had been in Afghanistan for five full days before I even saw a real-life Afghan. It was March 2007 and damp and chaotic. We'd left the UK charged up on the promise of romantic heroism, appetites whetted by 3 Para's adventures of the previous summer, thirsting after the tense ambiguity of Iraq for a good, hard fight, but the initial reality of southern Afghanistan was disappointing and disorientating. The long slog out through petty delays and RAF tea-breaks broke the spirit, a sense of time and place was lost as you squirmed on the hard floor at Brize or Akrotiri or Muscat or wherever it was the plane had broken down this time, trying to snatch some sleep so that you weren't completely exhausted when you finally got to Kandahar, which, of course, you were anyway.

Then it wasn't the unfamiliarity but the sameness which was a let-down. The airfield at Kandahar was the same bewildering, beguiling sea of blue, pink and green glo-sticks that Basrah had been. Humping unwieldy bergans* bulging with six months' creature comforts, we lumbered half-awake from plane to bus to tent and back again, tiny, grumpy cogs in the vast machinery of expeditionary war whirring efficiently all around us. Passing out on a stale mattress in the semi-dark, you'd wake to find yourself sweltering in a vast, 200-man tent. Stumbling, bursting for the loo, down rows of triple-decker bunk-beds, you emerged blinking into a choking fug; day and night seemed to come and

---

* Big army back-packs which under no circumstances did soldiers ever refer to as back-packs.

go randomly, the only constant the background cicada whirr of the struggling generators.

There were uniforms everywhere, but no guns; soldiers everywhere, but no enemy and no Afghans. Kandahar seemed to be almost wilfully disorientating: a Canadian hockey pitch in the desert, coffee shops next to the runway. Another coach, another wait, another plane and then Helmand, but the famous Camp Bastion was more of the same: damp and underwhelming. The Hindu Kush lay somewhere to the north, a looming jagged reminder that you were in the graveyard of empires, but we couldn't see it through the dusty fog which hung over the camp for days spent enduring introductory briefings, orientation briefings, Camp Regulations briefings, legal briefings, even, brilliantly, health and safety briefings. Hours and days of half-hearted 'Welcome to Afghanistan' from tired Marines at the end of their tour who couldn't wait to get the fuck out of Afghanistan. It was difficult to shake the initial deployment come-down: the heavy, first-window-of-the-advent-calendar awareness that you're only at the very start of an elastic and difficult period of time. There's the tantalizingly fresh memory of difficult good-byes and probably the last dull, dehydrated aches of the hangovers which preceded them. There's the new, stifling heat, if that's what gets you, or the jet lag or the anti-malarials – take your pick: Weapons briefings; Dari briefings; ground briefings; Pashtun briefings; cultural awareness briefings; Pizza Hut and NAAFI breaks; and still no Afghans. As the Royal Marines trickled out, so we trickled in to the more permanent tents and huts they vacated, the slow, awkward procession of the handover/takeover, not enough time to ask all the questions you needed to, too long spent on top of each other, uncertain as to who was coming or going. After a few days which seemed an eternity, those of us who would be working with the ANA finally made the five-minute move across the desert to the neighbouring camp which would be our home base for the tour, the Afghan garrison in Helmand, Camp Shorabak.

Shorabak was the headquarters and rear base location of 3 Brigade and home base to its three *kandaks*. It had been plonked in the middle of the desert next to Camp Bastion when the site had been picked by the Engineers for the water supplies beneath the ground and the flat visibility for miles around. Easy to defend, easy to survive in and with enough space for a decent runway, it would serve well as the primary logistics base for an expeditionary force, and so it has for the thousands of ISAF troops who have called it home in the five years since. Camp Shorabak was not, however, such a great posting for an Afghan. Other than the one enterprising local selling fags, sweets and pay-as-you-go sim-cards out of the back of a disused shipping container, the nearest market was 20 kilometres away in Gereshk. In fact, the nearest anything was in Gereshk, and you couldn't get there without manoeuvring across the desert for a bone-shaking half hour before taking your chances to dash down Route 1 without getting ambushed by the Taliban or, which was more likely, shot up by the jumpy Afghan National Police. Shorabak was probably the worst posting in the whole ANA, the garrison as unwelcoming as it was uncomfortable, the FOBs as dangerous as they were desolate. To make matters worse, unlike the ANA units in Kabul, who actually lived somewhere civilized, or the ANA units in the north, who were partnered with Germans, who didn't go out at night, or in the east with Italians, who took things a bit more easily, 3/205 was partnered with a bunch of gung-ho British units with high expectations and short tours.

We moved in to a little camp in the corner, technically part of neither Bastion nor Shorabak itself, which had been christened FOB Tombstone by the Yanks who built it, and for once (other than the dodgy painting at the front gate which was more Kurt

Russell than Wyatt Earp) they'd got it right.★ You couldn't imagine a more isolated location. Bastion was even named after the Hesco Bastion blast walls which are the building blocks of all expeditionary warfare. I guess it was a bit odd, giving a main base such a mundane, corporate name, like if Main Building had been named Camp Concrete or *Ark Royal* HMS *Steel*, but the stuff had saved enough lives and enough sandbag-filling man hours that it deserved the recognition, and you felt like you needed it out in the middle of the nothingness. With earthy eloquence the outgoing booties[†] had nicknamed the surrounding desert 'the GAFA' – the Great Afghan Fuck All; although you could have seen an enemy coming from miles away, the very space made you feel small and vulnerable.

We were even divided from the Afghans, our snug, corner camp tucked safely in behind an internal, wire-topped blast wall, the gate between us and our partners and allies manned by a permanent sentry. We slept and ate about a ten-minute walk from the ANA lines,[‡] in theory far enough away that we had to carry our rifles and some ammunition to go round and see them. It was a sensible precaution, but it made the whole process more

---

★ We assumed they had learned from the embarrassing precedent that had been set in Iraq where the Americans ill-advisedly, prematurely and sometimes downright misleadingly gave their bases names like Prosperity, Victory and Justice.

† Army slang for Marines. From 'bootneck', various theories abound, the most likely of which is probably something to do with the white gaiters the Marines traditionally wore over the tops of their boots.

‡ 'Lines' is Army for where you happen to live at any given point. At Sandhurst we lived in and rigorously polished the platoon and company lines and woe betide the cadet found after hours in the female lines. I suppose it derived from front and rear lines and similar battlefield terminology, but I liked to think it was because military accommodation was always in identical architectural blocks in nice straight lines.

arduous and formal than it should have been and heightened the sense of isolation. On my first night in Shorabak itself the sky lit up with a spectacular storm: thunder clapped across the desert and strobe sheets and piercing forks of vivid lightning cracked through the still, dusty air. We clambered up to the top of the Hesco to get the best view of the towering clouds and could see the Afghan camp spread out below; in the gloom and flashes I finally saw the Afghan National Army, soldiers creeping from the accommodation blocks in baggy T-shirts to stare at the approaching storm.

The first meeting was excruciating, like a junior school disco with the boys and girls lined up on opposite sides of the assembly hall, token disco ball throwing lame twinkles across the ceiling, everyone shuffling their feet and trying hard not to make eye contact. We made the first of what would be many hot walks across the dry helipad over to the long, low concrete huts that were both the offices and dormitories of the ANA. One of the outgoing Marines was accompanying us to introduce us to the soldiers we'd be partnering, and I wondered at his easy familiarity with the random ANA bods we passed as we went, was jealous of the incomprehensible phrases he chucked out and the delighted laughter he got in reply, but we didn't have time to stop, so I didn't really notice how small all the Afghans seemed to be until we got to one of the offices and there waiting for us, hovering expectantly around the door, crammed into the room and even peering in at the windows at the back, were our new allies, the *askar* of 1/3/205: the *kandak*.

There's a famous photo at a football match about a hundred years ago – the game was between a Public School XI and an East London Orphans XI or something similar – it's of the two captains shaking hands in the centre circle. They're both school-boys and were apparently almost exactly the same age, but one towers above the other. A tall, well-fed, athletic man with impressive Edwardian whiskers seems to be clasping the hand of a skinny child: no prizes for guessing who's who. I couldn't get it out of my head as we were introduced to our new comrades. The ANA *askar* all either looked incredibly, preposterously young or grizzled and incalculably old: the young-uns like Cruickshank's Dickensian urchins, the older, wizened sergeants with dark scowls and seemingly years of hard experience in thick lines on their faces. It didn't help that, being Queen's Company men, the Grenadiers were all over 6 foot tall, but even allowing for that we all towered above the Afghans, had to hunch down as we leaned forward to do that Louis de Bernières, typical Englishman thing of crushing the hands of every bewildered soldier we were introduced to. Giant, strapping, pink, all of us with similarly cropped hair, identically dressed, even probably stood in exactly the same way, at ease, feet unconsciously shoulder width apart, hands clasped behind our backs slightly behind our boss, the 'captain', as he did the introductions. I can hardly remember a thing about that first meeting beyond being overwhelmed by the sheer physical differences between us. Before a word was spoken by anyone, we all already knew we were from different worlds.

Time and time again, both on that tour and on subsequent tours, mentors of all nationalities and, for that matter, sizes, have struggled to get past just how different we all look. In recent years the mountain has come to Muhammad, the ANA kitted out in ever-smarter combats, absorbing the culture of uniformity and learning from the exacerbated shouting of dozens of successive British sergeants that there most definitely is a right and a wrong way to wear a beret. The peculiar psychological relationship militaries have always had with uniforms and appearance had always been amusing, but until we got out to Afghanistan I hadn't really noticed it was bordering on pathological. In the age of the internet chat-room, message boards on military sites are clogged with debates over whatever the current edict or fashion is: the latter invariably some form of flaunting of the former. I doubt much has changed except the forums and I like to think that grabbing a cheeky, cold fag behind a tent somewhere in the Crimea was a bunch of young officers complaining about having been told off for their beards not being big enough, but that hasn't made it any easier out in Helmand, as precious wasted hours and days are spent reconciling the cosmetic differences between two armies.

We stood on one side of the room and must have looked identical. Of course we were all wearing exactly the same clothes, that goes without saying; it's the detail, the nuance, or rather lack of it, that's telling. To a man we had our sleeves rolled up to four fingers above the elbow, the rolls themselves all four fingers thick, our shirts tucked into our trousers, trousers neatly tied at the bottom (but never, of course, tucked into boots), our boots laced up the same way, in our hands our carefully faded berets (removed of course because we'd stepped indoors, to be replaced automatically within seconds of stepping out again) practically rigid after long hours of dousing in cold water, sculpting tightly to our heads with our regimental badge just above the left eye and shaving.* The only differences between us were the badges of rank on our chests, the discreet crowns, chevrons and garter stars which signified most about us and even explained who was stood exactly where and even whose hair was subtly longer than whose.

On the other side of the room, gaggled around the guy doing the talking, who seemed to be the boss, but we couldn't tell because no one seemed to be wearing any rank at all, were 'the ANA', and it didn't matter whether you'd walked in with a

* To remove any fluff, obviously.

closed mind and were smugly having your prejudices confirmed or whether you'd started the tour with all the romantic good intentions of an international aid worker, you couldn't deny they were as scruffy as hell. It didn't help that their uniforms were old US Marine Corps hand-me-downs, most of which seemed to be two sizes too big for the few *askar* who were wearing them. The wazzing* berets perched on the back of the heads of the even fewer who were wearing headdress only added to the effect. They were sprawled on the floor, peering in through windows, talking over each other, in every combination of T-shirts, baseball caps, flip-flops and pyjamas; it was almost as though someone was playing a practical joke on us. The former Sandhurst instructors in the group practically fainted as we stepped in the room, and someone simply muttered: 'Fuck me, looks like the kids have been at the dressing-up box.'

As we struggled to learn the names of our new comrades, time and again you'd hear the lazy cry that they all looked the same. Of course they didn't, but they did all look different from us and, as Syed later told me, they thought exactly the same of us. Later, we would take photographs of all the *askar* and I would sit up with my laptop trying to commit a dozen a night to memory, just like I had done when I first took over my first platoon. Of course Nour Ullah, a fearsome-looking Hazara with piercing eyes and a neat goatee who you just knew was descended directly from Genghis Khan himself, looked nothing like Sar Dar, with his heavy beard and dark eyes set back above his big nose. I liked the idea of Mujib and Qiam sat up at the same time

---

* Pejorative phrase used almost exclusively to describe badly moulded berets, although I occasionally heard it more generally used to describe people in a mess. I'm pretty sure my platoon at Sandhurst, crashed out in the middle of the night with God knows what hanging lopsidedly out of our webbing and boots on the wrong feet, was dismissed by the company sergeant-major as a 'fucking wazzing space-cadets'.

on the other side of the fence, just like we were, scratching their heads and wondering who was training with whom the following morning: 'You're with Captain Smith, I think.' 'Which one was he again?' 'You know, the tall, white one, with really short hair.' 'They're all tall and white with short hair. Fucking Brits, they all look the same.'

Introducing ten of us to a room full of Afghans was never going to be easy with just one interpreter. The captain did most of the talking, and we just tried not to stare too much and smiled and nodded and shook hands as and when required. Despite the fact that all we had to look forward to that evening was weapon cleaning and watching DVDs on cot-beds in a tent in the middle of the desert, I've rarely seen a group so anxious to 'get back', the awkwardness of the first impressions augmented by the silent calculations we were all more or less consciously

Being welcomed to Shorabak by an unknown soldier from 1 Tolay, 1/3/205, April 2007.

making: how the hell were we going to train this bunch and, more to the point, who did we least want next to us in an ambush? 'Who were you talking to then, sir?' asked someone as we walked back to our little camp, blinking in the harsh afternoon sun and pathetically grateful for the immaculate turn-out and instinctive half-salutes of our own gate-sentries, order restored. What the hell was the answer to that question? The ANA, obviously, but beyond that? 1st Kandak, hardly: we knew the ANA was under-manned so we hadn't expected a full-strength, 500-man battalion to be waiting for us in neat rows, but that had just been a rag-tag bunch of guys in a room. The honest answer was that, for all curious staring and polite handshaking and nodding along to interpreters that had just gone on, we didn't have a clue.

Train Hard, Fight Easy

Given that our mission was 'MENTOR and ENABLE 1/3/205 Afghan National Army in order to ensure successful completion of their tasks', a week seemed like a long time to have gone without so much as catching a glimpse of one of the locals, let alone meeting the soldiers we would be working with for the next six months. MENTOR and ENABLE were brand new mission verbs, abstract words and unfamiliar concepts to British soldiers brought up on Falklands War stories and finely trained to DESTROY and NEUTRALIZE and SECURE. '1/3/205' was just a series of meaningless numbers designating the randomly selected and apparently brand new unit of a new brigade of a new corps of an army that had only existed for a couple of years, and the 'Afghan National Army', well, that was always just the ANA.

The ANA had been made an immediate priority for Afghanistan after the toppling of the Taliban at the end of 2001. UNSCR 1386,* which authorized the establishment of ISAF (the International Security and Assistance Force) to assist the Afghan Interim Authority in maintaining security in and around Kabul, is a typically self-important instrument of international diplomacy: its busy italics *reaffirming* this, *taking note* of that and variously *stressing* and *determining* all manner of good intentions

---

* United Nations Security Council Resolution 1386, which, much to the disappointment of many an online loon confusing things they don't like with things that are illegal, was the basis for the presence of foreign troops in Afghanistan.

in a detached and formal language which was a million miles away from the reality. Its three letters pronounced separately, like the RAF or the BBC and other more or less treasured national institutions, the term 'ANA' is, I suppose, correctly used in the singular. Through months of training before we deployed out to Afghanistan itself we spoke of 'the ANA' as a single body and of 'the Afghan troops' or 'Afghan soldiers' as the men who served in it: but something funny happened almost as soon as we got out there and actually met the guys. Firstly, they ceased to be 'Afghan soldiers' and became simply 'the Afghans', the distinction between civilian and military somehow evaporating in the relentlessly uniformed bases and battle-pocked desert. Secondly, lazily but expediently, 'ANA' became a more sweeping, general term meaning both the Army and its individual soldiers. *'These are the various units of the ANA you will be working alongside . . .'* was fine, and made perfect sense as the start of a sentence. Gradually, however, and then more frequently it was 'Oi! Someone get those bloody ANA off their backsides and up here' in reference to anything from three to three hundred soldiers, peppered with expletives and tempered in volume in proportion to the urgency of the situation.

Soldiers have more need than most for general terms for indeterminately sized groups. Through the fire-teams of four, sections of eight and platoons of thirty-odd which are the basic building blocks of any fighting force, up through the hundred-plus companies which made up 600-strong battalions and beyond, we had no shortage of specific terms for specific groups, but you needed something to shout at the gaggle smoking round the back of the cookhouse running late for a parade or, more pertinently to Helmand, something to scream at the huddle in the ditch across the field to get them up and moving. 'Men' was out of fashion for the twenty-first century: you couldn't hear it in your mind but in clipped, faux-Edwardian tones, uttered petulantly by a moustachioed turn-of-the-century public school boy. 'Bods' was a favourite in some regiments, and I always liked it, but it was, if you thought about it, tellingly impersonal, a Freudian slip of command. Short for bodies, it subtly reinforced the idea that we weren't individuals. Together we were bodies of fighting men, and the call for some 'bods' here or there surely hinted that it didn't matter who.

In any given barracks or base there will be a broad selection of more or less complimentary and descriptive general terms, from Guardsmen to grunts, Riflemen to REMFs.* Trying to tap into the undeniable Afghan fighting tradition, some bright spark in Kabul or Washington had favoured the literal translation of the Dari word *askar*, which was the emotive 'warriors' rather than just plain 'soldiers'. That was too much for us arch and ironic Brits, and we didn't know the Dari for 'blokes', so we made do with 'ANA' as if it was the plural: in the heat of the moment, everyone knew what you meant. It seemed dismissive, seemed to dehumanize the individual Afghan soldiers in a way I don't think it was ever intended to, but I don't know whether the ANA sensed the subtle grammatical slight, the casual indifference by which young and old, good and bad, Tajik, Hazara, Pashtun and Uzbek were all lumped together in those easy three syllables. If they did, I hope they also noticed the more subtle process by which, as we finally met them and worked and fought alongside them, the warriors, soldiers, men or whatever they should have been called somehow ceased to be 'the ANA' and became 'our ANA'. It would mean something eventually, but it would take a long time coming.

That it took five days in Afghanistan for me to meet an actual Afghan was not ideal, but neither was it surprising. When the

* Rear echelon mother fuckers.

British Army first moved into Helmand in 2006, the ANA was/ were little more than an afterthought. One year later, a whole battlegroup was dedicated to providing Operational Mentoring and Liaison Teams (OMLT), small groups of British soldiers who would work closely alongside the ANA and coordinate their training and operations. The good intent was there, the slick PowerPoint slides in staff mission briefings said all the right things, and we were well versed in the mantra that we were 'creating an Afghan solution to an Afghan problem', but the reality was miles away. Over the previous year in Helmand first the Paras and then the Royal Marines had been winning rosettes* and medals scrapping with the Taliban like the Great Game had never finished: fighting desperate skirmishes through the Green Zone and last-ditch defences of isolated platoon houses in towns like Sangin and Musa Qala which back then still sounded exotic and unfamiliar. We had a vague awareness that the ANA had been involved in some of these actions, but the rumours we'd heard in training were that as often as not they were fighting for both sides or simply ran away. The pictures we had seen of Afghan soldiers were mostly of doped-up *chai* boys with thickly kohled eyes and flowers in their rifles; these guys were barely men, let alone soldiers.

There were two vivid photos that someone had brought back from the Paras' tour, obviously both taken during the same fire-fight. In the first, an Afghan soldier on one knee is firing round the corner of a building, a burly Brit just over his shoulder, pointing out the target with a classic, four-fingered Brecon chop, silently roaring a target indication, the tension in his wide-open mouth speaking eloquently of the situation. This, we were told,

* The device added to an operational service medal to denote 'war-fighting' as opposed to just attendance.

was the theory of OMLT: nurturing, helping, directing the ANA up to and even in the heat of the actual battle. The second must have been taken barely a minute later. Presumably the same Afghan is now curled up behind the wall, eyes scrunched up with fear, AK47 discarded to the side while the Brit has taken up his position and is returning fire, still roaring instructions to his unseen comrades. This, we were told gravely, was frequently the reality of OMLT: doing the ANA's fighting for them.

Even in theory, this was problematic. Training to fight for yourself was one thing, training to fight for someone else was another. At Sandhurst we had learned the maxim 'train hard, fight easy'* the difficult way: sucking in great lungfuls of air, exhausted after log-runs and hallucinating on week-long, blistering, trench-digging, sleep-deprivation extravaganzas. Soldiers interviewed about heroic exploits invariably mumble the Pavlovian response that their 'training just kicked in', and so it turned out to be, but back in the UK on pre-deployment training we had no Afghans to train with, so laughably, worryingly, we couldn't train at all. Initially we just had to pretend: we'd push out on patrols on across the training area and get told off for driving too quickly because we weren't allowing for the imaginary six ANA vehicles we were meant to pretend were following our own. We knew that the language barrier was going to be a massive problem, so everyone took an aptitude test, and the bright ones went on intensive Dari and Pashtun courses – but the courses clashed with training, so we didn't see them again till we got to Helmand and, in the meantime, a pretend interpreter had to pretend to talk to the pretend Afghans.

* It might have sounded like a T-shirt slogan for wannabe cage-fighters, but it had actually been coined by Count Suvorov, the eighteenth-century Russian general and author of *The Science of Victory*, who had never lost a battle, so there must have been something in it.

When we finally got some demo troops they were cheerful, cheeky Yorkshire lads from the Duke of Boots* who had obviously just finished playing Iraqis for a previous exercise and spent the whole week pretending to be Jaish al-Mahdi,† running around the training area in tracksuits and dish-dashes shouting 'Ali Baba'. It would have been funny if it wasn't so surreal, British soldiers pretending to be Afghan soldiers but who'd spent so long pretending to be Iraqi insurgents that they kept forgetting whether they were meant to pretend to be fighting us or fighting with us.

On Salisbury Plain, being formally tested for our readiness to deploy in Quasar-laser vests with bleeping, blinking digital info panels which told you exactly where you'd been shot and what limbs you had lost, we were allocated a company of Gurkhas to 'play' the ANA. This was an improvement of sorts; the grinning Gurkhas had all been instructed not to respond to any orders given in English, to pretend they couldn't understand until whatever it was being said was translated into Gurkhali by a giggling sergeant. The problem was that the Gurkhas are just too damn good at soldiering; it's second nature to them and, try as they might, they just couldn't do it badly. The stories filtering back from Afghanistan were of soldiers who were lazy, soldiers who were weak, soldiers who would disobey orders and refuse commands. The British Army's official version of 'bad soldiering' involved wearing a soft hat under your helmet and not carrying your rifle properly. The Gurkhas would start off 'well', dawdling at the back and chattering when they were supposed to be quiet, but at the first hint of urgency, the first shouted order or pop of smoke from the training grenades, the instinctive soldier in them kicked in. The funny thing about soldiering is, while it can

---

* Duke of Wellington's Regiment, now 3rd Battalion the Yorkshire Regiment.
† The Shia militia who were the 'enemy' down in Basrah at the time.

be difficult to train in, it's almost impossible to train out. The Gurkhas could have stuck their underpants on their heads, two pencils up their noses and answered every question 'wibble' and it wouldn't have made a difference. When it mattered, they were still professional infanteers, still moved instinctively through the dead ground, spaced themselves out and at the first crack of simulated enemy fire got rounds down in the other direction and hit the deck. If we'd thought training with the 'Yorkshire ANA' was surreal, it had nothing on seeing a squad of Gurkhas getting bollocked time and time again for doing their job too well. In the end we nearly failed our test exercise by passing it too comfortably. The directing staff gave up trying to replicate the ANA and just reminded us at every opportunity that it wouldn't be like this out in Afghanistan. We'd look out over the plain, past the spire and red-topped gable-end roofs of Copehill Down, the mock East German village, and at the cattle grazing in the February drizzle in the distance, and bite our tongues: no shit it wouldn't be like this in Helmand.

At every stage of our training the Afghans themselves were dismissed. Most frequently they were infantilized: were children, boys, novices who needed hand-holding and baby-sitting. Sometimes they were romanticized: lip-service was paid to the orientalist tradition of the noble savage, the better-read officers in Brigade HQ entreating us not to forget defeats of yesteryear at the hands of wily tribesman, but doing so with a nod and a wink which meant that it was all good history but hardly relevant to the here and now. The knee-jerk military machismo didn't even know where to start with rumours of Afghan soldiers who held hands, wore henna and collected flowers on patrol, so they were brushed aside with a casual shrug and a joke about 'man-love Thursday'. Most worryingly, most dismissively of all, the Afghans were zoomorphized, reduced to animals by endless reference to the fucking advert with the cowboys herding cats.

There may have been some men and women in the brigade who hadn't seen the 'herding cats' video, but there definitely weren't many. The same guys just going through the motions, teaching the same lessons they'd taught to troops heading out to Belfast ten years ago, thought it was the funniest thing they'd ever seen and, to be fair, it's actually pretty good as virals go. It's somewhere out there on YouTube, of course, and we laughed along despite the fact that it was surely cobbled together by smug creatives, lounging on sofas in the sort of open plan, beer-drinking offices that, sweating our arses off in the desert, we all used to imagine that everyone in media or advertising worked in (and instinctively and jealously despised them for it). The plot is simple. Classic cowboys herd fluffy CGI cats in a sumptuous and gentle but knowing homage to the good old Wild West. Under vast skies, across sweeping plains and in massive hats, the humour is in the juxtaposition of the classic macho ranchers and the wide-eyed, meowing Persians. I think it's supposed to be advertising an IT systems provider of all things, and the fact that I can't remember for who or why probably didn't hamper the week-off coke-binge that the guys who made it rewarded themselves with, but then they probably didn't realize when they came up with the idea what its true legacy would be.

Over pre-deployment months of training during which we met no Afghans and a lucky one in ten of us got some rudi-mentary language training, through damp weeks practising drills and skills during which we barely touched the weapon and kit we would be using in theatre, and sat through interminable lectures delivered by instructors who'd never actually done operational mentoring or liaison, the one thing we knew for sure was that working with the ANA was like herding cats. We knew it because we must have been shown the damn film about 100 times. Even now when, thankfully, the piss-poor lessons of our own inadequate preparation have been learned and proper consideration is given to working with the ANA right from the start of training, 'herding cats' still gets trotted out to general amusement. Despite all the progress and good intentions it's invariably shown in an airless Nissen hut during a presentation on 'Working with the ANA' or 'Our Afghan Partners' or similar: probably during some lull in training to a group of soldiers, mildly grateful to be sat indoors, but not really listening to the brief, nodding dogs. They'll come away with the usual striking images stuck in their heads, soldiers on patrol with teapots instead of helmets, men in make-up, dangerous allies. Training, mentoring, partnering, OMLT, it didn't matter what you called it, that video perfectly captured the tone of everything that would follow.

I understand the rationale: any decent instructor breaks up lessons with a few movie 'funnies' to wake up an audience and keep them engaged, and it's a harmless bit of fun which makes most people laugh and which very few mistake for a serious critique of ISAF strategy. The problem was that it was the predominant image in everyone's mind; everyone knew we were 'herding cats' when they didn't actually understand what we were supposed to be doing. During one of the last checks before we flew out, stood in the queue behind a couple of junior Guardsmen waiting to hand in their passports, I couldn't work out whether to laugh or cry as I listened to them compare rumours. They'd just found out which *kandak* their company would be mentoring and were debating, inevitably, who'd be in 'the shit' first. There was a natural pause in the banter as the queue shuffled forward: someone up front was being barked at for not having filled in his next-of-kin forms. '2nd Kandak,' one of the lads in front repeated thoughtfully. His mucker nodded, another pause, twenty-four hours to go: 'And what the fuck is a *kandak* again?'

Duty – Honor – Country

When you join the British Army to become an officer you're subjected to such a sustained bombardment about leadership that if you're not careful you can become desensitized. At least we have an innate cynicism which tempers the call to duty, honour and vanity; from what I hear West Point* is considerably worse. At Sandhurst† instructors with straight faces invoked the great maverick generals before we were marched back down the hill for double ceremonial drill, but some of the lessons stuck. One of the basic principles we all remembered was leadership by example: successful fighting forces were rarely badly led; in fact it was the opposite: they were defined by their commanders. We spoke of the armies of Wellington and Napoleon, of Rommel's Afrika Korps and Bill Slim's 'Forgotten Army', so when it came to getting to grips with the ANA, naturally, we started off looking for the guys in charge.

The senior ANA commander in Helmand was the encouragingly imposing Brigadier General Mohaiyadin Ghori. If the ISAF staff planners thought he would be the kind to sit quietly in the corner and contribute his men to the wider battle, they were mistaken. Mohaiyadin cut a pretty fearsome figure whether in camp or out on the ground. Whip-smart, either shaven-

---

* The motto of the United States Military Academy is 'Duty – Honor – Country'. No prizes for guessing where the NATO staff officer who came up with the motto of the Afghan National Army, which is 'Allah – Honour – Country', studied.

† The finest leadership course in the world, so we were told. I guess that was because they didn't do log-races at Harvard Business School.

headed or bald (you wouldn't have asked), he looked like an Afghan Patrick Stewart but with a thick moustache and a glare that would have silenced the bridge of the Starship *Enterprise* even if it had been crewed by squabbling, mutinous Pashtuns. He was the brigade commander of 3/205, and Helmand in 2007 had been his party. Though our commanding officer was by comparison only a humble lieutenant colonel he was the only man in the province with the ear and confidence of the brigade commander, and what Mohaiyadin lacked in strategic nous and ISAF assets he made up for in presence. Interviewed at the very start of our tour, his proposal for dealing with local support for the Taliban was simplicity itself: 'I will punch them in the face and tell them to stop fighting us. Our plan is to show them force, then clean the tears from their eyes. Then they will know who is in charge.'[5]

He might not have been fluent in media-friendly, 'hearts and minds' speak, but of more immediate importance was that General Mohaiyadin Ghori was, at the time, the only senior

General Mohaiyadin with Brigadier James Cowan in 2009.

officer who instilled an appropriate mix of respect and fear into his men. The young ANA recruits responded to wily squad sergeants and, as we already knew, bruising junior commanders whose reputations went before them, but you never usually saw the Afghans get anxious about colonels and generals in that flapping way the British Army specializes in. You only had to see a formerly growling, murderous Glaswegian colour sergeant meekly and uncomplainingly ironing corners into a poncho tablecloth ahead of the visit of a random and probably, in the grand scheme of things, not all that important major general to realize how Western armies could lose perspective. The Americans, for once, were even worse than us. You could say whatever else you liked about the ANA but they never faked it for their own officers, unless General Mohaiyadin was prowling the front-line patrol bases with piercing eyes and a menacing, quiet word of displeasure to a looming nearby sergeant. This was a man, after all, who had been trained at Moscow's Frunze Military Staff Academy back in the 1980s while we were still in nappies and our majors and colonels were preparing to try and hold up the 3rd Shock Army as it rolled across the German plain just long enough for someone at home to fire off the nukes.* Now we were all on the same team.

Unfortunately, not all his *kandak* commanders came up to Mohaiyadin standard. The officer commanding our *kandak*, Lieutenant Colonel Shir Dil, looked great on paper. He was from the village of Chalarsnnod in the far northern, mountainous Badakhshan province. The biographical nuggets weren't as

* Just because the Cold War never got hot and most British Army of the Rhine casualties were from booze or clap didn't mean that it didn't have an edge. I remember being told by one of the lads who could still remember that, if it ever had kicked off, the life expectancy of all the front-line troops was about twenty minutes.

arbitrary as they seemed: a Tajik from the anti-Taliban, anti-Pashtun heartlands,★ Shir Dil was thought to be an ideal man to lead troops in the Pashtun-dominated south because his mother had been a Pashtun and, presumably, therefore, he was attuned to each side of an ethnic divide the complexity and depth of which we barely comprehended. We dutifully learnt the statistics – 42 per cent Pashtun, 27 per cent Tajik, 9 per cent Hazara, 8 per cent Uzbek, etc. – and garnered some supremely simplistic sense of the complex country. We knew that the Pashtuns with their own language were part of the largest tribe in the world, stretching over the notional borders of Afghanistan to the south and east, and had traditionally dominated; that the Dari-speaking Tajiks to the north considered themselves in some respects the original Afghans and tended to ally themselves with their northern Uzbek neighbours; that the Hazaras, the country's only Shi'a and said to be descended from Genghis Khan's invading army, were a fierce and traditionally persecuted minority; and so on and so on. Our training booklets were wonderfully bland: the country was 'highly diverse'; Afghan nationalism was 'relatively weak'; different ethnic communities lacked integration, but by far the most graphic and eloquent illustration of the fact that the country was basically an ethnic mess was a Freudian data slip: falling into the American habit of contextualizing the size of an unknown country by overlaying

★ The home province of Burhanuddin Rabbani, who along with Ahmad Shah Massoud – the Lion of the Panjshir – had been one of the most visible leaders of the Northern Alliance. Rabbani was assassinated by a suicide bomber at his home in Kabul on 20 September 2011. Men claiming to be Taliban representatives approached him to discuss 'peace talks' and offered him a hug while detonating explosives thought to be hidden in a turban. In the days before his death Rabbani had been in Iran calling on Islamic scholars to issue a *fatwa* against the practice of suicide bombing.

it with a map of somewhere similar,* whoever had drafted our background brief had used Bosnia as a comparator. On one level it made sense – many soldiers had been to Bosnia, and the visual was striking: Afghanistan was much, much bigger – but you couldn't help thinking there was a little subconscious at play – another country where the neighbours slaughter each other for reasons nobody quite understands.

Whoever Shir Dil was, however ethnically attuned he may or may not have been and however impressive his CV, unfortunately he wasn't actually there when we arrived. More worryingly, he wasn't there a month later when the whole *kandak* was rushed out on its first op, which was supposed to last five days, and he still wasn't there when his exhausted troops finally got pulled back into camp two months later. We only know he definitely existed because it said so on the paperwork and because my boss met him briefly – an awkward encounter since we'd spent the past few days dealing with the excellent Major Ataullah on the assumption that he was the commander and was just being modest; it turned out he'd been the second-in-command all along and just thought we were stupid. Ataullah was a burly Pashtun from Farah in western Afghanistan, a relatively peaceful province on the Iranian border but a sparse and hard part of the country which produced hard men with big families. He was technically the *kandak* executive officer rather than second-in-command, as the ANA followed the US terminology in that respect, but the jobs were effectively identical, and it really didn't matter whether he was the XO or the 2I/C. What mattered was that he was a good officer who had already worked with Soviets, the French and the Canadians as well

* Utterly confusing and redundant when the CIA World Fact Book helpfully explains that Armenia is 'slightly smaller than Maryland' or that Zimbabwe is 'slightly larger than Montana'.

as the Paras and the Marines and had such invaluable experience that he could have styled himself field marshal for all that we cared.

At least there was consistency in the confusion: the ANA had its own chaotic symmetry like some rare, green and brown, diesel-scented rainforest flower. My opposite number was meant to be the 3 Company commander, but it was far from clear who that actually was. Encouragingly, the Marines had prepared some background notes on the officer they had worked with; discouragingly they had been pretty scathing about the unimpressive Jagran S—, but as it was no matter, good or bad, Jagran S—, it turned out, was nowhere to be found.

The first time I walked into the sparse 3 Company office, already feeling the heat from the short walk across Shorabak even though it was only March, I ventured a hopeful 'Commander, Sahib?' The neat, bearded officer behind the desk got up, nodded politely and shook my proffered hand as I launched into the introductory platitudes I'd been practising all morning: such an honour to be in his country, looking forward to meeting his troops, learning from his experience, etc., etc. The 'terp rolled off the phrases like he already knew them, which he probably did. The bearded soldier behind the desk kept nodding politely and it was only when he said something about how he had fought many times with the Taliban and was looking forward to doing so again with me that I sensed something didn't add up. The Marines' notes on the commander had emphasized how much he stayed away from the fighting. There was something about the guy I was talking to, a hard edge which didn't chime with what I had read, but I could hardly pull out the folded piece of paper from my pocket, the one listing all his shortcomings, and compare the black and white thumbnail in the corner to whoever it was I was talking to. Now I was losing my train of thought: this long-anticipated first meeting was not going to plan. If this wasn't the boss then who was he and why was he in this office? Rather suddenly and surprisingly he pulled up his trousers to show me a gritty-looking gunshot wound deep across his shin: 'Taliban gun,' he said in English, helpfully miming someone firing a rifle.

I was about to ask him how and when it had happened, wondering why it wasn't mentioned in his notes and more to the point who exactly he was again, when we were interrupted by the arrival of a group of *askar* who ignored my presence and bombarded the officer with questions. There was something uncomfortable about the exchange; he seemed out of his depth, evasive. Avoiding the questions as if he didn't really know the answers or, more worryingly, any of the troops asking them, all of which would have confirmed the low opinion the Marines had formed of Jagran S——'s leadership if it hadn't been for the fact that none of these soldiers were referring to him as 'Jagran' or 'S——' or anything that sounded remotely like either. Jagran S——? I asked again when the room was finally clear. He shot me a look as if I was mad and said something quickly to the 'terp which was roughly and probably more politely translated as 'What the hell is this guy talking about and who the hell is Jagran S——? I'm just a lieutenant – Lieutenant Mujib Ullah.'

It was an inauspicious start, and although years later we would shake our heads and smile, I can still remember the rising sense of panic at the time, sat in the concrete office, on creaking plastic chairs, an empty table between us, the sort of anonymous room you could imagine CIA interrogations taking place in if it hadn't been for the ornate tray and tea-set on the side and the bright, rolled-up prayer mat in the corner. I was confused as to why the company commander didn't know his men; he was confused as to why I thought he was the company commander and had spent half the morning asking him about soldiers he'd never met and places he'd never been. For the whole conversation I'd been terrified, clutching in my hand a piece of paper which said the man was a coward, wondering why he didn't seem to have a clue about anything or anyone and thinking all the time that between the two of us, complete strangers, through a teenage interpreter, we had a month to conjure up a coherent fighting force from what still looked to me like a confused bunch of boys who'd been put in US Marine Corps hand-me-down uniforms as some sort of cruel joke.

There was something monkish about his appearance; he was skinny, but neat: neat beard, neat uniform, short hair with a high forehead, slightly balding. Briefing troops, he clasped his hands in front of him and tended to adopt an earnest, slightly pained expression which I associated with a sort of holy ascetic, but that was probably as much to do with the fact that he was the only ANA officer trying to help as it was anything actually outwardly monastic about him. I would have said he was older

Mujib Ullah, photographed later on the tour giving orders up in Sangin.

than me, but not thirty-six, which he was: the hardness I'd faintly detected even when I thought he was someone else was the product of growing up in the Khost wa Fring district in the far east of Baghlan province, strategically important and the scene of fierce fighting between the Soviets and Massoud in its narrow passes. This was the man I was to mentor, on whom I was to bestow the accumulated wisdom of my three years in a uniform: Mujib Ullah, son of Muhammad Rasoul, who had been fighting one enemy or another for sixteen years. Even though he had a rubbish beret.

Mujib's voice was low and considered, his speech deliberate and generally quiet which, maybe, added to the priestly thing, but around strangers and under stress he had a tendency to lilt up at the end of his sentences and the intonation sounded whiny. We had established that he wasn't the old commander, which was a relief in itself, but he never said that he was brand new to the unit, which would have explained why he didn't seem to know the *kandak* any better than we did. Knowing no better, we assumed he was one of the waste-of-space officers we had heard so much about in training and during our handover: clueless and complaining. My hardened West Country and mockney sergeants had been in the Household Division* for nearly fifty years between them, so clueless officers were the staple of their mess Apocrypha, but even they couldn't accept the idea that a lieutenant wouldn't know a single one of his own soldiers. Mujib kept shrugging and trying to explain that he had only just got back, meaning into the Army. We continued assuming he meant from leave, so that was hardly any excuse. The young *askar* of 3 Company, 1 Kandak kept watching us arguing through the windows,

---

* Comprising the Household Cavalry and the five Regiments of Foot Guards and, anecdotally, home to particularly strong sergeants messes (true) and particularly chinless officers (outrageous slander).

half smiling, half confused, but not bothered either way. Each time we gave up and just decided to do some training with whoever was there, whether we knew their names or not, a mysterious bell would ring, and the ANA would all disappear on cue – prayers, lunch, siesta, we never really knew to where.

As for Qiam, most of us had heard the rumours about him before we'd even unpacked our bergans. Qiam was unique in that, even in those very first days, he stood out, was a personality, an individual among the mass of unfamiliar, generic 'Afghans'. His was the first Afghan name we learned, and I'm sure it will be the last most of us forget, yet in a way he also came to represent not just the *kandak*, but the whole ANA itself, maybe even the whole country: he was Tommy Atkins, even more so when you recalled the last lines of Kipling's eponymous Barrack Room Ballad:

For it's Tommy this, an' Tommy that, an' 'Chuck him out, the brute!'
But it's 'Saviour of his country' when the guns begin to shoot

Over time I came to learn that his presence was something that you sensed first; he was like an express train that you could feel coming long before you could see or hear him. At his worst he was like the sudden heaviness before the storm, at his best he was the refreshing, crisp air afterwards and often he was the thunder and lightning in between; whichever it was, the effect was appropriately atmospheric.

In the dusty, disorientating days after we arrived in Helmand the medical centre had been inundated with ANA. The handful of British, pale-looking early DNV* sufferers shuffling

---

* Diarrhoea and vomiting, such an habitual curse of expeditionary warfare that the condition had been appropriated and paid the high compliment of being granted its very own military TLA.

uncomfortably outside the tin hut with the red cross on the door were joined each morning at 0755 by long queues of unfamiliar Afghan soldiers. From the cheeky grins of the more brazen who obviously had nothing wrong with them to the gritty dedication of those who paraded with self-inflicted cuts and bruises, it was clear that this had nothing to do with uniquely local health issues and everything to do with the fact that, unlike our predecessors, we had a female doctor. When word got round that one young warrior had turned up with a cracked jaw and refused to say how it had happened we assumed that he was another impressively dedicated admirer of the doc', but one of the interpreters had heard differently: the rumour in the Afghan cookhouse was that the young soldier had been thumped by an officer to whom he had answered back.

We weren't quite sure what to make of this. On the one hand, obviously, it was pretty bad for the guy with the broken jaw; not that he seemed to mind particularly as he sat wide-eyed, enjoying his treatment while his leery mates peered in enviously at the sick-bay windows. On the other it suggested that some-where in the extraordinary desert camp in which we found ourselves, somewhere among these through-the-looking-glass soldiers we were struggling to meet, let alone train, somewhere out there was someone with an instinctive grasp of old-school military discipline: somewhere out there was something as comfortingly familiar as the whiff of parade gloss and the dis-tant barking of a drill sergeant. The more senior sergeants' mess members nodded with quiet approval and warm memories of bygone beastings. Who was the mythical officer with the quick right hook? The answer, whispered fearfully or reverently by the suddenly shy interpreter, as if just to say the name would be to conjure him up in a ball of smoke and whirling fists, was *Jagran Qiam*.

A clip round the ear, an affectionate head-shove, even the odd angry slap, but no one ever actually saw Qiam hit one of his soldiers. Squat and powerfully built although even back then sporting something of a rear operations paunch, there was a touch of Stallone about Qiam, which was why the lads called him Rocky, but there was also a touch of Arthur Lowe: Rambo meets Captain Mainwaring. His voice was usually a growl, but his bark was invariably worse than his bite. What would begin as an angry shout would rumble low and menacingly before gurgling up into a roaring, Falstaffian, Simon-Callow-in-*Four-Weddings-and-a-Funeral* laugh. He seemed to exist in a separate world of his own: sometimes he was there, sometimes he was not; sometimes he was in the office where you had arranged to meet him, sometimes he would simply appear, uninvited, half-way through a patrol, when you had no idea how he even knew you'd be out, let alone how he'd got there himself.

At least Qiam officially existed. His name appeared on the virtually indecipherable spreadsheet the Marines had handed over to us on a dust-clogged USB stick containing the sketchy nominal roll. Qiam Udin was down at serial number 298, son of Mia Khan, ANA number 42C009. His position, so we were given to understand, was the commander of the Tolay Sekolar, the heavy weapons company which would have had the motors and heavy machine-guns if the *kandak* had actually had any mortars or heavy machine-guns. No one was sure if he was a captain or a major because he never wore any badges of rank on his uniform, just a fading brown issue T-shirt hanging out over baggy combats themselves, incongruously, always meticulously tucked in to a pair of lightweight desert boots he had blagged off one of the US contractors. Some said he was former Mujahideen; some said he'd been a senior officer under the Soviets, demoted for insubordination; some even said he was a Taliban spy, but never to his face. In another era, in another army, he looked like he could have been one of those annoying, fussy little men always minding someone else's business. He had a slightly camp, slightly too-long side-swept fringe which combined with his neat moustache and gut to undermine his warrior reputation. I can still picture him the first time we got ambushed together, flicking his hair out of his eyes, sweating unhealthily through the stained brown T-shirt and pausing for breath before grinning, breaking cover and charging towards the enemy.

The Marines hadn't sugar-coated the handover, but neither had they quite emphasized the extent of the problems facing us: the lack of unity and drive within the *kandak*; of any cohesion which started at the top. They had tried to explain that they relied heavily on certain individuals to get things done, certain driving personalities within the ANA sub-units which often had nothing to do with the rank structure: 'this guy *is* the company', they'd said, pointing someone out on the helipad who looked the same as everyone else. We'd nodded sagely, pretending to understand, but not getting it at all, and it would take us long and difficult weeks to realize that they meant guys like Qiam and Mujib. In a way, the *kandak* was the purest military unit you could imagine, it was just the men, but that made our task all the more difficult because it turned out the only way you could work with the ANA was to completely integrate with them, and that in turn would require a level of engagement, of cultural flexibility and social translation for which we were utterly unprepared.

Springtime in Shorabak

Symbolically located midway between our lines and the *kandak*'s, opposite the gate where neat ISAF Tombstone gave way to sprawling ANA Shorabak and overlooking the helipad where the Afghans played long, rolling games of football in the early-evening cool and watched bemused as we did PT in the mornings, was the interpreters' compound. Little more than a couple of rows of semi-permanent huts and one hard-cover bolt hole – a concrete shelter to provide overhead protection during a rocket or mortar attack. The 'terps lived six, seven, eight – we were never sure – to a room, a parody of student living, the heating or the aircon always turned up to max, a neat row of shoes at each door the only tidy thing about the dark, messy rooms which smelled unmistakably of young men and feet and always seemed to have someone snoozing in the corner despite a radio or TV blasting away in the background. Given the extent to which we utterly relied upon the 'terps, the ramshackle compound and chaotic management of our most precious resource was more than a little surprising. The 'terps were mostly young and nearly all friendly and helpful, but there were never enough to go round, and no one ever quite knew who was in charge of whom. A short, bullying Kabuli seemed to be designated 'head 'terp', and at first we were told to run all ad hoc requests for help through him. In theory each mentoring team would have had two interpreters, the same two interpreters to get used to working with. In practice, especially in camp, this never happened, and whoever was around and available, which usually meant whoever wasn't friends with the 'head 'terp', would get dicked for the job in hand. We quickly realized that unless a 'terp was in his good books, or more likely making sure he took a cut of his pay, he would get disproportionately picked on for the dangerous, uncomfortable missions.

Our first 'terp was a nice, scruffy kid called Shabir, which was too easy for the Guardsmen and immediately became Shabi. A Hazara with a big smile who looked about twelve years old and even younger with an enormous helmet wobbling on his head, perched on top of Wiley-X goggles he'd been given by a US Navy Seal and which he never took off. The first time we took him for training outside the wire Shabi turned up with a day sack he must have got from the dodgy kit man who had even in those early days set up in Bastion and was doing a roaring trade selling plastic pistol holsters to the sort of people who were never going to be using a pistol. Clinging on to each strap under a blue and neon-orange baseball cap, he looked for all the world like one of those Chinese exchange students that clog London in summer, ambling in matching yellow T-shirts in a disordered crocodile from the LSE to some dreadful West End musical, and in another life he probably should have been. He spoke English, Dari, Pashtun and pretty good French and wore a grin like that even when our fun day out was a long hot slog in the desert. Shabi was in the cheeky-chappy 'terp mould: everything was a joke, everything a bit of a game. It could get you into trouble, especially when the senior officers in the *kandak* thought he was being lippy, but at least you knew he was translating exactly what you were saying; in fact, the more upset they were, the more accurate the translation probably was.

Unless you were lucky and had one of the very few British guys who'd done the language course in your team or, even luckier, had an Afghan in the *kandak* who spoke English, you pretty much depended on your 'terp, and it was a nonsense that so little regard was given to recruiting, training and maintaining relationships with these brave guys, mostly little more than schoolboys, who were the lynchpin of everything we were doing. Shabi cheerfully told me that he was earning more money than anyone else in his family, but it still wasn't much once you factored in being out on patrol and getting specifically targeted by the Taliban, who knew how important you were. There was a big argument about whether or not 'terps should be allowed to carry their own weapons. Officially they weren't, but I caught a couple once or twice reaching for a pistol they'd obviously borrowed off one of the ANA when we were in a tight spot and couldn't help but think I'd have done the same thing in their shoes.

In a strange way, the 'terps' job was more difficult when we weren't fighting. Once we were out on operations the logic of a plan or the urgency of a fire-fight tended to communicate itself; it was the nuance of training and our attempts to justify doing things 'our way' which frequently got lost in translation. There was something ridiculous about how precarious the whole system was. If you had a guy like Nawroz, whom we were allocated at the last minute for our first big op, who was too young, too impressionable and too nervous, you never knew if what you were saying was actually being translated. It was not ideal that Nawroz was hopelessly nervous and would disappear at the first hint of trouble, but it was understandable – the guy was human after all. What was unforgivable was that we couldn't trust him; I later realized he would render my instructions into what he thought the ANA wanted to hear or, worse still, mistranslate ANA instructions he didn't like the sound of. He ended up getting too close to the squads he was working with, set up his cot with them when we would stop for the night and ceased to be impartial, and in the end we had to swap him for someone else. But for about a week out in the Green Zone our effectiveness was utterly and avoidably undermined.

It could go the other way, of course. Nawroz's replacement,

Sami, was both an excellent interpreter and impressively, nonchalantly fearless, but as time went on he allied himself so firmly with the mentors and British units wherever we were that he started picking up the casually disdainful, frustrated tension between us and the ANA and by the end of the tour was almost a parody of an intolerant British sergeant: berating the squads on his own initiative and getting into fights with the understandably resentful *askar* who knew perfectly well that he was getting paid far more than they were, and in precious US dollars. Even at the start of the tour, as we waited for five minutes or so each morning on our way over to start work with the *kandak*, you could sense that the guys lazing around the 'terp compound, squabbling over who had stolen whose radio and whose turn it was to come and help translate the new nominal roll, were way too important to have been given such scant consideration. You could have left dozens of us behind and devoted the time and resources wasted on Salisbury Plain to ensuring that each *kandak* had enough properly prepared, properly selected 'terps, and the whole thing would have been immeasurably easier. But nothing with the ANA was easy, not even working out who was who.

The Excel spreadsheet which was supposed to be the master *kandak* nominal roll had 342 names on it, but a different Word document we found on the same memory stick, given to us the day the last of our predecessors left, had only 248: we never managed to get the guys in one place at one time to physically count them ourselves. The latter list was the one that had been compiled more recently and ominously seemed to be more accurate, although we were relieved to be informed after a few days of frantic worrying that real numbers were only so low because lots of guys were on leave. Where, and more to the point when they'd be coming back, didn't seem to be questions anyone could answer, so we focused on our spreadsheets.

Columns in the table for 'date of birth' were largely blank or peppered with speculative and despairing question marks, Afghan names mangled by successive squaddie interpretations of how to spell Bismillah. In Welsh battalions they could distinguish the Joneses and the Thomases with their regimental numbers – Jones 32, 74 etc. – but of course because most of the ANA warriors either didn't have, had lost or preferred not to recall their own allocated soldier numbers there was no way to tell apart the twenty Muhammads in each platoon. Take an old soldier by surprise by asking him out of nowhere in a clipped and commanding enough tone for his 'name, rank and number' and even if he's spent only the briefest time in uniform he'll involuntarily sit up a little straighter and reel off an eight-digit number. Knocking around the laundry basket of anyone who's deployed on operations will be clothes with 'ZAP numbers' inked in to the labels. I'm not sure what is more tragic: that my old shirts still bear the legend HE2167, my own personal barcode, under the collar, or that with only the slightest of prompting (perhaps when the breeze catches the aggressive bark of a passing Glaswegian) I can even remember my Sandhurst number, 25181380, but both go to show how instinctive a thing one's 'number' is. Of course it's depersonalizing, of course it's part of the process by which we were stripped down, but it also happens to be an incredibly efficient way of organizing and referencing hundreds and hundreds of men and the fact that the ANA didn't do it was a nightmare. Only later did we stop to realize that this wasn't wanton inefficiency but a numeracy issue – if you couldn't read or count then a piece of card with your surname, digits and picture on it might just as well have been a passport photo.

It wasn't our predecessors' fault either. They had spent six frustrating months trying to get to grips with the ANA brigade administration, and even good ideas proved tricky. One intelligent Marine had obviously asked all the soldiers he'd tried to

catalogue for their father's name in an attempt to distinguish –
Muhammad son of Muhammad rather than Muhammad son of
Hossain Ali. It almost worked as a system, but things got a bit
complicated when one of our incoming clerks spent a whole
day confusing the 'father's name' and 'home town' columns, and
we only noticed when someone looking at the list asked why so
many Afghans were called Kabul. In two weeks of trying to
work out exactly how many soldiers were in 1st Kandak and
where they all were, we ran out of different colours to shade
uncertain data and imaginative ways to annotate our meaningless lists with the standard response NFI – no fucking idea.

The first few weeks we spent in the country were almost entirely
self-absorbed. We were so short of the vital kit we would be relying on for the next few months that none of it could be spared to
be sent back to England to train on, so we spent days cramming
on long-range satellite radios and grenade machine-guns and the
evenings testing ourselves on crib sheets, scared to fuck we
wouldn't remember how to call in the air support. It was essential, but I think we also busied ourselves with 'acclimatization'
training as displacement activity to put off the inevitable and
more daunting training that lurked on the other side of the Hesco,
the physical manifestation of all the barriers between us and the
ANA, Camp Shorabak's own little blast-proof Berlin wall. The
frustration of that disconnect was clear. With a predictability and
depressing laziness of which I'm more than a little ashamed, my
own diary entries in those first weeks jump squarely on the
unimaginative bandwagon. Of the day we met the *kandak*, the
same day the gloomy fog had lifted, I had written: 'Well, we did
see the hills, and the Afghans, who were pretty fucking insane . . .'
    At a sweep I had just dismissed an entire army, an entire
people in fact, as 'pretty fucking insane'. Like everyone else I
was struck only by the henna-dyed hair of the squad 'pretty

boys' and the 'insolent' smoking of hash. Insolent is an interesting word to have used. The beers being drunk up in Kabul presumably weren't being drunk 'insolently'. The female soldiers off duty over in Camp Bastion presumably weren't wearing their shorts and T-shirts insolently, but such was the presumption with which we arrived and so comprehensively did we carry our own world and social mores wherever it was we went that I obviously couldn't see the arrogance of sitting there on my camp cot in the middle of Helmand writing about the insolent Afghans in my pretentious black Moleskine.

Far more important than the contents of leather-bound, delusions-of-Hemingway diaries were our working notes, but they were no less gloomy. Organized and important officers carried waterproof Nyrex folders, A4 with clear pockets and zips and pen-holders. In general, the sergeants' mess still preferred the traditional credit-card-sized flip-book with a tiny pencil which resided as it had done since day one of basic training in the left breast pocket. The fashion at the time for junior officers was for bright-green, US-issue Federal Supply Service notebooks, which we presumably carried as some sort of disingenuous badge of having been on coalition ops, as if we'd been with the US Marine Corps in Fallujah as opposed to having stolen them from a giant base in Baghdad. The early operational picture was as bleak as my personal reflections. On practically the first page, under '3 Company, 1 Kandak', is a series of far from encouraging bullet points, even Mujib's name misspelled:

3 × NCOs + 1 × XO (Majhid)
9 Men (!)
Poss. 40 new draft
Poss. 30 on leave??
PKM + *Dushka* top priority
3 PKM broken, 1 *Dushka*

You didn't have to have done the full year at Sandhurst to know that an infantry company needed more than nine soldiers, three non-commissioned officers and a second-in-command. I'm ashamed now that I wasted ink on the superfluous exclamation mark. Forty new draft would beef up the numbers, but would have to be integrated and trained further, not to mention equipped – with what? We didn't know if the thirty guys 'possibly' on leave were on leave as in coming back or on leave as in we'd never see them again. Mujib had just shrugged when I asked. As for the machine-guns and heavy weapons, well, we'd worry about them if we ever actually got out of the gate, which with the state of our manpower it didn't seem like we ever would, or could. I'd obviously asked the XO what else he wanted me to look into, essentials for the *kandak*, and there follow even more depressing and almost existential notes, random scribbled words and despairing punctuation: 'Vehicles?' 'Bedding!!'

It was only later, walking around the *kandak* lines, that the true scale of what we were facing became apparent: bedding was an understatement. The shock of the first meeting with the ANA had been the physical differences between us; walking round the empty dormitories in which the *askar* lived, you realized how different our respective worlds were. Over on our side of camp we had been thrown together thirty men to a room, a few square feet of personal space around our cots with all our possessions in a bag underneath and just a mosi-net for privacy, but that was part and parcel of being sent on operations for six months, and we were still furious about it. The more appropriate comparison for ANA Shorabak would have been our barracks back home in Aldershot: far from luxurious but at the very worst junior Guardsmen living in four-man rooms with furniture, decorations and possessions. The ANA were in some cases living in forty-man dorms, bleak rows of metal bunk-beds on concrete floors with a few shared sinks and lavatories in a

Low-level training with 3 Tolay. Mujib and I are discussing something with Shabi;
the guy waving is, I think, Sergeant Nadir. Despite a few 'wazzing' berets on show,
encouragingly everyone is wearing uniform. Of greater concern seems to be that we
were obviously sharing one rifle between about five guys. April 2007.

small room at the end which felt more like prison blocks than a
barracks. My first, naive instinct was that the *kandak* was undergoing an austerity regimen, some sort of cathartic training
punishment in which personal possessions and splashes of colour had been banned along with duvets and anything comfortable
like we used to get at Sandhurst when we'd been naughty. Of
course this wasn't the case, Syed had explained later, smiling at
my assumption; it was much more simply that the soldiers didn't
have any possessions. They turned up from basic training with
the kit they could carry and were allotted a bunk-bed – home,
sweet home.

Babysitting in Kabul

Over the first few weeks we spent working with the *kandak* progress was painfully slow. My company had gained another officer with the arrival of Lieutenant Abdul Marouf, who was one of the originals and just back off leave. Marouf was a welcome addition, described by the Marines as having a 'methodical, logical approach to business', and I warmed to him the moment I read his profile, which recorded, simply and quite sweetly, that his hobbies were 'tourism and picnics'. His 'long-term aspirations', like seemingly every other officer in Afghanistan, were (sic) 'to be a general'. Most importantly, however, and unlike his absentee boss, the Marines had noted of the young Pashtun: 'does achieve results'.

Since returning to Shorabak to find a new set of clueless mentors, however, Marouf had worn an almost permanently grumpy, borderline suicidal frown. He assented to our draft training programmes with barely perceptible sighs and stood to the side of the early lessons we tried to conduct with a look of undisguised contempt. Monday morning patrolling formations, Monday afternoon PT, Tuesday on the ranges, Wednesday practising searching for IEDs – it was all laughably low-level, activity for the sake of it. Faced with a *kandak* which was so chronically undermanned we didn't have enough soldiers to do even that properly, we decided instead to try a little spring cleaning. The *kandak* armouries turned out to be a room with a metal cage and a haystack of AK47s in the middle of the floor: it looked like an arms factory had thrown up. From the state of some of the weapons it was clear that they weren't being cared for, so we started the soldiers who were there on basic weapon husbandry under Marouf's supervision and appointed Mujib and our sergeants to oversee the transformation of the stores into somewhere weapons and kit could actually be stored.

The first time Marouf actually smiled was when the news broke that the *kandak* was to get reinforcements, some 400-odd soldiers fresh out of training up in Kabul, to bring us up to full strength before our rumoured deployment out into the Green Zone. The gloomy lieutenant had an entire platoon up to that point consisting of just himself and Ismail, a striking Hazara boy from Daikondi who grinned the whole time but never spoke so was simply known as 'Smiler'. Smiler was always punctual and correctly dressed but by some established understanding which bypassed all the mentors he was never actually expected to take part in training or handle a weapon, and his chief duty, at which he excelled, was providing hot, sweet *chai* at a moment's notice.

Qiam was a peripatetic presence around the *kandak* in those days, sometimes in the office, sometimes apparently not even on camp, often someone would tell us, out at the market in Gereshk. Nonetheless he had been the first with news about the new draft and had told us confidently that someone would be sent up to Kabul a full twenty-four hours before the tasking was confirmed by our own Brigade HQ. Taking an interest and hands-on approach which we hadn't previously seen, he had gate-crashed one of my daily, slow progress meetings with Mujib and insisted that we should be the ones to escort the recruits back down to Helmand ourselves. As this was the first I had heard of any new draft I politely pretended to make a note in my little green book and dismissed it as another bit of nonsense, but he had been surprisingly firm: we must go up to Kabul and bring the recruits back ourselves, deliver them straight to him with our own Grenadier hands. What I took at the time for a touching faith in our pastoral care I later learned was more to do with the fact that the ANA brigade staff just assumed that whichever ISAF troops turned up to collect the recruits were the ones who subsequently 'owned' them, and the 1st Kandak officers were desperately and rightly worried that, if any other *kandak* got their hands on them first, we'd never see any of them.

The 475 newly minted pride of the Kabul Military Training Centre were probably and quite rightly supposed to be spread evenly across the weary and undermanned units throughout the province: 2/3/205, the 2nd Kandak, was haemorrhaging men in casualties up in Sangin and desperate for back-fill, as was 3/3/205, the 3rd Kandak, who at that exact moment were stuck out in a canal somewhere with the Inkerman Company chasing a drug dealer who had a feud with the *kandak* commander. 4/3/205, which was destined to be a combat support *kandak*, didn't even exist, so they probably needed a couple of soldiers. Instead, and unknown even to myself as I got the order that night to fly up to Kabul with a small detachment and escort the new recruits back down to Helmand, it turned out that we were on a mission to steal them all for our own *kandak* or, more specifically, for Qiam.

Fresh into Afghanistan, fresh on to Op Herrick VI, fresh to the idiosyncrasies of ANA, we weren't to know that our little adventure up to Kabul and back bore all the hallmarks of what had been and what was to come: one of those convenient microcosm stories so beloved of writers and with which Helmand was so generous. We set off with a clear and noble aim, too few in number, too brief in the planning, requiring the cooperation of various known and unknown agencies, not all of whom were singing from our hymn sheet. We didn't really know where we were going, didn't know the lie of the land and assumed, wrongly as it turned out, that all we really had to do was turn up at the gates of the Kabul Military Training Centre, sign for the new kids, form them up in a crocodile and get them to follow us, holding our rifles up like the rainbow umbrellas of Japanese tourist guides, all the way back down to Shorabak. The *kandak* commanders, our own battalion commanders, both the ANA and UK brigade commanders all thought we were doing something slightly different: picking up new men for the *kandak*, picking up new men for the Grenadiers to train, picking up new men to guard HQ in Kandahar, doing God knows what as long as it didn't distract everyone from whatever the Royal Anglians were up to. SNAFU, as they used to say during the Second World War: Situation Normal. All Fucked Up.

What was most prophetic and appropriate about that particular escapade, Operation Chaperone,★ was the way it nearly turned into a debacle and was somehow rescued by hard work, improvisation and sheer luck: cf. every previous and subsequent operation in Afghanistan. Of course the 'terps had all been told they were on an escort trip up to Kabul, but not that they had to come back down straight away. Two guys disappeared into the night as soon as we'd spilled disorientated off the back of a bumpy C-130 and into the pitch-black of Kabul International Airport and nearly walked across the runway instead of towards the terminal building. One-third of our Afghan-speaking power disappeared behind the roar of a couple of F15 E Strike Eagles. I couldn't really blame them: it wasn't that different from the time we'd been sent to London from Sandhurst to get our tunics sorted out by the tailors and had gone AWOL for a few hours ourselves – only difference was, unfortunately for us, the 'terps weren't on parade the next morning, hungover or not. Even so,

★ Sergeant T thought 'Op Trolley Dolly' would have been more apposite, but I thought probably not quite politically correct enough for the written reports, which, as it turned out, would eventually be wiki-leaked.

we did manage to find our charges. Nearly 500 bemused-looking Afghans weren't hard to find in an airfield throbbing with kitted-up and preposterously uniformed NATO partners mostly poncing about in the various kit shops; the problem was getting them on the planes.

The Belgians running the grandly and optimistically titled International Departures Terminal (a white tent by the runway) didn't want to let the Afghans into the tent and so when we found them they were all sat on their kit outside like puppies who weren't allowed on the carpet. If we'd had more time it would have been interesting to question the Belgians on what country they actually thought we were in, but the more immediate problem was how to get our new draft through the entry point to the airfield and on to the planes past the idiotic and uncooperative Brussels bureaucrat.* There's something persuasive about six foot and four inches of finger-jabbing gold-bloke,† and pretty soon we were shepherding the first of the warriors on to the tarmac, but it was once we started loading that chaos really broke out.

Not one of the 475 newly trained ANA warriors had ever been on a plane before: of course they hadn't. With the help of a couple of remarkably good-looking USAF girls enticing everyone in and demonstrating how to do up seatbelts, most of the guys went for it with good grace and in the spirit of adventure. A decent handful, however, watching the endless traffic of the runway in front of them, put two and two together and decided that they didn't fancy an airborne tour. Some called for the 'terps and requested to travel by road, but a couple just dropped their

---

* At least there was some consolation in the confirmation that the phenomenon of annoying jobsworths in Air Movement jobs was a truly international one.

† Because corporals in the Guards were called lance-sergeants and allowed to wear the three chevrons that denoted a sergeant to the rest of the Army, full sergeants in the Guards had gold as opposed to white chevrons on their tunics and were known in traditional Grenadier vernacular as 'gold-blokes'.

bags on the spot and started legging it back to the terminal and had to be scooped up by one of Belgians we'd co-opted as a sweeper. Even to the seasoned flier, transport planes are imposing: stripped of the thin cosmetic veneer and upholstery of a passenger airliner and, no matter who you are, there is something ominous about the slow closing of the rear ramp as the pitch of the engine roar increases. I suspect those who have done a lot of military flying associate it with the nerves of setting off, the start of a tour or an op; for the really bold it must evoke the thrill of knowing that the next time it will open you will be in mid-air and leaping out of the back. Thank God we weren't doing anything like that.

As it was, it was all too much for a bearded and senior-looking corporal who leaped out of his seat and made a dash to rival Indiana Jones himself out through the shrinking gap, but was bundled to the floor by a burly loadie and sat shaking in his seat as we roared down the runway and banked steeply up past the iconic mountains that ring Kabul. Perhaps these newly trained *askar* had long enough memories of when the airfield was a battered Russian enclave; perhaps some of them had even sat up in the snow in those mountains and fired off precious stingers and were now worried that one of these fat, slow birds would be their own coffin. Midway through the flight things were relaxed enough for the seatbelts to come off and everyone to stretch their legs and peer out of the windows at the clouds and beguiling desert landscape speeding below. I passed the time watching the sense of wonder on expressive faces, the tentative approach to the bright window as if one might get sucked out, the confusion and then realization of passing through streaky vapour clouds and grasping the reality of hills and rivers far, far below. Confusion gave way to a wondrous joy, innocent even on the older, gnarled and bearded faces of the more senior warriors, more than a few of whom shuffled back to their seats and offered quick and quiet prayers of thanks, and why not?

It would have all been too easy to simply fly straight in to Helmand, to land at Camp Bastion and form orderly queues for the quick ride to Shorabak. Instead we landed in Kandahar, where the recruits, only just recovered from their first flight, got what was clearly the first and equally troubling inkling of where they were being posted. Kandahar was the Taliban's old capital and the key to the south: the reporting papers might as well have just said: 'Do not pass Go, do not collect £200'. The problem with Helmand was that the massive C-17s couldn't land at Bastion: the runway hadn't been extended sufficiently then, and there was probably a rule about the wrong sort of dust. The German C-130s could have done, but the German mission didn't extend into Helmand, so the pilots dropped us off and, full of apologies, headed back to Kabul for a Thai takeaway supper. Being marooned in Kandahar presented a different problem. Once everybody was accounted for, sat as they had been hours earlier on kit bags outside another white tent – on the plane, off the plane – there was no more uncertainty about where we were taking them, and it wasn't a popular choice.

We were under strict orders from all directions to bring everyone straight to Shorabak, but with an overnight delay and nowhere for 475 Afghans to sleep in Kandahar airfield itself, we had to truck everyone over to Camp Shirzai, the 205 Corps headquarters just outside the airfield. The new 'heroes' got a briefing on arrival from a shambolic-looking colonel with a clipboard and, whatever it was he said, mayhem ensued. More experienced-looking soldiers started muttering darkly and those with any influence or cash instantly started trying to bribe whoever seemed to be around who looked like they could post them elsewhere. There was nothing new in this: the crisp dollar bills folded into the papers of the incoming GIs and discreetly handed to the posting clerk at Da Nang or wherever was a staple of Vietnam War mythology; then again you suspected that most of the ANA new draft hadn't come up on *Platoon* and *Apocalypse Now* like the rest of their ISAF allies.

Given that many of these young soldiers were only then getting the news officially that they had been posted to the most dangerous part of the country, the response was pretty calm. The disappointed, resigned faces of all soldiers are similar whether you're sat on your kit in Kandahar being told your R&R flight home is delayed, sat on a sandbag out in a patrol base being told that the tour has been extended a couple of weeks or sat on a rolled-up prayer mat in the dust outside 205 Corps HQ being told that you'll be spending the next three years of your life in Helmand, if you survive that long, but I was still impressed by how the Afghans took the news. My detachment, lolling over by the pick-up, sharing fags with the 'terps and wondering how to get one of the famous cinnamon donuts from Timmy Horton's, the Canadian coffee shop, before we shipped out, had all undergone months of training through Catterick. They were volunteer infantrymen who might have been lied to a little bit by the recruiting sergeant, might have expected a little bit more adventure training and a little less drill, but who for the most part had chosen their path and joined their regiment with eyes open and pride in their step in the hope and anticipation of just such a deployment as this. More to the point, they had all known that they would be spending the best part of 2007 in Helmand months earlier, had been lectured to the point of boredom on it, trained to the point of exhaustion for it and trusted that, if they stayed low and moved fast, they would be leaving it all behind again in a few months. Compared to them the ANA new draft had spent ten weeks up in Kabul being trained by an understaffed mishmash of foreigners through over-worked interpreters, making do with sticks for rifles while dealing with, for many of them, being away from home for the first time in their lives. Sure, if you asked them, they all hated the Taliban and were fighting for their country, and what better motivation did a guy need? But just like my boys, like any professional army, the reality was as much if not more about the job than the cause, about the paycheque as much as the payback. We left them to their wrangling and their newly discovered fate.

There was nowhere for us to sleep in KAF (as Kandahar Airfield was known), but that sort of thing mattered less: there was always a cot or a bench to doss on somewhere, and those large bases had their own twenty-four-hour rhythm, the tempo slowing perhaps a little at night when it got, if not dark, with the sea of glo-sticks marking out runways and piercing bright spotlights on in unsleeping repair hangars, at least darker, if not quiet, with the constant hum of generators and low thwock of helicopters and the higher-pitched peal of the 'fixed wings' coming and going, at least quieter. We managed to find a brew station at the back of the vast UK ops tent: even in the middle of the night a bustle of desks and phones and radio chatter and real-time unit info thrown up on digitally projected maps. Helped to the milk and sugar by a second-lieutenant so fresh out of Sandhurst you had to wonder if he wasn't finding it all as bemusing as the Afghans we had just left: weaving timidly between busy-looking loggy majors and thrusting J5 staff officers with PJHQ* patches,

---

* Permanent Joint Headquarters in Northwood. Staff officers were those working desks or plans or headquarters jobs (from back in the day when they had been on the general staff rather than with their regiments). A deployed planning job was hard work, albeit hard desk work, but a good and necessary step on the career path of an ambitious officer. Numbers were assigned by all NATO countries to different aspects of planning from 1 (Personnel) through to 9 (Civilian and Military Cooperation). Depending on whether it was an Army (G for General Staff), Navy (N), or Joint (J) post it would have a different letter, so SO2 G4 was a staff officer grade 2 (a major) in an Army post in charge of Logistics; J5 was the planning branch in a joint headquarters: a thruster's job if ever there was one.

he'd come a long way in a short time from final exercise in Cyprus or Brecon, where HQ had been a battered table and an OS map covered in pins behind the OC's* Land Rover. We were all out of our comfort zones one way or another and never more so than when I finally managed to get a line down to my own HQ and was told to hurry the fuck up because my 475 Afghans were no longer just good news on the manning tables and some more bodies for us to train, they were essential for the brigade's first big operation: 12 Mechanized Brigade's first all-singing, all-dancing, all-shooting, joint UK and Afghan, tell your grandchildren and mightily bored they will be offensive operation. Next week.

How many of the 475 did I think I'd actually bring back? I was sufficiently excited or nervous that night about the forthcoming operation that I didn't really think about what the consequences would be if I came back light. We were missing a couple of 'terps, but I had no command responsibility for the 'terps; in ISAF's eyes they were grown-ups who could look after themselves. Technically I had no command responsibility over the ANA either, and they were all grown-ups too, but if the whole escapade demonstrated anything it was the extent to which ISAF didn't consider them to be: the ANA were to be counted right into their dormitories and counted out again the next morning. I'd seen the frantic negotiations underway as we had left the 475 at Camp Shirzai for the night. I'd even seen the more nervous and more bold eyeing the flimsy perimeter fence and Kandahar beyond, maybe calculating the odds of slipping out and taking their chances with the looming mountains on the horizon. Now that there was really work to be done as soon as we got back I suspected that I'd be in some sort of trouble in inverse proportion to how many of the new soldiers I actually

* Officer Commanding, which in the British Army invariably means specifically a company commander rather than just anyone in charge of anything.

turned up with, but didn't hold out much hope for more than half, which seemed to be the going attrition rate at the time.

Bright and early the next morning 471 of the finest and freshest new recruits to the Afghan National Army paraded at Camp Shirzai to be escorted back to the airfield and onwards, to Helmand. I could scarcely believe my luck. Someone assured us that the missing four had been destined for Corps HQ all along, I was too glad to have the 471 that I did not worry about the missing four. We lost one further man, a casualty of his own greed and curiosity. One of the last chalk who had been sat patiently all day outside the transit tent (too messy, according to the pointy-sideburned twat, to be allowed to sit inside like British and Estonian troops waiting for the same flights, who – what – had all been to military finishing school?) who had been issued with the Halal MREs (the US meals ready to eat) and in his hunger had polished off not only the dubious veggie burger hash, pasty cheese and packet of Skittles but also the heating element with which you were supposed to warm the whole thing up beforehand. He was rushed off to the med centre, curled up with stomach cramps in the back of a pick-up, by a friendly US Marine who was passing: the first casualty of our tour, but sadly not the last.

Exhausted, hungry and even more apprehensive than we had previously been about working alongside an army we had now seen up close and in transit for the first time, we arrived back at Shorabak with 470 out of 475 new draft. One of the four 'terps had phoned ahead to tell his mates about the two who'd done a runner in Kabul: so much for OPSEC and COMSEC. As any information in Shorabak seemed to do, it got around the whole camp within about half an hour, so our welcoming committee was a mightily relieved couple of British officers, a bemused Afghan colonel, a delighted ANA S1 captain in charge of personnel with a table and clipboard at the ready, a faintly curious Mujib and a pissed-off Qiam. Behind the huddle on the helipad the evening game of touch rugby was underway, and the ANA shuffling back from evening meal seemed to be more curious about the strange game being played by their mentors than about their new comrades. In the end the *kandak* did get the bulk of the new draft. They would form the core of the guys we would fight with for the next six months, and I'd sometimes get a friendly smile from a faintly familiar face on patrol and realize that it was one of the lads I taken for their first-ever plane ride. Qiam even managed to squirrel away a couple of the leaner-and-meaner-looking old guys who we suspected he already knew from back in the day, so everyone was happy, but, if you stopped for a second and thought about it, the conduct of and indeed necessity for the whole little trip posed a few awkward, lingering questions.

There was the uncomfortable contrast between the Afghan new draft and that young Guardsman I still remember, deploying abroad for the first time. That nervous thrill of flying for the first time may have been the same for both of them, a mingling of apprehension and youthful excitement which felt hollow in your stomach and may have been why all the young recruits were hungry the minute we got on the plane – at least the RAF gave you a sausage roll. Beyond that, however, there was a difference in approach which said everything about how two armies treated their blokes. Recruiting in the British Army retained a regional element in some parts of the country, and there was no doubt that the odd recruiting sergeant played a little fast with the truth, but there was both choice and information all the way. Guardsmen knew they'd be becoming Guardsmen, which meant, like Riflemen and Fusiliers and Jocks and even Johnny

Gurkha, first and foremost they'd be infantrymen: colder, wetter, tireder and harder than everyone else. If you wanted to drive a tank, blow things up, cook, fly, teach or anything else the Army did, if you showed the desire and met the standard, that's what you'd be doing and you'd go through training for it, knowing ultimately where you were headed, who your regiment was, where it would be based and, subject to the ever-fluid tempo and requirement of operations, what you'd be doing. The odd fire-strike cover might come as a bit of a surprise, and when the chips were down with men deployed in numbers on two fronts, people's holidays took a bit of a battering and there was less give in the system, but you never got guys like Sergeant Ahmed who very politely and calmly tried to explain on the flight into Helmand that there must have been some mistake as he was supposed to be in the Artillery and, so he said, had been told in Kabul that he was being sent back to his old unit somewhere far, far away in the north to carry on training the next generation of Afghan gunners. Something had gone seriously awry when you were in the wrong trade, in the wrong unit heading to the wrong side of the country. I never saw him again.

More typical was a complete failure to provide any information at all. That only four of them had done one on hearing the news of their destination at such a late stage was surely comparable with the sort of desertion or refusal rates that any volunteer army deals with. Perhaps the flip-side of the failure to brief or prepare was that even at that stage the guys still weren't quite sure what they had signed up for. It was at times like that you remembered that the old Afghan Army had been Soviet-run, that many of the old-timers in the Afghan MoD had learnt their trade in Moscow and still copied the over-centralized, controlling Red Army model which abused its grunts and took them for granted even more than most armies. All soldiers are mushrooms sometimes – anyone in a uniform has been kept in the dark and fed on shit more often than they'd care to remember – but the amount of propaganda, half-lies and downright bullshit that was flying around Kabul and the way the average ANA warrior was treated by his country were and still are pretty shocking.

And if the whole exercise prompted some serious questions about the ANA, what about its ISAF partners? The most profound question I asked myself when I finally flopped back down on my camp cot to catch up with some *Brass Eye* was why? Why did twelve of us have to go up to Kabul at all? Why did the ANA need to be ushered through their own country by an ad hoc group of Grenadier glorified sheepdogs: grateful to be out of camp and enthusiastic no doubt, but you had to think, deep down, surely surplus to requirements. I decided it was because of the journey. Out of Bastion on a British C-130 to Kandahar, our stately progression had then been as follows: from Kandahar to Kabul on what I think was an American Hercules, but by then it was the middle of the night and without wishing offence the accents in the dark could have been Canadian; ushered back out of Kabul by stroppy Belgians and back down to KAF, our numbers now swelled by 475 (minus two) on a giant, definitely American C-17 Globemaster, the jumbo jet of military flying, but not without the assistance of a spare couple of German and Italian transport aircraft; finally from KAF on to the British-run air-bridge into Helmand, helped out by the Dutch . . . (catch your breath) . . . and none of them, not a single one of those nations, would have dealt with the Afghans alone. Nothing to do with the willing and often brave pilots who were mostly happy to fly whoever, wherever and did. When I asked the question, it was explained to me that it was ISAF policy not to allow 'unaccompanied' Afghans on to military flights. We were manning, equipping, training and fighting and dying alongside an army of soldiers we didn't trust enough to let on to the plane without holding their hands. It was as if the only thing missing at the gate of Camp Shorabak was one of those height restriction measures: a brightly painted, woodchip cut-out of a cartoon Taliban holding a tape measure. Bad luck, kids, you could die in a ditch in the Green Zone, but weren't allowed unaccompanied on the Helmand Experience Roller Coaster unless you were taller than 4 foot 11, or a foreigner.

Syed Meraj

Our trip to Kabul was an exhausting and in many ways dispiriting glimpse of the worst of ISAF and the madness of Afghanistan, but somewhere during those seventy-two hours something clicked for me, and you can even see it in the photos. Up until we went to Kabul the photos I have are all tourist snaps, mostly us posing with Gucci* kit, perhaps a handful of snaps of the ANA looking suitably exotic, but always separate, always taken as if we were on safari, an invisible finger pointing excitedly at the Afghans. Up until we went to Kabul we had woken up in our camp and walked across to Shorabak; even on our longest days of training we had only spent five or six unbroken hours with the ANA before heading back to our camp to dinner and bed. Up until we went to Kabul we had been facing the ANA, us trying to train them, them infuriating us. The first photos I have of us actually together, ANA and OMLT side by side, are those which were taken during the first seventy-two hours we actually spent in sync: what we had needed was a sense of common purpose.

What that trip also brought home in a way the glib videos and embellished after-dinner anecdotes of our training never could was the complexity of our relationship with the ANA; it was much more symbiotic than we had previously been led to believe.

---

* Slang for anything considered new or good. God only knows why it ended up being Gucci as opposed to any other fashion house, but there it was. Complimenting someone on their new Prada webbing would just have sounded stupid.

Sure, they depended on us for coordination, combat support, all the stuff that would win the battles, but without them we were just a handful of lonely guys lost in a big desert, protecting sceptical civvies back home from a threat I considered so long-since disappeared as to be faintly spurious – if we weren't making London safer, which I was pretty sure we weren't, we had, at least, to be trying to make Afghanistan better, and for that we needed the ANA as much as they needed us.

I always associated Sergeant Syed Meraj with that more difficult, more reflective but surely more important goal. Qiam always provided a spark, a brilliant, living cause for the fight and a potent reminder how mad and devoted and terrifying and magnificent the Afghans could be in that fight, but it was Syed who was a gentle but insistent reminder of why the fight was important in the first place, a vision of a better possible future. Where Qiam was all passion, Syed exuded smiling reason. Qiam was the guy you wanted at a party because he was so entertaining; Syed was the guy you wanted to be sat next to and have a decent chat with. He was my bullshit filter, maybe the one guy in the whole *kandak* who I knew had no agenda, was telling the truth, maybe the one guy in the whole *kandak* I could actually talk to, no artifice, no exaggeration, no lies and inconsistencies: by the end of the tour I wanted to fight with Qiam, sure, but I wanted to fight for Syed.

Syed was another of the originals; like Qiam he'd been with the *kandak* since its formation. He was on leave when we had first arrived. In his absence Mujib and I had struggled manfully with all variety of lists and nominal rolls, photographed all the individual soldiers we could find so we could try and fix who was who, identified the key non-commissioned officers who seemed to be able to motivate the lazy ones out of bed when we were trying to train them and even over the course of one agonizing and nerve-racking and sun-burning day on the ranges, just about worked out who could and couldn't shoot, but 3 Company, 1st Kandak was still a mess. Syed had turned up about three weeks after we'd arrived, another soldier back off leave whom we hadn't even realized we were missing, but, as it turned out, more than just another soldier.

Maybe it was simply the fact that Syed spoke better English than any other *askar* that got us off on the right foot: better English than some of the 'terps, in fact. He'd learned it from his father, an engineer who had been trained with the USAID money which had come into Afghanistan back in the fifties and sixties and which was why even in Helmand you still saw the odd part from an old John Deere tractor jerry-rigged to a generator and various other relics of a previous and less-destructive American presence. The pride with which he spoke of his father, of the regard in which he was held back home in Mazar-i-Sharif because of his engineering skills, his professionalism, was one of those things that briefly and tantalizingly made you think the whole country wasn't fucked – briefly. He didn't announce himself grandly like Qiam, he was suddenly just there, in the office, stood to the side watching training, chatting to the 'terps and to us and to his soldiers and calmly making things happen. Just in the nick of time, as it turned out: within days of his arrival, we began to prepare for our first big op, Op Silicon.

We tried to impress on everyone in the *kandak* that with the announcement of the forthcoming deliberate operation to clear the valley north of Gereshk we weren't just training for the fun of it. Fittingly, the reality of what we were doing was brutally hammered home as we took an afternoon off training to stand sombrely to attention at the first repatriation ceremony for the first fatality of the tour, standards noticeably improved. With less nagging than before, squads would be where we'd asked them to be, on time and fully manned. We thought these small but warming signs of progress were a response to the *kandak* finally having concrete plans; we might even have flattered ourselves that our mentoring was taking effect. It was actually because Syed was back from leave. Syed was only a platoon sergeant, but he seemed to have a disproportionate effect on the whole company as he took responsibility for squads that weren't his and dragged the other, previously anonymous NCOs along with him. There was never any doubt that the ANA had plenty of natural scrappers, but you still needed someone to sift through the new draft, someone to assign troops to task and get them out on parade, nearly all correctly dressed, the next morning. In camp we didn't notice because we were still living side by side, rather than on top of each other, but once we got out on the ground, fighting out of the patrol bases and living day by day, we realized it was Syed that did all that, he was the guy that made the trains run, and, as it turned out, he'd come back just in time.

After false starts and missions aborted and jealously watching other units and other *kandak*s charging around Helmand, 1/3/205's big moment had come with the planning and launch of Operation Silicon, the largest offensive operation the British had launched in Afghanistan in almost a century,[6] the first major operation to clear the treacherous Green Zone and, most importantly, the first large-scale operation which was to have independent ANA sub-units in the mix. Up until that point the ANA and their mentors had been force multipliers and mission justifiers, platoons here and there tagged on to the end for local knowledge or 'partnering' legitimacy and, when the chips were down and the plans had gone to rat-shit, useful extra bodies in the fight, but they'd never had responsibility in the plan itself.

Op Silicon was supposed to be different and, because we wanted so desperately to get out there, the obvious answer to any questions about the readiness of our *kandak* to be its main

ANA element was 'yes'. Yes they were raring to go, yes they were firing on all cylinders, yes they'd be able to hold their own. When the various orders were relayed to Mujib he just shook his head, caught between laughing and smiling: Ready? Willing? Able? It didn't matter really, did it, we were going to find out one way or the other. It was over the next few days that strange things started to happen. At roll call for orders and to explain the new and exciting plan there were twice as many soldiers as we were used to, completely new faces making a mockery of our painstakingly compiled photo boards. Syed later explained that once word had got round that there was a real op on, rather than just bullshit training, guys who had been hiding in Shora-bak or chilling out on leave, not quite AWOL but not exactly where they should have been, decided it was time to undertake the long journey back. We were so pathetically grateful that things were starting to come together we just accepted it.

Soldiers we did recognize, but who had spent the last few weeks in T-shirts and flip-flops, guys we'd been pestering the quartermaster to get boots for, were stood not exactly to attention but at least in full uniform. Body armour and helmets, of which we'd been told the *kandak* had none, started appearing in the lines, and there was that general sense of urgency which is standard military issue at home, but which we had so long given up hope of seeing that it almost caught us out. The first time I met Syed must have been when I was stood open-mouthed wondering if Shabi, the fun, young 'terp, had got it right, staring at this completely unfamiliar sergeant who was asking, in more or less fluent English, for more training. It was like a scene out of *Oliver*, the Army version. *More?*

After Mujib and I had gratefully accepted the encouraging new sergeant's requests and ramped up the training programme somewhat, pitifully thankful that someone, anyone in an ANA uniform seemed inclined to do some preparation for what by then we were all quite nervous about, Syed became more and more involved until he was the obvious man to go to with any problems, questions or ideas. In the frantic final days before we launched the big op, days when it seemed at any moment like the whole thing would have to be called off, or simply wasn't possible, and we all veered between praying that it would all be OK and secretly hoping that we'd get dropped because 'OK' was about the last thing the ANA were, Syed was a constant, calming presence. Invariably smiling and with more English than he even let on at first, he acted as a mediator between our increasingly frantic demands for the ANA to prepare more thoroughly and the soldiers in our company's stubborn refusal to do much more than clean their weapons and construct precarious-looking piles of gaudy blankets and pot plants, without which, we were alarmed to discover, they would refuse to deploy. I also noticed for the first but not the last time the calming effect he had on Qiam, a moderate counterweight to Qiam's fiery and unreasonable temper.

During the constantly changing planning of Op Silicon, as we tried to cobble together a coherent *kandak* that wouldn't embarrass us and itself in front of the rest of the brigade, Qiam flew into the room where Mujib, Marouf, Syed and myself were sat trying to work out who should command the respective squads, shouting angrily and clutching a scrunched-up sheet of paper. I recognized the poorly drawn pictures of generic 'cars' as my own crude attempt to portray the order of march for the ANA vehicles (more Model-T Fords with stickmen at the wheel than anything resembling either ANA Rangers or our own WMIKs, but it had seemed to work at the time). Qiam in one of his moods scared all the 'terps, which only exacerbated the situation as they stuttered their way through translating whatever it was he was shouting and my inability to provide a coherent answer because I didn't know what he was saying would anger him more.

Where in hell, it turned out Qiam wanted to know, were his vehicles? 'Where is the Dushka?' It was a perfectly good question, given that it was news to us that Qiam's Heavy Weapons Company had vehicles at all, let alone that one of the Rangers could be mounted with the 12.7 mm Dushka heavy machine-gun, all good news, but given that we had been trying to catalogue the *kandak*'s vehicles for the past few days, had been pleading with everyone who seemed to be in any way important in the *kandak* to try and build up a vaguely accurate picture of the vehicle state, and that this was the very first we had heard of the vehicles, hardly our fault that we hadn't included them in our planning.

I always liked to think I was better than most at keeping my cool, in general of course, but specifically with the ANA. You lost too much face if you flew into a rage and lost too much of your own energy and sanity in the process. Whenever our senior non-commissioned officers (invariably) or junior officers (less often but usually more pathetically and amusingly) lost their temper the reaction was always the same. The embarrassed 'terp wouldn't quite be able to convey what was being shouted, and the Afghans would just go very quiet, exchanging slight glances which seemed to say, 'Ooh, get her.' On this occasion, however, I was tired and frustrated and wasn't going to sit there and allow myself to be ranted at by a squat madman when, as far as I could tell, the whole thing was the madman's fault. As I was on the verge of launching a reply, which I intended to lace with quite a few choice words about how little effort and energy certain key members of the *kandak* staff were putting into preparing for an operation in which we were all equally vulnerable, Syed stepped in.

A quiet exchange, some raised eyebrows, a bit of pointed finger-jabbing on the crumpled sheet of paper, a soothing word and a hand waved airily over a map, some more eyebrow, reference to a list of incomprehensible numbers and Dari, which

I desperately hope is an up-to-date nominal roll, a pause and then a huge smile. 'Toran Padi,' said Qiam, breaking into a huge smile and pulling me in for a sweaty, musty bear hug, 'I *am* your Dushka.' A pause, and then with a characteristic laugh: '*Boom boom boom boom*,' and he stormed off out of the door, still making ecstatic heavy machine-gun noises as he went. Syed and Mujib exchanged a few further words as I sat down again and turned to Shabi to try and work out what the hell had just happened, but Syed got there first with the words that were to become his catchphrase over the tour and invariably music to my ears: '*mushkill nis*' – no problems. That was Syed and that was how we got everything ready for Operation Silicon.

Op Silicon

Turned out that everything else had been prologue: all that was good and bad, encouraging and bewildering about the operational element, actually fighting with the *kandak*, we learned in the first full twenty-four hours of Op Silicon.

First there was the pleasant surprise of the whole *kandak* ready to go, the last, tense phone-calls home – sorry, love, not sure when I'll be able to call again – and the nervy, sleepless night forgotten the instant we stepped out of camp and were confronted by the majestic, anarchic sight of the *kandak* in all its glory on the helipad in Shorabak. Days of increasingly pressured training had been ramping up to this moment. I'd lost count of the number of times I'd said to any Afghan who'd listen that this time we were doing it for real, this time if they said 90 *askar* were going to be there, then 90 *askar* had to be there, if we said we were leaving at 1600, then we had to leave at 1600. The encouraging noises and enthusiastic nods had been the same as ever, but we'd been here before and invariably been disappointed, so I'd patronizingly laboured the point. This wasn't another training session, I'd said to the collected sergeants and officers the night before, this wasn't something that, if we were late to or there weren't enough of us, then the worst that would happen is we'd all get a bit of a telling off. If we were late then we'd be leaving other soldiers vulnerable, if we got things wrong then we'd be putting other soldiers at risk. This was the real thing. I'd let everyone else go and grabbed a final word with Mujib and Qiam, reminded them in slightly less melodramatic terms that this was a big moment for the *kandak*, for the ANA, the first truly joint operation – we simply couldn't afford to screw it up. Mujib had looked serious, but was impatient to get to supper and waved me off with promises that it would all be fine, everyone would be ready to go tomorrow.

And first thing the next morning, the square was gloriously alive with men and vehicles, abuzz with excited chatter and revving engines. By ANA standards, three neat, long lines of Ford Rangers, one for each company, bristled with AK47s, RPKs, PKMs and RPGs. At the edge of the square an unmistakeable cluster of antennae and smarter vehicles and fatter-looking bods indicated that even the *kandak* HQ group (if obviously not the commanding officer himself) was ready to deploy. We could scarcely believe our luck. Rockets lolling like baguettes in baskets taped to the side of the wagons, oversized flags fluttering from radio antennae, flowers and tinsel lining the cabins, prayer mats and bulging, chintzy sleeping bags tumbling out of the back of the over-stuffed wagons. Warriors who had appeared from nowhere after our long month of haranguing and cajoling and desperately trying to find out who was who and where they were. Soldiers who'd spent the last few weeks sat uninterested throughout training sessions in shorts and T-shirts immaculately attired in various uniforms wearing badges of rank – corporals, sergeants, even bloody officers. Qiam and his heavy weapons squad revving up and down the square, grinning, piratical, in brand new body armour (where had that come from?) hanging off the back of the Dushka, wrapped in chain after chain of link, a cacophonous din of different jingly radio stations blasting out at top volume from half the wagons – we had to pause to take it all in, to try and work out whether we were relieved or appalled, delighted or terrified. In two hours we'd be setting out on the first deliberate op of our tour, on the first proper op of most of our lives. We'd spent the night fretting that we didn't have enough vehicles, didn't have enough troops, didn't have enough firepower – we hadn't been worried about how we'd control the *Mad Max* Army we found waiting for us, nearly 400 warriors in scores of vehicles hooting with impatience on the square.

It was the first time we had actually seen the whole *kandak* as an entity, a fighting unit, and it was more impressive than the sum of its dodgy parts. Infantry battalions form up all the time, in the gym for briefings, on the parade square for smart and shouty and at the very least in reluctant PT kit on a Friday morning. Platoons and companies have their own personalities but they can hinge on certain key individuals; a battalion is too big, and you only get a sense of it when it's all in one place, only get a sense that you're all subsumed into something with its own distinctive identity once you're amongst it, in it, part of it. For the first time the companies we were mentoring were more than arbitrary Dari numbers and long lists of names on scraps of paper, were more than the couple of regular faces we caught in the offices in Shorabak, they were proper units.

With the Captain, Major David, mentoring the *kandak* HQ and partnered with Ataullah the stand-in *kandak* commander, it was left to his three platoon commanders, mere team commanders under the OMLT tasking – me, Lieutenant Will Harries and Lieutenant Folarin Kuku – to mentor the *kandak*'s three companies: Tolay Awal (1), Do (2) and Se (3). Hand in hand with the officers, sergeants and warriors we'd spent the last few weeks first finding and cataloguing, then cajoling and tentatively training and now, we hoped, sufficiently gelled with to be able to operate under fire.

Lieutenant Harries would have his hands full mentoring his fussy *tolay* commander, the grey-bearded Muhammad J—, known universally to his own troops as 'the Lamb'. The Lamb was the worst sort of weak commander: hands-on but ineffective; never actively leading his company, but constantly whingeing and resisting all outside attempts to help; stubbornly refusing to

83

make plans but constantly interfering in everyone else's. He had a nasty habit of only remembering his rank when it suited him, shirking responsibility unless he was in a position to make a call which he liked, which was invariably that his HQ should go back to camp and leave the mentors and his men to get on with whatever the unpleasant task in hand was. His main preoccupation seemed to be an overdue promotion, which he no doubt hoped would elevate him safely behind a desk somewhere in Kandahar, and his constant gripe to anyone who'd listen was that he was supposed to be a colonel – well, who wasn't?

Lieutenant Kuku had a slightly easier job alongside the steady hand of Toran Hazrat, the efficient captain in charge of 2 Tolay. 2 Tolay was the best-manned, best-trained and most professional of the three companies, and even had proper platoon commanders: Gholam Nabi, who looked far too old to be a lieutenant, but by then we were used to the ANA either looking fourteen or forty but nothing in between; and Sharaf Udin, stroking his Charlie Bronson moustache and nurturing his sniper rifle, barely growling at his men but instantly everything was in order. We would banter Kuku after training that it was all a fix, that he'd been given the only well-led, photogenically ready-to-go company in the whole *kandak* because of all the press the MoD would shove his way during the tour, the token shining beacon of Household Division multiculturalism, cringingly paraded as our first black officer. He'd quite rightly tell us to fuck off and point out that it didn't matter to him so long as he had decent troops to work with and deep down we knew we had no come-back to that, because he was right and we were equally jealous of his impressive *tolay* and worried about our own.

As it turned out, I needn't have worried after all. A combination of Syed's influence, Mujib's growing familiarity with his new post and the fact that it was all about to happen for real had galvanized the *askar*, and on the morning of 29 April 2007 3 Tolay and the whole *kandak* alongside looked as ready as any of us could have hoped to set off for a scrap. Even my jealousy of Kuku and Hazrat was diminished by the lucky stroke of an invisible staff officer's pen which had attached Qiam and his Heavy Weapons Company lunatics to my team. The 'Heavy Weapons Company' was roughly the equivalent to what was called the Support Company in a normal British infantry battalion. Traditionally three specialist platoons of fitter, more motivated soldiers commanded by more experienced officers and sergeants, Support Company would provide mobility and firepower to a battalion commander, mortars and anti-tank capability and snipers and recce teams. Qiam's Heavy Weapons Company had the same swagger and confidence of a Support Company, but seemed to be more of a quasi-autonomous militia which had taken possession of the *kandak*'s heavy machine-guns, mounted them on vehicles and couldn't wait to get stuck in. Mujib and Syed, at that early stage at least, may not have exuded the same professionalism and military energy as Hazrat, but at least I knew that they'd be a calming influence on Qiam and his comfortingly fearsome crew.

It all happened over the next twenty-four hours: the terrifying and elating, the ridiculous and the sublime. Op Silicon was supposed to last seven days, but we had been warned it could extend. 'Possibly 10,' I'd written in my notes, which by the end of the op, over a month later, was a standard joke. 'How far out are we pushing on patrol today, sir?' 'One kilometre north,' pause, 'possibly ten.' Whatever, TIA, That Was Afghanistan. Those twenty-four hours, those seven days, those 'possibly 10' which ended up being whatever, they were the hours and days which bonded us with the *kandak* in a way no amount of training could ever have done. They were the hours and days during which we finally stopped thinking in terms of ANA and British, stopped thinking in terms of them and us and became simply us.

The first time I wrote about it made it sound easy: 'And suddenly we're on the dam,' as if the tense move through Gereshk and the chaos and thrill of the ambush on the start line had been inevitable. For all our superior ISTAR capability and meticulous planning, no one had expected the Taliban to open up on us so brazenly, still daylight on the afternoon before the op was supposed to start as we trundled the *kandak* into its starting position on the outskirts of Gereshk. One minute we were rolling slowly up the towpath, using the canal as our axis towards the police checkpoints where we planned to spend the night, more worried about whether the ANA vehicles were following on behind us and whether or not we were on the right route, the next minute an RPG roared from somewhere to the left, not that far over our heads, and with perfect comic timing Pricey and I looked in at each other *beat* back out where the shot had come from *beat* raised our eyebrows *beat* and then crack, a shot, and another and then what seemed like hundreds peppering the path in front of us, and so it began.

The Taliban had chosen the spot for the ambush well: the two forward companies of the *kandak* were strung out along either side of the canal, vulnerable on the raised towpath and restricted from firing across each other for fear of hitting our own guys. About 100 metres down the path was a dam and a flimsy-looking ANP checkpoint, and our best bet was to push forward and coordinate the response from there: 100 metres never seemed so far. In the checkpoint itself was an ancient police commander with wild, white hair and fear in his eyes as if the threat of the incoming rounds zipping over the flimsy corrugated roof was somehow more imminent than the threat of old age, despite how comically old he looked and how comically inaccurate the incoming fire was. Even in the midst of that earliest of introductions to the way time plays with itself in a fight I seemed to linger for endless seconds in wonder at how old the dude was, like Godfrey in *Dad's Army* when I used to watch it at Grandma and Grandpa's, laughing but conscious of never having actually seen someone that old in real life, secretly terrified that he'd die on screen any second.

In Afghan culture, I dimly remembered, great deference was shown to old age. If we hadn't realized it already, we could have noted there and then that Qiam didn't do respect. He jumped into the checkpoint and started boxing the old man around the ears for his spinelessness while his squad, or the remains of it, crouched in foetal positions behind the Hesco, hands over their ears, eyes scrunched up, knees getting damp in the remains of their tea. As the other mentors made their way breathlessly up the flank Nawroz the 'terp explained to me that Qiam and the old policeman were arguing about kit. It was all very well, the cop was complaining, for the soldiers with their helmets and body armour and mentors with Apaches, it was they who were the cowards. Turned out Qiam also had a touch of the Marty McFly about him, no one called him chicken. I was automatically going through radio drills, pinching myself to have finally fired the rifle, which suddenly felt weightless with adrenalin in my hands, grateful for the experience and nous of Colour Sergeant Yates and Sergeant T marshalling things up at the rear, and staring incredulously at this punchy, paunchy Afghan who started stripping off his clothes to prove, screaming at the policeman, that it was nothing to do with helmets and body armour and Apaches, he'd take the Taliban on naked. Pulling at his shirt with his hairy gut hanging out over the top of the cotton long-johns he wore under his combats, dripping sweat in the crowded, stinking sentry box. Sergeant Gillies was up with us by then, and you could tell he'd never seen anything like it in his life, and he'd seen plenty. Qiam raging at the cops, raging at the Taliban, practically flecking at the mouth as he threw his own weapon at another ANP guy who was whingeing about a stoppage, picked up an enormous wrench from the floor and charged out of the position.

There was a word Qiam often used to describe himself, half-boastingly, half-apologetically: *kharkus*, it sounded like, and although none of the 'terps could ever quite translate it, we all knew what it meant: crazy and brave. There is no word in English I can think of that so perfectly captures the grey area where courage and madness overlap. I only found out much later from a linguist that it was actually Dari slang, an 'unacceptable' rude word which I guess must have been literally 'ballsy'. Qiam was often *delawaar*, simply 'brave', and at times he was downright *dewana*, 'crazy', but *kharkus*, was what he would always say, either slapping me on the back of the head after an assault or peering across a ditch, thumbs up, grinning even in the middle of a fire-fight: *kharkus*, a mix of the two, crazy and brave: ballsy. It made perfect sense in the context of that moment, the balls-out moment that set the tone for the rest of the tour, for the rest of the war. Incongruously even as it was happening I recalled the moment in *Notting Hill* when Hugh Grant realizes despite his Englishness and everything else he's going to have to follow Julia Roberts over a fence: *kharkus*. That must have been the moment I'd read about Tim Illingworth having, read about Hugo Farmer having, read about Dick Winters and Sidney Jary and even my grandfather having, come to think of it, the 'fuck it' moment when you have to go to and hope to God Lance-Sergeant Rowe is popping up enough UGL bombs to keep the enemy's heads down in the time it takes you to grab the lunatic and haul him back. Except, of course, you don't have to, because it's Qiam, and the moment he breaks cover, the firing stops, and everything is suddenly calm.

Syed and Mujib also showed their true colours: the weight of RPG and PKM fire which the ANA had poured back at the enemy the moment the ambush started and bought us enough time to get up on to that dam in the first place hadn't come from nowhere. A couple of hundred warriors who had never paid the slightest bit of attention when we'd tried to train them had broken the ambush immaculately and there, smiling with a fresh pot of tea which was the most thirst-quenching thing I had ever drunk, were Syed and Mujib, quietly getting the *kandak* back into shape, not breathless and nauseous with excitement like we were because, of course, they'd done this all before.

We posted sentries and settled down for a tense night holding what was to be the following morning's start line, hoping in vain for at least a couple of hours snatched sleep but instead cursing the same soldiers we'd been congratulating earlier. It was as if, having acquitted themselves well in the ambush, the ANA had an obligation to cancel out the good performance with the sort of ill-disciplined nonsense we'd naively hoped they had left in camp. The night was peppered with angry shouts and nervous, random shots at ghosts and shadows. The warriors, unhappy at spending a night on the ground, fought with locals and tried to occupy their houses, fought with dogs, even fought with each other. It was only months later I found out from a giggling sergeant that at least one squad had simply waited until it was dark and buggered off back down the road to Gereshk. I'd been too busy getting everyone in position the next morning and too gratefully hungry to wonder where the hell the delicious, warm, fresh bread had appeared from. And then it began again.

In the Green Zone

First thing the next morning, Kuku, Hazrat and 2 Company got their chance, and it was the same story: the brave were brave, the good were good, and the foolish were lucky. As dawn broke up on Hamilton Hill the elements of the *kandak* who had missed out on the opening dust-up started taking incoming mortars, and it was Hazrat's turn to prove himself an effective, if gung-ho, commander as, tasked to provide a screen on the flank, he got a sniff and charged for the enemy. Barely waiting for the rest of his troops, let alone any sort of plan, he had to be pulled back by Kuku. They cut a funny pair, the forty-year-old battle-scarred veteran from Takhar and the twenty-three-year-old fresh from the factory second-lieutenant from Nigeria via Harrow. Worlds apart and bonded in those instants when the mortars came in too close.

At about the same time, deep in the lush Green Zone, which had seemed comparatively peaceful at H-hour just before the sun rose but was by mid-morning an angry and confused mess, Qiam and I had our definitive moment. From Zumberlay to the north-east, where the BRF were doing their thing with Kuks and Hazrat all across the line of advance, to the Scimitars jockeying out in the desert to our west, Silicon had started properly by then, and pockets of violence erupted sporadically as different units moved forward at their different tempos. My ears were burning hot with the uncomfortable headpiece and the shouty, urgent chatter of the busy net. On the hill on our right flank, less than a kilometre away but it might as well have been ten or 100, Kandak HQ and the Captain's mentor group were still getting hammered with mortars. To my immediate left the Royal

Anglians, correctly but cumbersomely kitted out in heavy helmets and body armour, weighed down with full fighting scales of ammunition and carrying ladders and all the other extra kit we thought was essential, but which the ANA disregarded so that they could fight through nimbly and preserve their energy, made slow, sweaty progress through compounds and villages which melted into each other while half the *kandak* moved serenely down the centre, handing out sweets to kids as if you couldn't even hear the fighting all around. Only eight hours had passed since our ambush on the move in, four of them in fitful half-sleep, swinging in my hammock between the two WMIKs, being haunted by the call to prayer wafting over Deh Adam Khan village at first light and wondering if the knot in my stomach was the come-down from the contact we'd just had or fear ahead of the inevitable next one. That morning I'd been enchanted by everything – the sunrise, the hospitality of the locals who offered water to us as we passed which was quaffed by the ANA and politely refused by the mentors, how much more fun we seemed to be having than everyone else.

You can find meaning in anything if you look. There was the tortuous slow progress the Royal Anglians made in those first hours because they were trying to do it 'the British way': everything done correctly and well, but to what effect? Then there was how much more naturally it came to the ANA, patrolling through their own back-gardens, chatting away to the few farmers still cutting around in the fields and generally far more at home – which of course they were – but how they would never have been there in the first place, couldn't possibly have pushed out on an op like this nor lasted more than five minutes if they hadn't been being supported and guided and pushed and pulled and over-watched by mentors and dollars and helicopters. There was how it was supposed to last a week and ended up being months, how quickly we needed more men and more kit than we had first thought. How when it went well it seemed to go brilliantly, the grateful welcoming smiles of villagers and quick easy *shurahs** as we pushed through, and how when it went bad it teetered on a knife edge.

Too focused on the mission, the heat and fatigue and the strain of trying to follow the flow of the battle through snatches of radio traffic and the occasional buzz of an Apache overhead or the plumes of smoke popping up ominously in the distance, what almost passed me by was what a strange and foreign land we were actually in. It's not surprising that the *Lonely Planet* details got lost in the narrative, when you had fought to take a compound for four hours, finally bust through the main wall with an explosive charge and a couple of grenades and lived to tell the tale. The compound itself wasn't the story, but like the cultural and ethnic differences between ourselves and the ANA, so fundamental that we simply ignored them, no one had prepared us for how different a place Afghanistan actually was.

There was a story we get told at Sandhurst about the importance of being observant, probably only half true, but it stayed with me, and I caught myself using it with my own soldiers, an overly simple but effective illustration of why every man on every patrol needed to stay alert. The absence of the normal or the presence of the abnormal was what all routine patrols were looking for, and so it was that a sharp-eyed Guardsman patrolling a familiar residential street somewhere in deepest Bandit Country[†] noticed that a house which always usually had one

---

* Arabic for 'consultation': down at our level, a meeting with local villagers and elders.

[†] As South Armagh became known during the Troubles. Above the entrance to the OMLT room up in FOB Inkerman in Sangin, the walls chipped by incoming and a massive hole where an SPG-9 had punched through, inches over Lance-Corporal Perry's snoozing head, an Ulster veteran had written: 'Welcome to Bandit Country'.

empty bottle of milk outside suddenly had two and reported it to the patrol commander, who reported in turn to the intelligence officer, who fed it back to whoever it was who monitored and acted on these sorts of things, and sure enough the place was a terrorist safe house, and someone nasty was staying over. So simple it can't possibly have been true, but we spent the next few days on exercise scouring every nook and cranny of Copehill Down village* for just such a vital clue and a pat on the head from the DS.

The same principle should apply in somewhere like Gereshk or Helmand, except that the whole fabric of an Afghan town is so utterly unfamiliar that the close, hectic market and the open stone compounds had more in common with the disorientating texture of a dreamscape than any towns or villages we'd ever been in before. When every face and building and street was as unfamiliar as you could imagine, how on earth could you spot the milk bottle clues? I wish now I had been able to press pause on that first morning of Silicon just to try and absorb more. It wasn't the hot desert and harsh mountains and dense Green Zone which were difficult: they presented their own challenges as terrain, but we trained for different terrains, we had harsh mountains of our own back in Wales, had some pretty recent desert experience and had grown up on the tense jungle folklore of Vietnam films. The Green Zone was surreal in places, patrols snaking through beautiful fields of swaying blue poppy so high that all you could see was a procession of helmets like mushroom caps floating across an opiate sea, but it had nothing on the compounds and villages that we were supposed to be clearing through, not to mention gathering intelligence from on the way.

Like mazes was the only way to describe them: thick,

* The mock village in the middle of Salisbury Plain which is the Army's largest FIBUA training site, FIBUA being 'fighting in built-up areas'.

stone-walled labyrinths twisting and turning along and over the deep *karez*, which were the irrigation channels dug out from the canal and the Helmand Rud, snaking through the province to which it lent its name. Impossible to control the movement of troops through; once you entered one through an ornate, brightly coloured metal gate, usually with an unnerving pair of painted cat's eyes watching you from each door, you were lost in a world of low, cool rooms. On Op Silicon, as we pushed north from Gereshk for the first time, most were deserted. One turn might bring you into a courtyard, chickens picking at rubbish on the floor, perhaps a tethered goat or nearby barking of a guard dog where a family had only just pulled out ahead of the heavily publicized operation. The odd teapot or children's colouring-in books were the only signs of more modern life. If you ignored the very twenty-first century kit we were all carrying, you could look around you and see nothing, literally nothing that wouldn't have been around in a similar state 200, 300 even 500 years ago. As Lloydy pithily observed, Iraq might have been a shithole, but even they had TVs. Taking a pause to gulp down water and let everyone take their helmets off for a few, precious cool minutes, I found myself compulsively peering through every stone aperture and stooping through the low carved doorways, reminded again of the physical differences. Syed was mortified by our curiosity, would later spend long evenings explaining that Mazar was nothing like this, that the Helmandis were peasants, and maybe there was something in that; maybe my squad would have been disorientated patrolling through isolated Scottish Highland villages, but not to the same extent. This wasn't just a foreign country, it was a different world.

But not, of course, to the ANA. Listening in to the net, I could hear the frustration of the solely British units being pestered to up the tempo of their patrols. Sat in front of a map-board in a tent back in Gereshk, the Brigade HQ staff couldn't understand why it was taking them so long to clear through the compounds which we thought we had 'marked' by splodging digital numbers on top of Google Earth maps. Of course it was taking them hours, the compounds sucked you in and melted into each other, a cluster marked as three on our maps might well be home to ten families and might just have been one big one. Even assuming the compounds were deserted, each one could have taken a conscientious team of soldiers hours to clear because they had no idea what they were or weren't looking for. Absence of the normal, presence of the abnormal? We were overwhelmed, but not the ANA. Rotating their eight-man squads skilfully through the buildings, one team pushing through and securing, one sweeping through and searching and one at the rear, the *askar* knew which homes were long abandoned, which recently and which were suspicious, and on that long hot morning I could have kissed every single one of them for the way they got on with it.

When it was good, it was good, but when it was bad, it was horrid. Ducking through the opening in the thick wall of another impenetrable maze of compounds, negotiating between the animals and occasional vines which made the whole Green Zone seem more like something out of the Bible than the counter-insurgency manual, catching the occasional glimpses of the large, brown eyes of stunning children peering out from behind windows and the off flash of a brightly coloured veil, I came suddenly across an unwelcome scene. Qiam's men had somehow identified this particular compound as one we'd been shot at from the night before, had started a half-hearted search and uncovered a couple of AK magazines and ammunition. Qiam had a youngish guy by the scruff of his neck, bent over in the courtyard screaming blue murder at him, and a wailing old woman in the corner. The young, gold-toothed warrior who rides the Dushka in Qiam's wagon who we've named Goldie for obvious reasons (we've no idea what he's actually called, as we only saw him the first time yesterday) gave me a huge thumbs-up and flashed a glittering smile: '*Talib*.' He nodded towards the cowering young man. Qiam was growling something at both of them, and, trying at once to size up the situation and work out what I should do, I motioned to Nawroz to tell me what the hell was being said.

'It is not good, it is not good,' Nawroz was muttering, clearly upset: something of an understatement. Qiam was clearly demanding to know where the weapons were hidden, but, according to Nawroz, the young guy didn't know. 'These people do not know,' Nawroz said to me, almost pleading now. 'This is not good. They have sworn on the Holy Koran, and we must believe them.' None of the ANA looked like they believed them, and I glanced around for Syed or Mujib, whose judgement I'd trust more in this situation, but the only soldiers were from Qiam's own squad, and even Pricey, the nearest mentor, was on lookout at the gate, a good 20 metres away. There was another unsatisfactory answer as Qiam fetched a stinging back-handed slap across the young guy's face and, to my horror and an increase in wailing from the old woman in the corner, pulled out a pistol.

I put a hand on Qiam's shoulder, and he whipped around as if I've struck him, eyes gleaming as the mood changed and the warriors suddenly all looked in on me as if to say 'What the fuck do you think you're doing?' I pulled Nawroz in close and told him to translate exactly what I was saying, exactly. 'I thought you were supposed to be brave,' I tried, desperately, 'a famous *delawar* warrior? No true warrior would strike an unarmed boy. This is doing us more harm than good. This is crazy, not brave. Are you some kind of coward?' There was another pause, maybe he was going to hit me. This was our 'moment', his 'incident'. He looked at me as if at a child who had no understanding of what was going on and just laughed and cocked the pistol.

And the first thing I noticed was that the old woman's screaming had stopped. She sighed, rolled her eyes and pointed Qiam and the squad to a haystack in the corner, from out of which they fished another cache of weapons and ammo and even little, grubby assault vests: turns out even the Taliban like their Gucci kit. I was utterly bemused. We didn't even arrest the young guy, who was apparently just being intimidated into hiding the kit. The old woman gave all the ANA a friendly slap on the forehead as they leave the compound, which Nawroz said is some sort of good-luck gesture. Surreally, improbably, we'd gone from war crimes to hearts and minds in the time it took to cock a pistol, and before I could mull over the strange and puzzling, Qiam pulls me in close, no trace of anger or even 'I told you so' on his face. 'Toran Padi,' he began, schoolmaster in tone, patiently explaining that he would never have shot the boy, but that force was the only way to deal with liars and, more pertinently I suppose, as we kicked on to the next compound of the day, 'how on earth will we have time to search all the compounds in Helmand?' An Afghan solution to an Afghan problem.

Good, bad, sublime, ridiculous. We had seen the good, the awesome response to that first ambush, the unhesitating fighting spirit of the *kandak*; we had seen the bad, the ambiguous world in which we operated, the uncomfortable fine line between robustness and abuse; we'd been going twelve hours and we weren't in Kansas any more. A four-hour lull while the *kandak* took lunch in the shade of an irrigation ditch and we battled our way across to the Royal Anglians to find out what was going on might have seemed ridiculous at the time, but judging by the state of panting Brits, hooped* to a man and still a good way short of the D-day objective, the ANA lunch break seemed

* Exhausted, probably deriving from the tendency to use hoop as a synonym of arsehole.

pretty sensible. And the final push, up the canal to capture the sluice-gates – that was sublime.

Every witness to an event remembers it differently, a phenomenon amplified by the heat of battle and the fog of war, so I can forgive the Royal Anglian platoon commander whose only recollection of the *kandak* that day was that 'they were supposed to follow up on that flank but had not yet pushed forward'[7] – he was busy enough at the time. The enthusiasm of 1st Battalion the Royal Anglian Regiment, 'the Vikings', was understandable. They were the first 'normal' infantry to be the main fighting battlegroup in Afghanistan and were keen to show the Paras and the Marines that you didn't have to have a special badge or silly-coloured beret to be able to do the job. It was perhaps more understandable from their perspective that Silicon was 'about 240 Brits altogether, with the ANA in the rear'.[8] Still understandable, but far less acceptable, is the account of Op Silicon that emerges from the Royal Anglians' quasi-official history of their tour. Penned with the benefit of hindsight and perspective, *Attack State Red* was written by a Royal Anglian for the Royal Anglians, so on the one hand it doesn't set out to, nor does one expect it to, focus on the role of their Afghan partners. On the other hand, the sixty-odd ANA warriors of 3 Tolay, 1/3/205 who were crashed forward in a frantic panic in the middle of their lunch on the afternoon of that first day of Op Silicon might justifiably feel aggrieved not to merit a single mention over the twenty-page account of the events of that day. Zadiq Ullah, shot through the eye storming the Taliban positions which had pinned down B Company, 1 Royal Anglian and were preventing them from reaching 'Report Line Purple', might feel pretty pissed off that his company's frontal assault up the towpath is somehow missed out; Sergeant Nadir, who broke cover and drove the Dushka wagon right up to the front line with bullets pinging off the bumper, and Goldie, whose steadfast refusal to ever wear a helmet nearly cost him when he had his beret shot off while firing his beloved RPGs, would be mightily pissed off to read that the ANA had been kicking their heels safely back in Gereshk all afternoon while the plucky Brits did all the fighting.

Of course you can't tell every story and you can't show every picture. In the grand scheme of things the *kandak* was involved in two noteworthy actions that day, one mildly embarrassing for the ANA, one mildly inspiring. Right on H-hour, Hazrat had nearly led 2 Tolay and Lieutenant Kuku's OMLT into a trap which could have jeopardized the whole operation, but made wet-dream copy for the MoD Media Ops team, who could run Black-Guards-Officer-in-Afghan-Partner-Saving-Baptism-of-Fire stories on the website to their hearts' content. Lieutenant Colonel Stuart Carver, commanding the Vikings and running the battle, was forced to deploy his mobile reserve in an unwelcome and risky, but ultimately successful, move allowing 'the battered and bloodied ANA to pull back into line with B Company'. History records that a near-disaster had been averted and that the ANA had almost diverted the whole battlegroup 'away from its main effort in the Green Zone':[9] so far, so Afghan, and we all smile apologetically and shrug and make the right noises about enabling and move on.

Except that the main effort that day was for the Royal Anglians' B Company to reach the five-five easting* by last light and form a defensive line, and what the book doesn't mention is that they were only able to do so because of the ANA. At about 1500 Lance-Sergeant Rowe and I had just scrambled back from

---

* Eastings (running north to south) and northings (running east to west) were the lines with which we divided up our maps. Because the ANA didn't have maps we tended to have objectives which were both real geographical features as well as map features. The five-five easting was also a road, which was probably why the ANA looked at us as if we were mad when we talked about Report Line Purple, or whatever it was.

B Company's position, not that far short of the five-five easting which was our joint objective but nonetheless pinned down under heavy and accurate enemy fire and with a decent number of Taliban in between. The hasty instructions from B Company's no-nonsense commander, an excellent Aussie who didn't mince words but got the job done, were to get the ANA up the fucking flank pronto and do something to relieve the pressure. So we did.

Mujib and Marouf prevailed at first, methodical and careful, noting the vulnerability of the raised towpath, which would have been the obvious route for the vehicles, but on which we would all have been ducks in a fairground shoot. At a rate and with an energy and enthusiasm which I hadn't previously believed possible, on hearing that their British partners were in trouble the ANA Sergeants Syed Meraj, Zadiq Ullah and Nadir got amongst the troops in a way that would have made the drill sergeant weep with pride. Nadir was another squad leader who had kept an almost invisible profile when we had been in camp but as soon as we had rolled out on Silicon had slapped his chevrons on and with a smile and a cool pair of shades led his men calmly and efficiently throughout the fight, and I was barely able to keep up in the WMIKs as suddenly we were bouncing from compound to compound, rolling up prepared defensive positions with gusto, seemingly impervious to the mortars and RPGs whizzing in both directions. It was good, but the tension on the net suggested it wasn't good enough. Up to the north of the Green Zone Colonel Carver launched his A Company to assault the village of Habibolah Kholay. It was meant to be an objective for tomorrow but such was the need to relieve the pressure on B Company that all options were being considered.

Further south, unremarked and, as it turned out, unrecorded, 3 Tolay, 1/3/205 were launching their own desperate last gambit. Marouf's rapid assault through the compounds had been slowed by his own, self-inflicted injury. A cry had gone up to our right, incomprehensible, strangled, neither Dari nor Pashtun nor English, but unmistakeably and universally 'MAN DOWN! MEDIC!' Marouf was pale and sweating but hopping and upright when I scrambled up out of the ditch and into cover behind a wall to see what the fuss was about. His jaw was clenched tight and tears streaked from the corners of his eyes, but he was man enough to attempt a grin and point down at the clean hole in his boot, blood darkening the dust beneath and perhaps as impressively man enough to admit straight away that it was his own fault. We called T3 over the net and asked for an estimate on the IRT,* and you could almost hear the stifled sniggering when Zero came back to ask for a description of the injury and I had to reply, 'Gunshot wound to foot.' Never mind that Marouf was brave enough to want to push on, but there was no sniggering to be done minutes later when two young warriors struggled round the corner dragging Zadiq Ullah by his armpits. The bulky Pashtun was limp, his face bright scarlet, blood dripping from his thick beard. You feared the worst immediately, but he groaned, and without thinking Syed heaved him on to the back of the nearest Ranger, bundled Marouf into the passenger door and barked instructions at the driver, who was wheel-spinning back down the towpath before Nawroz could begin to translate. 'Quicker,' shrugged Syed, and off we went to try and regain the lost momentum which, from the calls on the net and the angry presence of the Apaches overhead, B Company still needed.

Down an influential commander, a sergeant and the squad detailed to charge back down the canal to Gereshk with them

* Incident response team. Nowadays they would call it the MERT, medical emergency response team. Different TLAs came and went but they always meant the same thing: incredible brave men and women saving lives every which way in the back of a Chinook.

for treatment, it was finally Qiam's moment. Bugger the risk, bold as brass, silhouetted up on the raised towpath for maximum impact, Dushka blazing away to the front, Qiam charged. There was no mentoring or liaison going on by then, no partnering or advising, just the frantic, tight grip of a rider in the Palio, dashing bareback, barely in control over Siena's ancient cobbles, terrified of where the horse is taking him but knowing that the only thing worse would be falling off. The last kilometre was a grim, relentless, teeth-clenching breathless pincer with the Taliban finally caught on two sides and the veteran members of the *kandak* coming to the fore, experience showing,

Syed Meraj posing in front of the dam his boys had captured the day before.

sensing the kill and flushing the enemy out with ruthless fluency till suddenly the sluice-gates, the five-five easting, Report Line Purple, call it whatever you want, the end was in sight, and we fixed bayonets for the final dash across a hundred metres of open ground to the line. What felt like minutes had been hours, and no one would have disagreed with the B Company commander's assessment that it was a fucking good scrap and a fucking good day. Good, bad, ridiculous, sublime, twenty-four hours and bravery and silliness, nerves and relief, but let the record show that the *kandak* stood shoulder to shoulder with the Vikings on that final push to the line, accounted for more than its fair share of the Taliban who had been causing B Company such problems that afternoon and were sat, brewing up *chai*, on the secured objective five minutes ahead of schedule.

Mowing the Lawn

It was two months since the start of Silicon, and it felt like we had spent that whole time up and down that valley, fighting in and out of villages, running the gauntlet past Jen-i-Deen and down the towpath to FOB Price for a quick hot shower and a couple of hours gorging on Pringles and popcorn and Gatorade and Nelly Furtado on the TV in the NAAFI before heading back out to the dam – the dam which we had captured ourselves and which became as close to home in Helmand as we'd get on that tour. Harries and Kuks had both been flown home injured, and the hastily reshuffled *kandak* was suffering split personality syndrome, with half the men under Qiam and Syed achieving more than we could ever have hoped for, and the other half under the still hopeless Lamb living down to his nickname and every clichéd low expectation of ANA foolishness. Only the night before, all of us collapsed exhausted in the middle of a marathon village clearance, licking our wounds and counting the cost of another couple of guys back in the hospital in Bastion, the Lamb had threatened to mutiny, muttered darkly that he would refuse to soldier and would order his men to do the same. We ignored him and hoped that the rest of the *kandak* would too, told him what time H-hour was, and there we were the next morning, waiting on the line of departure when the lead warrior tried to shoot a dog, missed and shot himself through the foot and his commander in the gut with the ricochet. So horribly sad, why is it we felt like laughing? Another story for the mess bar at home about how the ANA were so bad, except that story wouldn't tell you what the rest of the *kandak* were doing.

Qiam in his element, telling stories to the kandak *while we wait for another H-Hour.*

While we waited for the medevac Qiam, basking in the successes of the last few days, reflected even more brightly by the woeful shortcomings of his counterpart, had the other half of the *kandak* sat around in a lush green hollow, alternating between peals of laughter and rapt attention as he lectured them on life, love, history and God knows what else, because I couldn't get much out the 'terp, who was giggling along with the rest.

It's one of my favourite photos of the hundreds of the tour. It must have been Sergeant T who took the shot because the jpeg reference is his camera's, but I could have sworn he was elsewhere at the time. It doesn't matter who took it or on whose camera or when or where, there's a photo which captures perfectly an idyllic scene of togetherness in the middle of the mother of all scraps: us and our *kandak*. Qiam is holding court, bedraggled with his shirt open, in his element. Syed sits neatly on his kit at his side, efficiently rehydrating, the perfect platoon sergeant. Lloydy and Mizon are sat on the wall, letting the foreign words wash over them, unaware I think of the photo being taken and that their faces were being captured gazing blankly into the middle distance: not quite thousand-yard stares, but a telling state of exhausted calm; Mizon cradling his beloved GPMG, half smiling, both of them clearly a million miles away. The rest of the guys, some flecks of colour and the odd bandana here and there but mostly a leaner and greener fighting force than that which had rolled out of the gate, unrecognizable as having been fashioned from the confused and bedraggled shower which we had taken over from the Royal Marines.

Over those months we had had close shaves and bad moments. There had been genuinely difficult times: taking our first casualties and being pushed out on what we sometimes felt were fools' errands devised in seemingly far-flung ISAF HQs by planning officers with fat fingers and small maps. There had been ridiculous 'Afghan' moments too, when a couple of the soldiers got high and drove one of the Rangers straight into the canal, but my overriding sense is one of a strange contentment amid the chaos and violence, a sense that having bonded in combat with the *kandak* there was a brief and treasured period of harmony. To look at the photos I have of us swimming, apparently carefree, sat chatting away over *chai* at sunset or mucking around in the base you'd barely know we were at war. It was only if you looked hard that you saw the rifles close to hand, the mortar tubes in the background, the sandbags piled up around the sangars.*

It's important to treasure the memories like that because they're not necessarily burned in with the same intensity as the

---

* General military term for a protected sentry post, appropriately enough picked up by the British Indian Army when they were in Afghanistan a couple of centuries before us.

memories of fighting. Syed popping up on my shoulder during the crazy first day of Op Tufaan and dropping the other sharp-shooter with a smile before following me, Lloyd and Mizon across the open ground when no one else did. Poor Noor Ullah, a scrappy Hazara shot in the face on the first day the BBC embedded with us when it felt like the Taliban were doing it on purpose, the horrible sight of his head flipping open like it was hinged where it shouldn't be as he paused mid-run before the momentum switched and he dropped back, never to be seen again as we finished the assault and his body had already disap-peared, another Afghan casualty who'd only even get a one-line mention at the bottom of a web-page if one of us got shot, which we didn't that day. Nazim, who wouldn't ever take off his bright-red bandana, stood bolt upright in the line of fire trying to rescue a donkey before the airstrike came in and we assaulted through Kakaran. Hazrat wreaking fury and vengeance on the Green Zone after Kuku got blown up by an IED. You had to make the effort to remember the rest, not because those were bad memories and you wanted good ones too, but because those were only half of the memories and you wanted full ones.

It was our own brigade commander who said of the uniquely free-flowing violence of that summer that it was like 'mowing the lawn',[10] the grass always grew back. With manpower and assets that the Paras and Marines before had lacked, 12 Mecha-nized Brigade punched its way around Helmand all summer. Perhaps unwittingly the phrase also captured something else, a sense of a comfortable routine, going through the motions not unpleasantly, in the back yard, in the summer, with a beer. If we were honest, we enjoyed mowing the lawn. The enemy, perhaps flush from the excitement of the previous summer, was still fighting in the open, yet to adopt the IED heavy asymmetric tactics that would grind the province to a slow, attritional halt. In that way we were lucky. We charged around in unprotected vehicles, fearful of neither the invisible menace of the hidden bombs nor, particularly, of an enemy we knew we had the beating of. The *kandaks* too were starting to come together, growing into their roles and learning from a year of experience, not yet too knackered to try or care. As successive brigades grew in size and were supplemented by ever more Americans, the operating areas grew smaller and smaller so that today, recounting the story of the time we drove from Bastion and Lashkar Gah, through Gereshk and straight up to Sangin and back in a handful of WMIKs, you might as well be talking about a different conflict.

The softer moments are harder to recall, but maybe more important; the laughs and the japes which meant more than the assault and bombardments. Remembering Ali Ahmat not as the youngest soldier in the *kandak* to get killed but, as Lance-Sergeant Rowe nicknamed him, the mischievous tree-frog who rode a bicycle up and down the line between the PBs delivering M&Ms. Qiam not just as a scrapper but as a host. After the fighting phase of Silicon, when we occupied the new bases on the new front line and settled in for long weeks of cat and mouse, Qiam painstakingly built a colourful shelter on the dam and hosted the villagers for long lunches. Bustling around officiously checking the flow of people and cattle through the only crossing point on the Noor-i-Bugrah north of Gereshk and knowing more about what was going on in the area in five minutes than we could glean from the slow and painful hours of cross-legged, pins-and-needles *shurah* we sat through with the elders. Syed had spotted that most of the OMLT didn't join Qiam for his lunches: greasy *ghost* and salty *pilau* mopped up with yesterday's stale *naan* wasn't to everyone's taste, after all. He'd asked Sergeant T what British soldiers like, and the cheeky old Scouser had told him with more than a hint of wistfulness in his voice 'fish and chips'. That night, after a frenzy of activity in the broiling waters down by the sluice-gates and some highly unauthorized stun fishing with the under-slung grenade launchers that had been magicked up by Corps HQ in Kandahar for the *kandak* as a reward for its performance on Silicon, Syed had beckoned us all over from the PB for a delicious supper of pepper-fried *mahi* and chips. It wasn't beer-battered cod, and the chips were a bit skinny, but it might have been the best any of us had ever had.

Almost inevitably, good times would give way to bad, achievement to frustration. No one could spend six months working across the cultural and linguistic divide between the British and Afghan armies without losing their cool from time to time, not least because everyone was spending most of that time getting the minimum amount of sleep and trying not to get blown up every day. A handful of senior non-commissioned officers, brilliant career soldiers who had successfully marched and trained their way into very comfortable round holes, seemed to spend their time with the ANA perpetually on the verge of a nervous breakdown – the poor old things quivering with rage and exasperation midway between Michael Douglas in *Falling Down* and Mr Creosote in *The Meaning of Life*, one wafer-thin bit of Afghan tomfoolery away from reaching for the baseball bat. One of the worst times I ever lost my temper with the ANA Brigade Headquarters, ranted and raved at embarrassed 'terps and nonplussed staff officers and implored my own chain of command to start rattling cages up in Kabul, was when I came back from my two weeks' R&R, slightly more than halfway through that formative 2007 tour, and learned that Qiam had been demoted from major to captain.

By then we had spent four months together, and in the fortnight before I'd gone away for R&R had all fought on one of the most sustained and ferocious operations the *kandak* had hitherto conducted. Both the ANA and our own Grenadier mentoring team had been severely depleted by casualties, so we had gone old-school and formed the *kandak* up into two nearly full companies instead of three under-strength and ineffectual ones. The plan was simple: two-up, nothing in reserve, straight down the middle with bags of smoke. Qiam had been instrumental in keeping the thing going, his bullish, shouting presence driving his company when it lagged, his softer side, all enthusiasm and old war stories, keeping spirits up when we were static. His counterpart had downed arms on more than one occasion over the operation, threatened to pull his company back when it needed to go forward, deliberately ditched his rations in an attempt to bring the whole thing to a standstill and whinged throughout in poor Rob's ear in the most abject display of leadership.

Two weeks later, inexplicably, Qiam had apparently been demoted and the Lamb, the hopeless, bleating Lamb, had been promoted. I had lunch with Qiam in the big kitchen in Shorabak, the recruits from the newly formed 4th Combat Support Kandak eyeing us suspiciously as they came bustling through, unused, it seemed, to seeing the ISAF mentors eating in their cookhouse.* Over the months I had seen Qiam raging, I'd seen him throwing himself and his men forward in the heat of battle and I'd seen him seething with dangerous anger confronted with stonewalling insurgents and unrepentant detainees, but I'd never seen him sad. Over lunch he had been dejected and resigned, snorting incredulously when I suggested formally complaining. 'What does it matter?' he had asked. Part of me was cross that a cowardly commander's wish had come true and that he was out of harm's way, but the other part realized straight away that such anger was counter-productive, that at least he would no

---

* And not without good reason after one of our mentoring teams went down with violent DNV after taking an Afghan lunch without realizing that the meat preparation area behind the kitchens back then seemed to double as a rubbish tip.

longer be a hindrance on the battlefield and a danger to his troops, probably comfortably sidelined behind a desk up in Kandahar where no one made bleating noises as he walked by. At the same time what would Qiam have done with a promotion? He was only ever going to be a front-line soldier, and what difference did it make whether he was a captain or a major in an army where no one wore their rank slides and where lieutenant colonel commanding officers refused to deploy on the ground with their battalions.

I later heard that Qiam's demotion was the result of an internal investigation the ANA had done into bribery on the front line. Those of us who were living with the *kandak* day in day out found it pretty hard to imagine any sort of internal investigation taking place, and the whole thing stank of someone better connected having had his nose put out of joint and wanting revenge. Qiam's fighting spirit impressed his mentors despite the culture clash between the ANA officers and their British counterparts. The former were predominantly remnants of the old, Russian-trained Army. They were steped in a culture which was a blend of the Soviet centralizing ethos and the even older imperative of looking after number one. ANA officers, especially the more senior ones, rarely led from the front, and the idea that they should put their men or their mission before their own comfort and safety was an absolute anathema. Those former Northern Alliance fighters like Qiam, who were non-commissioned officers at heart but had rank in the new ANA, or those officers fresh out of ISAF training up in Kabul like Mujib were different and clearly better, but their performances and the pointed praise they earned from the ISAF troops working with them reflected poorly on the old school, whose hump was up and who had a vested interest in keeping the new and better generation in their boxes. My suspicions were only heightened when I learned that Qiam had managed to negotiate that he'd get a pay-rise as well as a demotion.

Sangin

The news I got coming back from two weeks' mid-tour R&R was not good. It wasn't just that we were being sent to Sangin, even then the most difficult posting in Helmand, nor even that my team was being sent to FOB Inkerman, the most isolated and dangerous base in the area, it was that the mentoring teams were being reshuffled and we were being split up. 3 Company would be 8 kilometres down the road in the Sangin District Centre, but it might as well have been 800 because you couldn't drive down the road without getting ambushed: we would have to forge new working relationships with unknown Afghans, and, worst of all, I'd have to see out the tour without Syed or Qiam or Mujib.

The reluctance of most of the ANA deploying up to Sangin was less to do with the reconfiguration of personnel and more to do with the fact that they'd been there before. The *kandak* had spent a miserable winter up there with the Marines and weren't happy to be heading back so soon. Just getting there was difficult enough: the journey overland meant the long and dangerous slog up Route 611, which was little more than a hopeful line on a map and the occasional rutted track. Back in 2006 the first major casualties in Helmand – Afghan, US, French and Canadian – had all been sustained in ambushes on the route up to the town. By the time we made the journey ourselves the fishhook, the long curve which slung up towards the safety of FOB Robinson, the main logistics base just south of Sangin itself, was infamous, the approach dotted with the rusting hulks of burned-out vehicles which hadn't quite made it.

Robinson, known as FOB ROB, appeared on the horizon as a welcome sanctuary, but it was bleak even by Helmand's Spartan standards; coated in a fine moon dust which got everywhere as if the very sand was making life difficult for you. The very first mentoring teams had lived like slum-dogs in a couple of ISO containers by the helipad, roasting in the sun and freezing in the cold nights, a short dash to the tense sentry positions overlooking the town itself. The ANA had a designated compound slightly down the slope from the blasted helipad and dust-silhouetted sangars where the handful of ISAF troops lived, but many of them set up makeshift camps in the small nooks which had formed naturally in the steep, cliff-like sides of the deep-cut path which ran down to the river. Huddled together like the Italian peasants of Matera in their Sassi mountain grottoes, the ANA at FOB ROB led an extraordinary, semi-troglodyte existence in caves hollowed out of the sandy stone.

It was tempting to read too much into the contrast between the westerners living on top of the hill in metal boxes, gathered round a couple of straining little petrol generators and struggling for communications under frail, reaching antennae, and the Afghans living in the ground itself, like hobbits on the steep, cracked path down to the river which snaked up towards the town. While the sentries on top of the hill kept watch out over the desert for the faintest signs of hostile movement and tracked the incoming helicopters bringing vital supplies, the ANA would change out of their uniforms and casually meander up into the town centre to buy drinks and bread from the local market. The ghetto carved out of the hill seemed sparse and miserable at first glance, but whichever *kandak* was down there was left mostly to its own devices, which suited the soldiers just fine. They may have been uncomfortable, but the ANA preferred the caves at FOB ROB to everywhere else in Sangin because at least they didn't go hungry and thirsty. Most ISAF units rotated in and out of places like Sangin in shifts and wore their endurance and beards with a soldier's pride – the longer and stragglier the hair, the harder the stint had been – and we all took perverse pride in making do with grim rations, going unbroken weeks and in some cases months of only eating boil-in-the-bag Lancashire hotpot. The ANA hated rations, the British ORPs even more than the US MREs and kept only the tissues from the former and the M&Ms from the latter, simply giving or throwing away whatever else they contained. The big issue for the ANA in Sangin wasn't how dangerous it was, it was food. The frequency with which *kandaks* refused to deploy anywhere out of range of a supply of fresh rations seriously limited their fighting capability and seemed to be another affront to professionalism, but they were measuring their expectations in years, not weeks, and there was no doubt whose suppers tasted better.

Up in FOB Inkerman, isolated 8 kilometres north-east up the road to Kajaki, we had more pressing things to worry about than scoff. When you're static, the psychological impact of perceiving yourself even slightly under siege colours everything, and, despite the fact that we were stuck in one place, our life more ordered and less nomadic than it had been down in Gereshk, the time we spent in Sangin still seems to have been something of a blur. We pushed out and engaged the Taliban, gave as good as we got and better, but the novelty was wearing off, the sense of adventure was diminished, and whatever it was that had seemed so perfect before I'd gone on R&R was missing. We had grown used to how 3 Company worked, the reassurance of having Syed on patrol to hold things together, or knowing Qiam was on hand to motivate and cajole. Now we were exposed to another inherent difficulty of the mentoring strategy, the extent to which each different sub-unit, each individual commander and soldier, worked slightly differently. What had been natural and easy with Mujib had to be learnt anew with Toran Hazrat; the tasks we had come to trust 3 Company and the Heavy Weapons boys with weren't necessarily those which 2 Company were as comfortable performing. As it turned out, Hazrat was as natural a commander as any in the *kandak*, and his company in some respects more organized and effective than the others, but going through the learning process all over again was no easier, and conditions in FOB Inkerman didn't help.

One of the key differences, more subtle and less dangerous than the mortars and rockets which rained in on the FOB but no less harder to adjust to, was that we were sharing Inkerman with a proper British company. I had long since fallen into thinking of the ANA and my OMLT together: when I said 'we' in the meetings, O-Groups and briefings which maintained a vague rhythm of the days, I meant my boys and the ANA equally: C Company, 1 Royal Anglians, ostensibly our fellow countrymen, were firmly 'them', and although they were perfect hosts, we were conscious of being guests in their camp when it should have been the other way round. Even allowing for my posture, part being a good mentor but if I'm honest a little bit the fun of the moral high ground, of being entitled to, required to, adopt a difficult, junior officer-ish position, even allowing for my own immaturity, we were still in Afghanistan after all; surely it was Toran Hazrat who was hosting Major Messenger and not vice versa, surely the relationship shouldn't have been defined only by who had the biggest helicopters?

As FOB Inkerman came under sustained indirect fire the ANA, whose living space in the compound was on the exposed forward slope closest to the enemy positions, took a number of serious casualties; it didn't matter that in reality it was simply to do with resources being stretched, but the ANA perception was that it wasn't until we started losing British limbs that our calls for engineers and precious Hesco were heeded. When the hospital at Bastion got full and there was a temporary lock-down on patrolling it was suggested, not maliciously but at least unthinkingly, that perhaps I could ask the ANA to continue patrolling. My anger wasn't just righteousness bristling at the unattractive implication that an Afghan casualty was a lower priority, it was also self-interest, how infuriatingly quickly the rest of the brigade seemed to forget that with every ANA patrol there was a mentoring element. Tempers frayed towards the end of the tour: the pressure of being up in Sangin, the fact that we were all tired, had all just realized that we were within shouting distance of getting home in one piece and didn't want to be taking unnecessary risks. We had a visit to the base in our final weeks by the deputy commander, and it was politely but firmly suggested to me that there was concern in some quarters that the OMLT had 'gone native' – we wore it as a badge of pride.

Hazrat's 2 Company were easier to work with because, it turned out, they were far closer to our expectation of a 'normal' rifle company. Hazrat was the boss and very obviously a good boss. He led from the front, knew his men and calmly took instructions every night over the radio from Kandak HQ down in the Sangin District Centre. Hazrat had been an engineer and had some experience with explosives. One of his frequent party tricks was to grow impatient of waiting for ISAF expert disposal teams and stroll out to wherever something suspicious had been spotted and attempt to detonate or defuse it himself. Fortunately for all of us, the devices he invariably encountered were not at all sophisticated. It was not to be recommended and it frustrated the hell out of the experts, but he always seemed to get away with it. I had my ear bent on one occasion by a Royal Engineer officer complaining that unless I could get 'a fucking grip on my Afghans' then we were losing valuable evidence that could be turned against the enemy, not to mention taking unnecessary risks. I could have told him that he should have had a little bit more respect for the ANA's innate ability when it came to IEDs. By the end of those two months up in Sangin we'd found more than thirty of the bastards, and by 'we' I mean the Afghans: of the thirty-seven IEDs found in the area in those two months only one had been IDed first by a British callsign. The Sapper was right about the evidence but made the point a little too aggressively. Hazrat understood, but the burly sapper was missing the point: I was a very junior captain, and 'my fucking Afghan' was a very senior and experienced major. On one level of course I thought of them as 'my ANA' – we all did – but I could no more give a direct order to Hazrat than I could

Hazrat up in Sangin, walking softly and carrying a big stick.

have ignored the guy now shouting at me – that was how armies worked.

There was something else being missed, something more subtle but nonetheless important. It was one thing for the locals to see us crash out in force when they reported a problem, reassuring up to a point to know the huge blast-proof Mastiffs and body-armoured, goggle-wearing ISAF giants that rode around inside them were just up the road; it was another entirely for them to see Hazrat strolling down the road at the front of his patrol, smart but casual with his Rad-Op trotting along behind him. Hazrat carried a walking stick out with him in Sangin, where no one else moved without their rifle and preferably an Apache buzzing menacingly overhead, and I'm sure his confident strolls up and down the road did more to win over the locals than if we had stationed an entire brigade in the dust at Inkerman. It didn't stop us getting hammered the whole time we were up there and it annoyed the hell out of the protocol-bound units that couldn't control the ANA and couldn't understand that it wasn't my job to, but it was more of an Afghan solution to an Afghan problem than you normally got to see.

Hazrat was helped by having as near to a full staff as any company commander I ever saw in the ANA. Sergeant Muhammad, his company sergeant major, clearly hated Sangin, hated Inkerman and hated having to share his camp with the British as much as they found it difficult sharing with him. The morning the Royal Anglians' CSM came to see me, furious that the ANA were flogging his soldiers cans of Pepsi from down the road for the rip-off sum of a dollar a can, Sergeant Mu' was already in with me, furious that the Royal Anglians had been encouraging his men to go out on 'shopping' trips. He was a proper company sergeant major with a firm grip on the nitty-gritty, taking care of rations, ammunition, manpower and somehow keeping the little things which were daily dramas in many other units under control. We had fewer instances of soldiers who would dis-appear and crop up again unexpectedly a few days later, partly of course because there was nowhere to disappear to except the hostile Green Zone yards out of the front gate or, for the really foolish, the 8-kilometre IED rat-run into town, but also because, for all that they gave them hell and worked them hard, between them Hazrat and Muhammad ran a decent company.

Where Qiam had been required to drive his boys on with sheer force of will and shouting, sometimes manic leadership by example, Hazrat was able to direct things more centrally, not least because in addition to a good CSM he had two senior pla-toon commanders up there with him: Gholam Nabi and Sharaf Udin. Gholam Nabi ran his platoon with quiet efficiency, the classic 'grey man';* the ANA needed a few more of those com-petent, methodical operators. Sharaf Udin led his platoon and patrols like we'd like to imagine we did, and had lent me his spare Russian tank commander's hat for the grand occasion when, like a pair of lunatics, we test-fired the captured SPG-9 and nearly collapsed the roof: he was serious but he laughed then like he used to laugh picking the enemy out of the trees with the Dragunov. It felt odd to be a captain marching out alongside these men, twice as old and infinitely more experi-enced, but junior lieutenants in the ANA, just as it felt somehow fraudulent to sit in with Hazrat and have to weigh in with more clout than you merited because yours were the radios that talked to the air support and yours were the colleagues who actually had the vehicles.

The other reason why we came together so much more up in

---

* It was often said on courses like Sandhurst that the ideal candidate to be was the grey man: neither so good that too much pressure was heaped on your shoulders, nor so bad that you invited the unwelcome attention of the angry staff.

Inkerman was surely because we had nowhere else to go. Throughout the months we had spent in the Green Zone and patrol bases down in Gereshk there had always been the hope and promise of the odd rotation, an unscheduled couple of nights in an air-conditioned pod in FOB Price, three cooked meals a day in the mess and a glut of sugar and salt and MSGs from the NAAFI. In Price, just like further back in Shorabak, the ANA had their own, separate camp, and so after weeks of living side by side we would have a little distance, the breathing space in the intense relationship forced by us having to gear up to walk ten minutes round camp to see them, or vice versa. Sat with a brew on one of the picnic tables in FOB Price or zoning out after dinner, the chatter which washed over you was in various accents of English, and while those little breaks kept tempers from fraying too much out on the ground, they slightly reset the relationship each time. Other than that, the ANA were slightly down the hill and we were slightly up it, there was no distance at Inkerman, was no literal or metaphorical fence for each of us to retreat behind, and we were forced into even closer co-existing with other Brits who we could only define ourselves in opposition to. There were incidents when things were strained, not least when it was suggested that the ANA take over patrolling when we were temporarily locked down because of overcrowding in the hospital in Bastion, a clumsy order which made far too obvious how the ANA were prioritized as casualties. Hazrat took these with little more than a raised eyebrow, and my admiration for him only grew.

By a twist of the calendar our last weeks would be the first of Ramadan. Handling the period sensitively was a big issue across the whole country, and it was the first time the ANA got cut some slack, the patrols matrix juggled to acknowledge the fact that, on top of everything else, the *askar* would be out on their checkpoints and tasks all day without eating or drinking. In the evenings the small hill towards the back of the base would be crammed with soldiers phoning home with the free minutes the mobile network operators credited everyone with as a Ramadan gift. Sergeant Muhammad had acquired one of the strange-looking fat-tailed sheep from a local farmer which was being saved for a celebratory feast. The Brits in the camp kicked up a huge fuss about the inhumanity of slaughtering the beast, but in the end one of the squad leaders, Karim, had taken such a shine to it that he had persuaded half of the company that it was good luck, and the beast seemed to have been adopted as a pet, prompting the same guys who'd wanted it saved to complain that it was living on camp.

There was an equally grumpy response to the slight increase in celebratory gunfire which seemed to accompany sunset at Ramadan, and I was sent off down the hill with my own fat tail between my legs from the evening briefing to ask Hazrat to tell his boys to cut it out. He nodded politely and paused before saying something in a voice so low it was almost inaudible, but which prompted a wry smile from Muhammad and a sarcastic snort from Sharaf Udin, who were sat either side of him. I had looked over at Sami the 'terp for explanation, and he had given a little wave of his hands, half shrug, half conductor's gesture, which I think he had picked up from watching *Friends* on DVD back down in Shorabak. At least, for once, they are firing at nothing.

On our last day in Sangin, Hazrat, Sharaf Udin and Sergeant Mu' had come up the hill with a going-away present for me, a brand new set of ANA combats. The gift left me speechless beyond the obvious generosity from a sub-unit that didn't have enough kit to dress itself. The whole *kandak* was in a massive, collective grump, sensing that the mentors they had finally got used to and comfortable with were all heading home, knowing that they were being left behind to spend a tough winter going through the whole painful learning process again with an arbitrarily selected brand new set of foreigners with different badges and customs and accents and peccadilloes. It was noticeable in the way the warriors had been playing up in front of our replacements. The incoming OMLT battlegroup was 2nd Battalion the Yorkshire Regiment, the old Green Howards, who'd recently been more prosaically designated 2 Yorks. Suddenly, the ANA started showing off and being almost pointedly ill-disciplined in an effort to live down to the new mentors' worst expectations. It made me wonder whether the worst we had seen of the *kandak*, now nearly seven months earlier, hadn't perhaps been similarly exaggerated, part of a pantomime, the only way the powerless *kandak* could register its displeasure.

Hazrat had been calm and subtle about it, but I sensed a reproach in his generosity, the lavish Ramadan feasts laid out for us on coloured plastic picnic rugs down in the snug HQ room at the back of the ANA compound. Sharaf Udin would sit quietly with a cup of *chai*, waiting for everyone else to eat. Gholam Nabi with a glass of sweet milk would tuck in and tell jokes with his mouth full, while Sergeant Mu' dished out the rice and pushed huge portions in my direction. For all the fun and individual flair of working with Syed, Mujib and the charismatic unpredictability of Qiam and his Heavy Weapons boys, by the end of the tour I probably genuinely preferred the more functional, less stressful atmosphere in Hazrat's 'ops room', where I could let the Dari chatter wash over me, away from the buzz of the C Company HQ and the questions and the banter and, I suppose, to a certain extent briefly the responsibility.

Hazrat could see that I liked chilling with them. He always made a point of coming up to fetch me, pretending it was another urgent ANA muddle that I had to solve so I could slip out as if to work and sit back and relax over cool watermelon. In those last weeks he didn't change the routine, would still appear at dusk and invite us down the hill for dinner, but was a bit more distant, sat in the corner occupying himself through the meal with the radio or a list or something; we were both part of but on the outside of a circle. I suppose it made the parting and the carrying on that bit easier, but you couldn't avoid the keen sense of frustration that, just as things were starting to come together, so the *kandak* would have to start the whole difficult process again.

My last substantive contribution to the tour was preparing the handover notes for our incoming replacements. Up in FOB Inkerman the manpower couldn't be spared to fly back down to Bastion and break the new guys from 2 Yorks in gently, so the handover /takeover was going to be quick and dirty: the new guys would fly in, we'd have about forty-eight hours together, and then we'd be on the next chopper out: a hot HO/TO. Trying in vain to condense the experience of the previous six months into a couple of PowerPoint slides and some easy-to-remember checklists was impossible and pointless. Forty-eight hours. It had taken us a couple of weeks to get used to Afghanistan, and a couple more weeks to get used to the ANA, and then about another month to get used to actually fighting and working with them. By the time we had just about started to build up trust, get a sense of each other's strengths and weaknesses, bods were being hauled off the frontline for R&R, and then by the time we were back up and running again, we'd just started to really synch, were just starting to feel like some sort of progress was being made, and BUZZ – time's up, prepare your notes for the next brigade, and we'll start again at the beginning.

Maybe we could have done some good in six months if we'd just spent them in Shorabak getting the *kandak* into a decent shape, imparting institutional knowledge and sowing the seeds of good practice so that the next lot that came in would maybe be able to request a nominal roll without so much fuss and bother. We might even have been able to achieve something in six months attached to an already functioning unit and going to war with them, helping coordinate offensive support, organize logistics and the other complicated stuff still slightly beyond the reach of what was basically a Soviet-legacy, Third World army and tried to teach the finer points of counter-insurgency as we went. What there was no doubt couldn't be done in six months was precisely what we were trying to do: both together, the beat and the chorus at the same time.

In the queue for scoff in Kandahar on the way out I had to check myself when the twat in front started mouthing off how he couldn't wait to get home and back to proper soldiering instead of mentoring 'fucking rag-heads'. After everything we had been through alongside these men in this country was it possible that this cretin could have maintained the perfect integrity of his own pig ignorance? I must have tensed up because I felt a hand on my shoulder and a look from an older and wiser head behind me which said 'let it go': it wasn't worth kicking off over blowing off steam at the end of the tour. Ugly, sad and pointless pub racism was the same in Shorabak or Shoreditch, but I couldn't work out why this guy in particular hadn't got past it.

I thought of Sergeant Azim, young, wise-cracking and ambitious with an amusing smattering of American slang and a treasured denim baseball cap. How he had insisted, jokingly at first, that he would smuggle himself back to the UK with us, would do some reverse mentoring of his own. He was only nineteen years old and, as the days passed and our chuff charts were nearly complete, each time he repeated the joke his laughter grew more brittle. I tried to joke back, explain that Aldershot

124

was not that much nicer than Sangin, but the jokes fell flat against a desperation that I suspected uncomfortably was not particularly to come with us, nor particularly back to England, but simply not to be left behind, not again, not there.

In 2007, in the last days before we left, Hazrat told me with an unerring certainty that I'd be back again. I honestly can't remember the exact words Sami used to translate what was said, but I can remember the chill they sent down my spine, a strange mix of *déjà vu* (or, more accurately, *déjà entendu*) and the more disconcerting feeling that something uncomfortable, something a bit too close to the bone, was being said: they sicken of the calm, who knew the storm.

Hazrat had said it was a bit of old wisdom from the north. The sort of thing I imagined Massoud had bantered his young fighters with every time they said they'd had enough and were going home. Hazrat grinned knowingly as he said it; Qiam would have said the same; both of them knew that, if it was true, there was a sadness behind it. Both were family men, a long way from home, who'd spent the past few months teasing me for my youth and lack of heirs – but what they were saying was that they were trapped, that we were trapped. That I could try and escape, but that I'd want to come back. I had politely smiled and agreed at the time, took it for a back-handed compliment and thought privately to myself: fuck that, I'm going home.

Maybe the only thing scarier than being under siege in Patrol Base Inkerman was being cossetted at home in London and realizing that Hazrat was right. The phrase was Dorothy Parker's, and I'm pretty sure that neither Sami nor Hazrat had ever so much as heard of her, but in the Afghan dirt about as far away in all possible senses from the Algonquin Round Table as it was possible to imagine, either the hard-as-nails *tolay* commander or the plucky 'terp had synched with poetic accuracy:

This level reach of blue is not my sea;
Here are sweet waters, pretty in the sun,
Whose quiet ripples meet obediently
A marked and measured line, one after one.
This is no sea of mine, that humbly laves
Untroubled sands, spread glittering and warm.
I have a need of wilder, crueller waves;
They sicken of the calm, who knew the storm.

Staring out of the back of a Chinook fast leaving behind it a brown fuzz which had been home and a couple of watching green specks, I was numb. I was touched by Hazrat's parting gift of an ANA uniform, saddened that I had not been able to say a proper goodbye to Syed, curious as to what had happened to Qiam, but I was tired and stiffened and dirty, and the only focus I had was on home. Right then and there I thought I'd had enough of Afghanistan's wild and cruel waves and I was really, really looking forward to the untroubled sands of home.

PART II
After the Storm

Life after Helmand

I've never been much of a crier. It's not that I'm one of those heart-of-stone types, unmoved by human suffering. I'm not a sort of vacant, face-mask-peeling, Patrick Bateman psychopath, and certain music, in particular, always moves me in certain ways, but I've never been one of those people who cry at films and TV shows, except with one exception. At the very end of Spielberg's *Band of Brothers* we're finally told who the wrinkly old talking heads who've introduced each episode are. As you follow the series through, it's not hard to guess which measured veteran is the awe-inspiring Dick Winters or which cheeky laugh is 'Wild Bill' Guarnere's, but there's still something incredibly powerful about the moment that finally connects the real people to the characters you've shared ten stomach-churning episodes with. Winters, who passed away this year, a model for all junior officers, can't help but choke up slightly as he recalls a letter a fellow Airborne veteran had written to him which said: 'I cherish the memories of a question my grandson asked me the other day when he said, "Grandpa, were you a hero in the war?" Grandpa said, "No . . . but I served in a company of heroes." ' Tears. Every time.

It's brilliant TV, and Winters was and is an almost impossibly perfect hero, but that's not the only reason why it moves. *Band of Brothers* took its title, of course, from the St Crispin's Day speech, the lines of which are still scribbled in black biro in the front of one of the now brittle and yellowing notepads I've kept from Afghanistan. 'From this day to the ending of the world / We in it shall be remembered / We lucky few, we band of brothers / For he who today sheds his blood with me / Shall be my brother.' On the one hand it's the sort of self-indulgent nonsense, albeit in polished prose, which it was probably for the best in the long run that we didn't all have tattooed across our backs the moment we got home,* but it means something if you'd been through it, and who you'd been through it with means something too. March to September of 2007 is a pretty small chunk of the brief few years I spent in uniform. Looking at it in a cold, statistical light I only spent a few months living literally side by side with the *kandak*. We fought hard that summer, but not every day, so maybe to have such a heightened consciousness of that time, that place and those men is disproportionate; but then maybe it isn't, maybe it comes from the intimacy of comradeship.

Now before the world comes crashing down on me, I'm not suggesting for a second that there's any comparison between the *askar* of 1/3/205 ANA and the legends of Easy Company, 2/506 PIR, 101st Airborne.† Those guys liberated Europe, fought tooth and nail for a year across a continent without knowing when or if they'd ever get home; many of them didn't. There's no comparison between their deeds and anyone else's, let alone ours. Except . . . except that when it's your mates being blown up, when it's someone shooting at you it doesn't really matter whether the incoming rounds are being fired by a central casting Nazi villain, a tabloid anti-hero woman-hating Talib or a random villager with a grievance who wants you to go away. 7.62 × 39 mm of

* Except for the 3 Company guys who did get their proud Fleur de Lys tattooed on their arses, justifiably proud of what they'd achieved, but at least one of them without having realized that the particular heraldic device was also his old school crest: no one enjoyed their sixth-form days that much, even at Eton.

† 2nd Battalion, 506th Parachute Infantry Regiment, 101st Airborne Division – *currahee*.

high-velocity copper-plated steel does the same damage to flesh and bone whoever pulls the trigger, and your wounds don't know whether they were sustained in the great fight for civilization or some nasty, post-imperial dust-up.

It didn't matter whether you've held that line for 107 days* or 107 hours as long as you've held it together. Didn't matter whether you'd liberated Carentan or Kakaran, it was the fact that you'd fought for something which bonded you and shared tea out of the same stinking greenie as you caught your breath afterwards. In Patrol Base Inkerman in Sangin, my little band of brothers watched the eponymous series on a scratched DVD, running a cheeky line off the generator at night while the battery charger got an hour or two off to stop it exploding. A half dozen or so grimy and, by that stage, tired and hardened faces seemed to relax in the pale-blue glow of the familiar episodes. Hazrat and Sharaf Udin had come up the hill one night to see if we wanted to come down and share some fruit they'd managed to barter off the locals on the road. Even Sami the 'terp was so into the series by then he wanted to stay and find out what happened instead of getting some fresh watermelon. I'd thought that they would laugh at us or ask why, after another gritty day in the Green Zone getting shot up, we were relaxing by watching a bunch of actors pretending to be soldiers pretending to get shot up. Hazrat understood it instinctively just like he knew we'd get bored at home. It helped us to feel part of something bigger, for our actions to have been part of a wider story, helped to process the contrast between the morning's violence and the evening's uneasy calm if it was all part of a wider, just fight in a broader, just war which, in turn, was easier to deal with fitted snugly into the wider narrative of the wars of our fathers and grandfathers.

* As A Company, 2nd Battalion the Royal Regiment of Fusiliers had done up in Now Zad on Op Herrick IV.

For all the friction and shouting and exasperating roll calls and near-miss green on blues and even the deliberate moments of madness and murder when the ANA would turn on themselves and their mentors, most of us feel a kinship to them that outweighs the mere time we spent together. In direct proportion to how far the partnering went, skewed towards how hard the fight had been, you were closer than you would ever otherwise have been, closer even than to other British troops. Another Sangin veteran wrote elegantly and poignantly of the moment after a close shave when, out of nowhere, one of his soldiers called it what it actually was:

> we call it respect because it's easy to say. It's not soft and it's not embarrassing. But Matt has called it by its true name, love. Simple platonic love. This love that motivates men to do the most touching, brave, selfless things for their brothers . . . And sometimes, out here, you get a glimpse and you understand. You understand why soldiers charge machine-guns or hold out to the death while others escape. Love.[11]

It's the only explanation for whatever unlikely bond formed between mentor and mentee. We didn't have time to get to know each other properly and had no common ground. We'd deployed out thinking that we were all soldiers and had spent the first two months in the country dizzy and stunned, overwhelmed by the vast gulf between us, infuriated by the fact that the very thing we were supposed to have in common was one of the main sources of division. But it turned out that on another level we were all soldiers and there must have been something in the chemical cocktail that was released as we fought that overcame those differences: the complete strangers who became best friends after one night together on the best pill they ever had – whatever it was, Silicon was far more than buying 10 kilometres of breathing space for Gereshk, far more than a dozen less Taliban pestering the valley, it was crossing the Rubicon: FOB Inkerman was more than the place where close shaves were survived, it was where you discovered things about yourself that couldn't be unlearned. No one was saying that after six months and some shared bittersweet moments of loss and triumph we were suddenly Easy Company, but it went some way to explaining why the memories stayed so fresh and the sense of something special, something to be treasured out of what should have been horrific, was so strong and so difficult to let go.

We returned home from Helmand in the autumn of 2007, bursting with boastful stories of being 'the hardest' this or 'the most' that, protective of the memories, even the lexicon, of the war which was just then gaining in ferocity and growing in the public consciousness. Deep down we knew that some of 'our' soldiers had been trained by Marines and Paras before us, and by the Americans before them, and even some by the Russians before them, but we ignored it and carried on telling ourselves that no one else could know 'cause they weren't there, man. Returning from post-tour leave, we were sent straight out on to Salisbury Plain to lecture units under training on the lessons we had learned; the dos and don'ts of working with Afghans. Out in cold Wiltshire wood blocks and in mock-up Thetford bases, grumpy to be back in our drab green smocks, we thrust our hands in our belt loops like all good directing staff and flung around pidgin-Dari phrases like bragging sailors as we tried to project and maintain ownership of what we'd experienced, snobbishly correcting the pronunciation of the smallest Afghan villages like crushing gap-year bores back from Laos and signing off lessons with a smugly knowing 'Of course, you can't really know what it's like until you're there yourself.'

For a while it remained recent enough to dine out on without fully missing, but the more distant the experience got and the more we settled back into a soft and easy routine, the greater the itch seemed to get back out. Over tea and toast on a lazy afternoon in Aldershot or stuck in traffic inching back into London for another same same but different weekend you'd hear a tune on the radio which had been playing on an iPod somewhere deep out in the Green Zone and be right back in the heat and the dirt, wondering what on earth Qiam was doing now, whether Hazrat was still stuck up in Inkerman, whether Syed had ever got his leave. Restlessly, perhaps even a little compulsively, scanning the papers and website for news, not of Helmand *per se* – there was always plenty of that – but of the ANA and of 1/3/205 specifically. Friends on R&R, staff officers popping back from in-and-out visits would sometimes bring the whisper of a similar-sounding name or a vague message from the 2 Yorks, but such snippets proved more frustrating than informative, and monitoring the *kandak*'s progress from back home was more tantalizing than satisfying.

The vague and disconcerting sense of purposelessness and unfinished business was exacerbated by the surreal visit we received from the old ANA brigade commander, General Mohaiyadin himself, smuggled into the Home Counties for dinner in the mess during a visit to the UK. Over the course of the tour, Mohaiyadin and our own CO had bonded as closely as anyone. Their respective seniority meant that they hadn't exactly been storming compounds side by side, but they had closely shared the frustration of their own men, both Mohaiyadin's ANA and Hatherley's mentoring Grenadiers, being consistently overlooked in various HQs, and nothing unites soldiers more quickly than the perception, valid or not, that they're being shat on from above. Those of us who had spent most of the tour out of Shorabak had missed out on the politics back in camp: out in the patrol bases life had been sparse, but at least we had avoided a difficult atmosphere back in the headquarters at Shorabak and Bastion, tempers flaring in both camps and grievances flying between the two bases and across to the Brigade HQ, which was awkwardly out of the way in Lashkar Gah. It was a different type of adversity, but it bonded the ferocious old brigadier and his occasionally quixotic counterpart – they were both men who cared deeply about their men, and perhaps they had that in common most of all.

It was natural that they would want to catch up, and the invitation to a handful of ANA top brass to come and address the next brigade deploying to Helmand provided the perfect opportunity. There was a worry that the MoD or the Foreign Office or someone somewhere would have wanted to make a big deal of the visit of a high-ranking Afghan officer, and there was a risk we'd be up to our necks in protocol and bullshit. Our boss just wanted to have dinner with his mucker so with a stroke of junior officer genius he arranged for a couple of us to pick Mohaiyadin and a couple of others up from the airport when they arrived for the start of their trip: nothing official, no pomp, just the chance to pay the tough old brigadier back for seven months of hospitality. Despatched with a colleague from the late Victorian, Grade II listed red-brick splendour of the Lille Barracks officers' mess in full ceremonial evening finery down to Heathrow to escort our illustrious guests from the stunned Terminal 3 arrivals lounge and back to Aldershot, our strange little party drew some curious glances. An overweight Guardsman nonchalantly swinging the minibus keys and counting his extra-duties pay in his dark-green combats flanked by two young officers in gold-braided forage caps and long, grey coats from which flashed preposterously scarlet-striped mess dress trousers and gleaming wellingtons, all towering above a huddle of bewildered-looking Afghan men, older and far more delicate it seemed to me, seeing them for the first time out of uniform in brilliantly if unwittingly retro, shiny *Scarface*-style suits; hard as nails old warriors all three, but stunned by the alien bustle and colour and endless coffee shops of an airport terminal.

For one weekend only we all caught up over long dinners in the mess (which nearly killed the poor 'terps who'd come over too) and during trips to the usual London landmarks (which I suspect our guests endured politely). The undoubted highlight of the weekend was the visit to the giant Tesco's by Sandhurst: men who had known nothing but real fighting were hardly going to be that impressed by a visit to the Guards Museum in Wellington Barracks, but there was nothing in the whole of Afghanistan which could have prepared them for aisle after relentless neon aisle of all things shiny and sweet, and it rendered them speechless, these fierce, proud men who had seen and done what those shuffling past the discount DVDs could only dream of.

The highlight for the rest of us was the bandying around of familiar names and the sharing of memories and stories which even then were passing into regimental folklore. The namedropping and 'of course you remember the time when . . .' suggested, even if only out of politeness, that we hadn't been forgotten. The *kandaks*, it was said, sent their regards. And how was Qiam, of ours? An eloquent shrug from the old general and a polite smile from his interpreter: 'Still Qiam.' We all laughed, but should we have? I felt with a slight pang like there had been a moment of betrayal, it was a bit too distant and somehow a little unseemly. It had been all right to laugh at and with Qiam when we were both stuck in the same ditch, waiting for an airstrike and the next chancy move; it didn't seem OK from the plush, upholstered comfort of the smoking room. It had been fine to sit and talk through the night with Syed, to try and pick apart all that was wrong with his army and mine, with his country and mine, while gazing out over the hostile valleys, living through our respective shortcomings. But, under the impassive, oil-painting stares of highly decorated royals and flushed colonels of yesteryear, I felt more than usually like a pathetic armchair pundit, my right to comment and critique forfeited in comfort and safety.

It was nice to think, as was graciously being suggested, that the *kandak* sat around their *chai* and Mirinda* recalling us as we used to get drunk and shouty and remember them; but I was reminded of the sense of pathos watching a friend, returned to university on his stag do. The streets and colleges no more remembered us than they did the thousands of others who had lived, loved and learned in them for centuries. Drunkenly he insisted that despite the passage of time the kebab van owner would remember him and his favourite order:

'Hassan, it's me,' he waved and slurred as we approached, 'X from Y College. You remember? You always used to make me cheese and chips.'

Hassan had only taken a moment to adjust his bored stare and beamed back: 'My God! X from Y College, I remember you. Cheesy chips, right? Coming up!'

X had smiled delightedly as he spilled the chips down his front and stumbled through the lodge; and who were we to begrudge him his deluded, drunken contentment on that night of all nights? Poor guy was getting married, after all. Hassan was a good salesman and depended on the profligacy of vain and drunken students for his livelihood; good luck to him. But you knew deep down that he didn't care any more than he actually remembered, and I always sensed that, similarly, the Afghans were more anxious to be polite than anything else.

The ANA knew who paid its bills, and a bit of flattery didn't do any harm. It was nice to think that, out of dozens of British and American units they had worked with over the years, the *kandak*

---

* Super-sweet, super-addictive version of orange soda which the ANA loved. An acquired taste, but there was nothing better after a long, hot slog than finding one hidden at the back of the medic's fridge.

would have remembered us, but it was more likely they'd quickly checked who we were just beforehand and were saying what they knew we wanted to hear. It didn't matter whether it was in a mess in Aldershot, a FOB in Helmand or on the pavement in Broad Street, no one wanted to be the well-meaning but drunken guy, trying to recapture former glories, eating a portion of chips.

And after a while, it faded. With each fresh six-month rotation of Op Herrick, each fresh clutch of proud medals and sad litany of casualties, the resentment at having to share those formative experiences lessened; the feeling of something missing dimmed. Occasionally I'd bump into someone recently returned from Helmand who had run into soldiers I had once mentioned or who would drop names that would ring distant bells. 'Do they remember . . .' I would begin excitedly, but remember Hassan and stop myself. The reality was that, despite the odd letters, pictures and emails sent more in hope than expectation, invariably to an obsolete address or a British unit which might or might not have crossed its path, the memory of what I still thought of unconsciously as 'my' *kandak* was already fading. With distance and the passage of time the men I had lived and fought alongside for mad months back in 2007 had begun to exist in that twilight zone of the collective memory in which shared Facebook photos were increasingly the only evidence of the time we'd spent together. I suppose it is the animal nature of combat to imprint certain things indelibly on the memory so that, even as I realized I couldn't recall how many children Qiam had, I could vividly remember his laugh in the middle of a fire-fight. Keeping full and rounded memories, rather than adrenalin-soaked snapshots, was increasingly difficult. Sometimes I would catch a glimpse of a familiar face in a dispatch from the front, but rarely more; it felt as though in London newsrooms the ANA made good photo copy, but you still needed to be wearing a British uniform to qualify as a hero, and when the Afghan forces did make the headlines, it turned out to be for the worst possible reasons.

Blue 25

During R&R, at home from both Iraq and Afghanistan, I could never go for longer than a day without checking the internet for news from Baghdad or Helmand, obsessively clicking the links on the BBC website like a reflex. Everyone wanted and needed the break, but in two weeks you never really left the front, you couldn't fully relax into the overwhelming and unfamiliar world of home so instead you worried about what you were missing out on and hoped and pleaded and bargained with invisible brokers that no one would get killed while you were away. Perhaps it was a brief and unpleasant taste of what we all inflicted on friends and family when we went away, but I hadn't realized how difficult it was being the ones left behind until the battalion that had been my family for five years left for Herrick XI.

Six months after I had left the Army, the Grenadiers deployed back, into the mess of Nad-e Ali to walk IED tightropes while I stayed at home in air-conditioned shiny libraries, obsessively opening the MoD homepage in the fervent hope of not seeing that grim, tri-service crest that announces before you've even read the ominous 'With deepest regret . . .' that one of your mates has died.

On 4 November 2009 I got a phone-call from an unrecognized number as I was walking down Chancery Lane, I have no idea why. Five guys had been killed in Nad-e Ali, three of them Grenadiers, it seemed by one of the Afghan National Policemen they were mentoring. One of them was Daz Chant, the sergeant major, the senior soldier in the battalion, one of the most important men in the regiment, a good bloke, a friend.

Check Point Blue 25 is a small base sitting on a crossroads just south of Shin Kalay, maybe slightly closer to the road than some I've seen but otherwise like many other slightly more modern compound buildings in southern Afghanistan: concrete, boxy, low, maybe slightly more ornate, the hint of an ambitious por-tico on the roof now run with razor wire and sandbags. I was there in summer, and relatively thick trees splashed a vivid green canopy over our patrol as the vehicles slowed down as we passed by. It doesn't matter really, there are no good or bad places to die. Daz Chant, Sergeant Matt Telford and Guardsman Jimmy Major were killed along with Corporal Nicholas Webster-Smith of the Royal Military Police and one other by a policeman called Gulbuddin. After all the work done to dispel the myths five good soldiers had been shot by a bullying, stroppy policeman who'd flipped for some reason or other after a patrol. The Taliban claimed him straight away as one of their own, but once the dust settled the attack seemed neither planned nor strategically motivated. One of the survivors told the inquest: 'All I could hear was gunfire, scream, gunfire, scream, gunfire, scream, and then it all stopped.'[12] The coroner found that the men had been 'unlawfully killed'. Weren't they all?

Chant and Qiam had met once, I mischievously remembered. Poles apart of course but on one level kindred spirits, pure sol-diers both of them. I've got a photo of them, arm in arm, grinning and dirty the morning after the tumultuous first day of Op Sil-icon, both of them in their element. Chant's unrewarding job at the time had been to liaise with the British Battlegroup HQ, and I'd overheard him once, I don't think he realized I was at the door, going toe to toe with an officer who was talking down the ANA. Only minutes before he'd given me a good-natured bol-locking about the state of the *kandak*, lunatics on bicycles when they should have been on stag, the usual stuff, and all of it quite right. Now he was tearing strips off a Royal Anglian captain for presumptuously short-changing us, for mistaking the difference between constructive criticism and just slagging off guys you didn't know. Chant had high standards and fierce loyalty. He'd have beaten the crap out of Gulbuddin, no doubt, but he'd have gone straight back out on patrol with the Afghans.

In the media frenzy that ensued, the naysayers vindicated by the ultimate betrayal, the trenchant optimists seeing only a rogue setback, symptomatic of nothing more profound, and the rest of us in the middle, numb and frustrated, a lone sensible voice could be heard over breakfast. Captain Andrew Tiernan, back on his R&R and grieving for Chant as much as anyone, a true Ribs man like Chant who had also taken the young officer under his wing (so to speak) as a fellow airborne soldier, had managed to get himself on the *Today* programme and wanted to direct the discussion away from what had happened at Blue 25 and to look at the bigger picture. He was, by then, on his third tour of Helmand, so Humphries wasn't going to worry him, but he had a go.

'With great respect,' the veteran presenter ominously began, 'you're a brave, highly trained officer in the British Army but you know nothing about the kind of lives those people lead and we know are leading. I mean, we know that a very large proportion of the police force are on drugs. We know that they can effectively buy their way in: they've only got to have a couple of friends vouch for them, senior officers pay £100,000, $100,000, to become a senior police officer. In those circumstances, knowing nothing about the culture of the place, knowing nothing about the tribal relationships and all the rest of it, how can you, however good you are at your job, train those people?'

Tiernan had replied: 'Well, how foolish would it be to go about any kind of operations in Afghanistan without being alongside the Afghan national security forces? If we were just there on our own we'd be far less effective. For instance the Afghan national policemen who I work with have saved the lives of my men by finding improvised explosive devices in the ground. They were metres away from where I was standing but I would not have noticed them because I don't live there. The Afghan desert to me looks pretty similar . . . embedded partnering,' he explained, 'means completely working hand in hand with the Afghan national security forces . . .'

'Living with them?' Humphries interrupted.

'Living with them.'[13]

Chant's funeral was difficult: harder than I had expected. It was the first time I had been back in barracks since leaving the Army, the first time I had seen former comrades, rather than specific friends. There is an awkward celebrity that attaches to grief, I remembered how we used to resent hangers-on, and I felt my civilian status like a visitor, conspicuous in a suit, rather than a uniform: part of something but not part of something, everyone sharing a grief that was, at the same time, intensely private. The wake was in the sergeants' mess bar and, sat under the impassive stares of black-and-white VC-winners and glittering framed medal collections, the very walls of the bar a faint reminder of your own insignificance and a comforting reminder that you were once part of something so much bigger than yourself, the potent mix of mourning and celebration and cheap booze kicked in. Wild schemes were plotted, drunken ideas seemed sensible. None of the Grenadiers asked me if I missed it; they looked me in the eye and told me that I did. I recall speaking to Tiernan, before his radio appearance; he'd been buzzing about Nad-e Ali. 'You've got to see it,' he said. 'It's very different from when you were last there.' What had changed, I wanted to know. 'The manpower, the strategy, everything.' The Afghans? I had asked. 'Yes. But, in a good way.'

There was a regimental saying, appropriate for a sad occasion like the sergeant major's funeral, 'Once a Grenadier, always a Grenadier.' So it proved. A couple of months later I was back in Helmand, in Nad-e Ali, 'visiting friends'.

PART III

An Afghan Christmas

Bastion II

I had heard that a lot had changed by the end of 2009, but it didn't seem like that at first. It didn't matter whether you'd arrived that morning via Dubai on a luxurious Emirates A380 or knackered from Brize Norton on a venerable RAF Tri-Star, the final leg of your journey was still half-snoozing in body armour, uncomfortably propped against the netting in the back of a dark, noisy military transport. It was only on landing in Camp Bastion itself that you began to see it. I glimpsed a sign as the bus made its way from the runway to the onward dumping point, 'Bastion II'. In two years the place had more than doubled in size: it had been a big camp to begin with; now it was massive.

In 2007, Bastion already had the feel of a growing town, was gaining a softness and blurred edge to its perimeter reminiscent of KAF but without the threatening proximity of the hostile city. When I was first there it had the coherence of a defined military base even though it was already the size of a village. Nowadays it is a vast military city: the size of Reading, apparently, if Reading was encircled in 40 kilometres of razor wire. Not thousands but tens of thousands of troops come and go: numbers fluctuate with the RiPs and ops, but the population these days can peak at 30,000. Shorabak itself is no longer an empty home to a couple of undermanned *kandaks* with the fittings ripped out and on sale down in Gereshk, it is the new ANA 3/215 (Maiwand)* Corps

---

* The Battle of Maiwand being the notable defeat of British forces in southern Afghanistan in 1880. The new name for the new corps delighted the cognoscenti and the Anglophobes, but I think the *askar* had preferred being 'Heroes'.

Headquarters. They still play football on the helipad. Bastion is the largest overseas British base since the Second World War and conjoined with the US Leatherneck becomes an unprecedented behemoth, a desert-cam favela bigger even than the massive US airbases now growing weeds in Vietnam. If you took it literally that Bastion was a corner of a foreign field that was forever England, that made it, by some estimates, the country's third-busiest airport:[14] Heathrow, Gatwick and what? An eight-figure grid reference in the middle of the Helmand desert, 15 kilometres west out of Gereshk down the A1 and hang a left at PR 154 308, an unmarked dirt track putting Stansted, Manchester, Birmingham International and the rest to shame.

Apparently, since the US Marines moved in and started trying to sneak across to the British dining rooms, there are thorough ID and finger-scrubbing checks conducted at the hand-wash stations by retired Army chefs who've handed in their berets and picked up KBR* baseball caps and headed straight back out. Hit by a comforting wall of heat, familiar sachet racks of ketchup, mayo, horseradish, mustard and mint sauce. It's not that our food is better than theirs or vice versa; something different is always better in the strange world where days and nights and on the job and off the job merge into one six-month- or year-long haul where twenty minutes on rickety benches with a curry or a Sunday roast is the closest you'll come to a rest. Back in Iraq bored Guardsmen would happily volunteer for extra duties if it meant a trip to a US FOB with a big D-Fac† on the way back in; soda fountains and Ben and Jerry's versus the gallant Royal Logistic Corps fish-fingers – no competition. The Yanks trying to sneak into the Bastion's cookhouses had had enough of their cardboard burgers and were trying

* Kellog Brown and Root.
† As the Americans insisted on called their dining facilities.

to satisfy their craving for something different even if that meant poppadums and warm squash. It was still growing when I returned, more dining rooms being erected for the hungry Marines, two vast chow halls of over-sugared, not-quite-enough-like-home BBQ flavoured ribs and endless packets of free jerky, which have the Brits sneaking in the other direction and somewhat put Pizza Hut and the determinedly quaint NAAFI coffee shop in the shade. Even the reassuringly shabby market stalls selling pirate DVDs and hacking, fake Marlboros are set to be eclipsed by 10,000 square feet of PX, the US Military's relentless travelling malls. For good measure they were also throwing up a 200-seater chapel for the devout or the curious. I wondered when I heard that whether a mischievous contractor had planned those two modern American cathedrals purposefully side by side, two giant shops selling salvation and underpants. I'll bet on which will exert more of a pull on bored and sceptical, kit-hungry and spendthrift young British soldiers, but you never know.

In Bastion it's quite easy to forget about Afghanistan altogether. It's on everyone's minds, of course: no one is under any illusions that they aren't a long way from home and the creature comforts stocked by the NAAFI are few while the local stalls selling cheap military accessories and fake shades for the aspiring special forces Walts* are many. It's not that you can forget that you're deployed, the sense of bustle that intensifies outside the ops rooms and joint operating centres hangs too thickly in in the air and the new Tannoy system all too frequently barks out gloomy calls – *all on duty anaesthetists to the operating theatre* – it's rather that the deployment could be anywhere. You're at war, and if you look carefully you might catch a glimpse of a half

* Named after the eponymous, day-dreaming hero of James Thurber's 1939 short story 'The Secret Life of Walter Mitty'. These fantasists tend to be found in greater numbers the further one gets from any real fighting.

Union Flag, half Afghan Tricolour flash Velcroed to the shoulder of an internationally minded badge hunter, but otherwise there's nothing particularly Afghan about it. All manner of helicopters buzz around the expanding pan:* transport and cargo and even passenger planes hammer relentlessly up and down the runway while everything from monster armoured vehicles to one-man quad bikes churn up the dusty roads and curse the monkeys† on speed gun duty. There's no particular sense of danger, much to the disappointment of an enthusiastic crew of young reporters from a regional paper who've come out without the right insurance and aren't allowed outside. Periodic incidents – a mine-strike close to the gate, a speculative attack on one of the area clearance security patrols which potter around the desert – keep everyone honest, but it could be any bustling rear operating base in any hot and boring war. Afghanistan itself is somewhere over the mountains looming in the distance.

Perhaps this is why there is a subtle difference in the way people seem to behave and even think back in Bastion. Despite the privations being less and the threat negligible, there seems to be more casual whingeing around the camp than out in the more vulnerable patrol bases, and perhaps because Afghanistan seems to be something 'out there', and the Afghans are just the locals selling knock-off DVDs and kids scrabbling for brass at the back of the ranges, there's more ambivalence about the mission and a more dismissive attitude towards the ANA. Maybe only the more embarrassing stories filter through, colouring the

---

* Helipad.

† General term for Military Police common to English-speaking armies. More specifically Americans tend to use the abbreviation MPs, which is considered equally derogatory (and which some cynics might say translates just as well). The Royal Military Police are only rarely referred to by the rest of the Army as Red Caps, which lacks that crucial, pejorative edge.

perceptions of those who don't themselves deal with Afghans in or out of uniform.

The ANA constantly trickles through Bastion, a gentle reminder of the war and one of the only authentically Afghan things in camp, although the warriors don't like the attitude in Bastion and mostly they keep to themselves in Shorabak. You no longer need to take precautions driving from 'ANA' Shorabak to 'ISAF' Camp Bastion. Once we had donned helmets and goggles; now they have both been swallowed by the ever-growing sprawl, and what was once a mad dash through the sparse desert is miles and miles of confused driving through ISO* mazes and up to dead ends of strange reservist camp tents and huge pallets of stores abandoned in the dust. Where once there were clearly two camps, adjacent but separate, now there is just a steady flow of ANA trudging to and from the helipad, attracting curious glances from the newly arrived US reservists and being shooed out of the ISAF shops by officious contractors.

In a scene that must play itself out hundreds of times on every tour, within hours of landing and waiting for my onward transport, I watch a small gaggle of ANA warriors waiting for their own airlift forward to the FOBs: squatting quietly in the gravel, inviting curious stares from the rest of the ISAF troops. The mover gives the brief for the chalk getting on the next Chinook and then looks askance at the louche interpreter shambling towards him in a purple T-shirt and plastic wrap-around shades, more Bollywood than Babaji. One of the Jocks from the current designated 'partnering'† battlegroup rushes in from finishing his

---

* International Standards Organization, the designation given to the metal shipping containers, no fewer than 10,000 of which are the cupboards, walls, offices and bedrooms of Afghanistan.

† 'OMLTing' was out of fashion by the time I went back to Afghanistan. Even 'partnering', which was what the 1 Scots were doing, was being phased out for 'advising' – they all involve exactly the same so far as I can tell.

cigarette to intervene, noticeably protective of 'his' Afghans, and I remember the familiar, proprietary logic with a warm glow: it was all right for those living and working hand in hand with the ANA to slag the guys off, but it was not OK for some bloke in a plastic hi-vis vest to do the same. The mover, in no position to argue with the man in the faded UBACs,* is persuaded to give the brief again to the interpreter and chops the sentences up, dropping conjunctives and enunciating each word like he's talking to a Labrador. The ANA look in with vague interest, which might have as much to do with the female lance-corporal behind the loadie as a desire to know the relevant safety procedures for mounting a CH-47, but you wouldn't have to speak either language to know they're being talked down to.

They could be from any one of a dozen units which now comprise the beefed-up ANA presence throughout Helmand, but it's strange to think again how out of place they look. It's their country, it's really their war, but in Bastion life is about getting people and supplies to where they need to be, keeping birds in the air and soldiers in hospital alive, about getting a fresh scoff and a decent night's sleep and supporting the main effort – it's an essential place, but whatever Afghanistan is it's miles away, and the Afghans might as well just be bullets, beans or any other cargo loaded up and flown on to the FOBs. We waited patiently in our line until the Shawqat chopper was ready, grabbed whatever boxes of mail and resupply needed to go forward and off we went.

* Under-body armour combat shirt, issued primarily to front-line troops and if being worn around somewhere like Bastion probably denoting someone who had just come in from, or was just heading out to, somewhere a bit spicier.

Shawqat

This time round the Grenadiers weren't the mentors; the battalion was the main battlegroup in Nad-e Ali with its own area of responsibility, its own HQ and its own little camp built up around the ruins of an ancient fort: Forward Operating Base Shawqat. The very idea of the fort at Shawqat, overlooking the main market at Nad-e Ali, is almost too good to be true. A perfectly versatile metaphor cited by all sides in the vociferous debate about Afghanistan as comprehensive proof that their contradictory theories are correct. The regular journalists, the in-out commuters with more time in Helmand under their belt than many soldiers by now, are bored of hearing from every captain and above how, when the British first consulted with the locals in Nad-e Ali where they should put the base that was to bring security to the area, they were directed with a wry smile to the one which they used 'last time'. For those who think the whole game in Afghanistan is doomed to failure and a waste of time there's something irresistibly poetic about the British operating back out of a base which was abandoned years ago in what they will insist was defeat then as surely as it will be defeat again now. It suits the Taliban narrative as well: the foreign invader reoccupying the site of his past oppression. The clichéd Afghan memory may not as be as long as the orientalists love to insist: in 2007 I rarely came across any Afghans who 'remembered' or had even heard stories of the bygone British embarrassments at the hands of their ancestors, but the stories about the British burning down the bazaar in 18-whenever-it-was have been retold enough times in the last two years for everyone to pretend they always remembered.

On arrival at Shawqat, invariably by chopper, you become aware for the first time of being in a warzone. Bastion is too big and chaotic to be owned by any one organization or unit or, these days, nation. It feels like the international transit hub and sprawling logistics base it is; it just happens that nearly everyone is in uniform. The reason arriving at Shawqat feels like arriving in the Helmand you've heard about and seen on the TV is the same reason the units that live there prefer it to most other postings in Helmand and why journalists and visitors love it: you're out there, in the thick of things, mere miles and kilometres in various directions from the fluid front line and slap bang in the middle of the real battleground in the evolving counterinsurgency, the centre of mass of population. It is a perfectly located and perfectly sized base: big enough for cooked supper, not so big that there's a KBR cookhouse to lull you into a false sense of security; big enough to plan and launch proper operations from, small enough that it still feels like a real tactical HQ, a real fort.

It's a credit to the Victorian engineers who built it that you can't fault its construction or appointment, although its ruins serve as little more than a curiosity and shell in the middle of the now sprawling FOB home to nearly 1,000 ISAF and ANA troops. The sentry positions, sturdy brick towers up spiral staircases that have fared better than the walls, were used back in 2006 and 2007 by patrols passing through, spending tense but not unpleasant nights harboured up in their cool shadows. Now the camp perimeter is pushed hundreds of metres out, and the walls and towers serve to screen the tented accommodation from the incessant dust and grit thrown up by each thundering incoming Chinook.

In the time it has been home to the *kandak*, Nad-e Ali has been the six-month base of four successive British battlegroups and the occasional motel of itinerant US Marine Corps units, vast columns of M-RAPS and IED-rolling tractors; shady, non-uniformed advisers to the NDS, the Afghan security services, living out of mythically luxurious Portakabins and driving around in beefy Toyotas; scores of visiting journalists; even politicians and the V-VIPs with their twitchy-fingered, shade-wearing, earpiece-tapping, black-body-armoured escorts. The engineers who first made the camp liveable threw up a handful of HABs with their usual, impressive, Hesco-filling speed and lined up the neat rows of tents in which everyone would sleep with further blast protection. In the winter it is cold and muddy, in the summer hot and dusty. Only the ops room and Battlegroup Headquarters have air-conditioning units, and the bustling kitchen which chucks out breakfast and dinner every day for whoever is there is still under canvas. After about six months it gained another FOB rosette with the addition of three ISO-container washing stations, the luxury of nine flushing loos and nine hot showers (strictly no shaving before 1000, as if that is ever going to be hard to enforce).

Not long after that the welfare machines, sturdy desktops for checking Facebook and retro, Amstrad-style typewriters for e-mailing home, got their own dedicated container down by the quartermaster's area of camp, where the more enterprising had already set up a mini-NAAFI flogging essentials like Haribo and Pringles and Help4Heroes wristbands to those with dollars to burn. When I first visited over Christmas the last thing on anyone's mind was sweets; even the *kandak* soldiers were groaning with sickly appreciation under the astonishing weight of chocolate, toiletries and gifts generically known as 'welfare', which the combination of free post out to Afghanistan and the frankly humbling generosity of folks back home, fed up of seeing the taut faces of young sisters and wives and mothers trying not to cry at funerals, had sent avalanching into Helmand. Abashed, eighteen-year-old Guardsmen on their first tours smiled and then winced as their mates tore into weekly parcels from their mothers, guessing before they were even open exactly what would be in them, while section commanders growled good-naturedly: 'I thought I told you to tell your fucking mum that we prefer salt'n'vinegar.' Outside the cookhouses two vast bins stood full to the brim of toothpaste, toothbrushes, deodorants and soaps as much of which found their way, presumably via the ANA and ANP, out into the market as into the soldiers' wash bags. The Army had always been 'pongos' to the Navy and Marines, but it seemed the wider public had really taken the lack of hygiene out in patrol bases to heart and decided the British Army needed urgent and fragrant talcum powdering. Forget hearts and minds, we could have washed Helmand there and then in lavender scrub. The excitement was the occasional triumphant cry of a passing sergeant who had spotted something premium like a set of Mach 3 razor blades or a new and exciting 'posh' shower gel and emerged triumphant from the ensuing scrum, leaving the rest ferreting around in the hope it wasn't a one-off.

Under the roar and exhaust fumes of the Merlin, running out on to the Shawqat helipad, you're directed by screaming sergeants to kneel up against a nearby wall. An efficient and well-choreographed procession of quad-bikes and soldiers simultaneously loads and unloads: mail, ammo, wide-eyed new bods, resigned-back-off-leave bods, scruffy going-home bods, blue-helmeted journos, suitcase-wheeling interpreters and even bomb-sniffing dogs and ANA chickens are quickly shuffled in and out while you wait, the least of everyone's concerns, kneeling against a wall in the dust. There is something reassuring about this, something deeply impressive about finally being sufficiently far forward that operational priorities – the chopper must be on the deck for not a second longer than necessary – trump all other considerations. Hurry up and wait is a familiar mantra to all servicemen and can be as comforting as it is frustrating. In contrast to the tragedy of the commons, Shawqat feels demonstrably owned, a base with the authoritative stamp of a strong regimental sergeant major, home to a unit with a quiet and determined sense of collective purpose. The chopper safely off, you're marched without ceremony to the Battlegroup HQ and pulled in: take out your notebooks, sirs, ma'ams, gents, 'scuse rank, etc., etc., for a proper briefing on how the camp runs; meal timings, actions on indirect fire attack, emergency muster points, first aid drills and so on. This is a working Forward Operating Base – or at least one side of it is.

Running down the middle of the camp is a dividing Hesco wall topped with a token concertina of barbed wire. One end marks the back of the helipad, the last marker for an approach to landing and take-off which still manages to cut it quite fine and nearly take the roof of the tents which overcrowding has huddled up too close to where the wheels of the Merlins and Chinooks scrape inches over the wire. Along for a couple of hundred feet it marks the back of the vehicle park; neat lines of an incredible cornucopia of off-the-peg armoured vehicles mock those returning to Afghanistan from the unrecognizable past of only two or three years back, when you were lucky with your WMIK. Huge Cougars and Mastiffs tower like lorries above the fence, their protected turrets and automated weapon systems the stuff the boys were only dreaming off last time they were here as they were issued flimsy panels of plastic and elastic ties to 'protect' their Land Rovers, highly mobile Jackals with enormous mine-proof wheels and Panther command vehicles brimming with electronic wizardry all stand in the correct order for whatever the next likely crash out is and hide the desert roses which are the more rudimentary pissers and remnants of a time when Shawqat was a little more basic. Beyond, the drainpipe urinals, still hugging the dividing Hesco fence, the planning tents and HQs ops rooms are linked by durable plastic walkways and sit in a horseshoe round the simple, effective memorial to the British soldiers who have died operating out of the base, new names carved diligently in the wood by each outgoing regimental pioneer sergeant, each incoming regiment adding its own sad flourishes. Almost unnoticeably the plastic walkway snakes off in a narrow gap between two of the squat structures, bustling twenty-four hours a day with officers and senior non-commissioned officers and watch-keepers and signallers; a soldier minding his own business, keeping out of the way of trouble and rank, might not even know that it leads past two welfare telephones and the dense wire and metal forest of the antenna farm, through a gap in the Hesco fence, to the other side of the camp, the Afghan side.

The difference is not noticeable at first. The plastic walkway continues past an identical Hesco and canvas ops room to the ones on the British side; tall antennas out the back hint at the planning and battle direction going on inside, the constant flow of digital traffic out and back from the patrols and units on the ground. And as you come round the corner, a neat row of accommodation tents and open dining and relaxing area strewn with improvised weights and dilapidated canvas chairs is identi-kit British in Helmand. Further beyond, however, things start to look more foreign – or less foreign, depending on your point of view. Original concrete and mud buildings, shunned by ISAF as vulnerable and structurally unsound and usually ignored or built around, sprawl with life and colour. On the flat roofs of some, touching distance beneath the bellies of the Chinooks thundering in, camp beds and mosquito nets have been erected, and pairs of boots stand, airing in the breeze. Corrugated-iron 'car-ports' shade the gaudily painted Humvees and battered Ford Rangers, which seem tiny next to the monster Mastiffs next door but remain the workhorses of the ANA. Some new buildings house cool, open rooms with carpeted floor and small televisions in the corner. Variously, chaotically, soldiers come and go with ornate kettles and small glass cups of *chai*, sergeants sit cross-legged arguing over nominal rolls, and officers snooze. The atmosphere, though more haphazard, is much calmer than on the British side, and in the middle of the main concentration of huts and buildings and beds which is the closest thing to HQ, about where on the British side in the corresponding arrangement you find the simple cross and memorial and the battalion flags of the current battlegroup, there is an immaculately tended garden.

Khoja Wakil posing in front of the ANA garden at FOB Shawqat. The HQ den is behind the lace curtain.

Depending on the mood of the mentors, the ANA garden in Shawqat is a microcosm of progress or futility, gradual, hard-won success or inevitable, tragic failure. Head-shaking, sarcastic Brits can't believe the effort that goes into tending the garden, a soldier posted on watering duty like clockwork even while sentries neglect their duty on the outer security sangars. An ornate and lovingly assembled picket fence marks off the dazzling green grass square, lined with bright pink roses when I was last there, with even a cute little door frame opposite the *kandak* commanders' room which might one day be wreathed in creepers. After a particularly bad week for casualties a few months back it was decided to do an intensive batch of refresher training in counter-IED drills and mine-clearance exercises. From Shawqat all the way out to the most distant patrol bases, the *kandak* commanders and the now-whatever-OMLT-was-called sub-units rehearsed the life-saving drills in the scorching sun and coached the non-commissioned officers through a series of further lessons they could go through with their squads in their own time: how to identify the threat, to mark it and then to plot a safe route back with bright-orange mine tape. A couple of days later a request came in to the company sergeant major from the *kandak* supply sergeant: could they have some more supplies of mine tape? Significant looks were exchanged and smiles played on the lips of the trainers: the sobering lessons of the casualties were starting to sink in. Of course they could have some more mine tape, gladly. Except there didn't seem to be any further training being conducted, and the fatalistic attitude to basic drills remained. The mine tape appeared a couple of days later, meticulously wound round the picket fence as a colourful addition to the decorative garden border.

The *kandak* XO didn't see this in quite the same way as the exasperated mentors. He laughed at the unfortunate coincidence of the request and training, but why wouldn't his soldiers want to make Shawqat more bearable, with gardens and mine tape and beds on the roofs if they so wished. The mentors all flew home at the end of the tour; our beds and gardens were thousands of miles away. The difference between the two Shawqats was that one was never going to be anything other than the efficient, temporary, operational home of a transient force with a keen eye already on R&R and the homecoming parades, the other was where the *kandak* were expected to live. Only one side of the camp may have been an effective, recognizable Forward Operating Base, but only the other side of camp was expected to be a garrison, a home.

I had been told the story about the garden while organizing my trip so I knew that there were ANA based in Shawqat, but no one had mentioned which unit. 'We've got a couple of surprises for you,' I was told on arrival by the grinning ops officer as he walked me round to the Afghan side. Gathered around the garden and sat on rugs in the ops room were the men of 1/3/205:

Reunited with Qiam in the middle of Nad-e Ali, December 2009.

Syed Meraj was in the corner, poring over a notebook, Sergeant 'Jimmy', who'd driven with me up to Sangin, stopped on his way past with a double take of recognition, and from over by the vehicles there came a familiar voice, followed as he rounded the corner by a familiar grin and a familiar shout – of all the FOBs in all the world: *Toran Padi!* roared Qiam, and he enveloped me in a hug.

Friends Reunited

I don't know what I had expected from that trip, but I genuinely hadn't expected to see Qiam and the boys again. I'd made a couple of enquiries before heading out to see the Grenadiers, but Helmand was a big place, Afghanistan bigger, and no one seemed to know with any certainty which ANA units were where, let alone who the individual troops were.

The surge of warm feeling and happy coincidence was overwhelming on my part and seemed genuine on theirs. ANA soldiers I am certain I had never seen before in my life appeared from behind low stone buildings and arrived in vehicles and enthusiastically joined the huddle, and the frenzy of backslapping and handshaking that ensued was only broken up by the timely roar and downdraft of an incoming resupply. Everyone had somewhere else to be, so I promised to come back and join them for supper that evening and went off to sort my kit out, completely distracted, buzzing with an excitement which stayed with me for the rest of the day.

Sat cross-legged on dusty blankets, smoking in the HQ room later that night, a trickle of low, Dari chatter in the background, it was like the past two years had never happened. 'I wrote a book about you.' I told Qiam and Syed excitedly. I wasn't being deliberately disingenuous, it felt like I had. Some poor young second-lieutenant on the British side had been sent a copy by a well-meaning uncle. Someone fetched the dog-eared paperback, and we all sat huddled over it, pointing with the thrill of recognition at the photos of me looking younger and thinner and the Afghans all looking the same. Later, when it was just the two of us, I realized as I flicked through the pages, trying to find some good bits for Syed, that I hadn't written a book about them after all; like all first-time writers I had just written a book about myself.

Syed was too polite to say anything. He told me later that the whole idea of being written about at all, seeing his own name in print, 12/14.75 Monotype Bembo, was so alien that he had struggled to get his head around it and hadn't even noticed me skipping apologetically over two-thirds of the book. Qiam noticed though. Already deeply unimpressed that I was no longer a soldier, he had spent the evening telling me that I should have been carrying a gun, that I would get bored if I wasn't a soldier. He peered suspiciously at photos of Sandhurst and Iraq as if it was a betrayal to have been anywhere other than Afghanistan, have done anything other than fight with him. Qiam dropped the orange book dismissively to one side and interrupted the 'terp who'd just returned with instructions from HQ: 'Hey, Padi. Do you remember our first battle with the Dushka?* This was our best action ever, a hard fight. I want you to write this in a story.'

We all looked at each other, at the book Qiam had tossed to one side, at the Dictaphone one of the younger soldiers was playing with – I'd got it out to illustrate 'journalist', to deflect the accusatory questions about why I didn't have a rifle any more. I couldn't work out if it was a request or a challenge, but it hung in the air until one of the mentors stuck his head in to fetch me and the 'terp back across to the British side for orders. The ops officer had promised me a couple of surprises. The

* Apparently the Russian translation for the heavy machine-gun's nickname was roughly 'darling', which was a pretty accurate summary of the affection that Qiam obviously had for the weapon. Fair enough, the number of times it had got him out of a tight spot.

ANA was one, the other was getting out on what sounded like it was going to be a punchy little fighting patrol first thing tomorrow morning. I asked the 'terp to explain that I had to go and get my kit ready and began to leave.

Outside the fug of the HQ room the night was sharp. I realized with a shiver that I had never been cold in Afghanistan before, that winter was as unfamiliar as being a civilian. Patrolling out tomorrow with a camera instead of an SA-80 surely fell within Qiam's favourite idea of *kharkus*, crazy or brave. There had been genuine reproach in his voice, and he wasn't wrong: he had been, all the ANA had been, little more than flecks of colour in a breathless, youthful memoir. I stuck my head back in through the flap of cloth that passed for a door and extended my arm, clasping the Dictaphone in a clenched fist into the room. 'When I get back tomorrow, you tell me everything you want in a story and I will write it.' The 'terp had already gone back across, but Syed smiled and nodded, translating for Qiam, who grinned. Tomorrow evening. Syed promised to make chips, my favourite. We had a date, but first I had a patrol.

Two years and three months after I had watched Sangin receding from the back of a Chinook, exhausted, empty but happy, I found myself waist-deep in a cold ditch, watching the bright-pink petals detach from the flower I'd been handed minutes before by the smiling, toothless old villager who'd warned us not to come down this path and realized with a shiver that could have been cold but was more likely excitement just how right he had been. If you forced yourself to poke your head up long enough you could see the muzzle flash from the corner of the building, about 100 metres to the front, but the hedges themselves were shaking violently with the weight of incoming fire, and the hyperventilating of the young guy curled up next to me dragged me away from the mesmeric effect of the petals, floating calmly, mockingly delicate in the brown water around my waist.

Shouts rang out up the ditch, grit flew as those stuck out in the open scrabbled and slithered towards the safety of the cover, willing their bodies low into the frozen, rutted track and silently making trade-offs that they'd never again complain about sore knees and leopard crawls in training. I realized two things at the same time, my Dictaphone, foolishly stored in a trouser pocket for easy access, was probably ruined, and, which was worse, I was completely unarmed. For a second I felt a rising panic, bile in my throat, scrambled around in my grab bag, felt the weight of an utterly useless knife and reached round for a camera, something, anything to do with my hands. At the front the patrol commander was barking out instructions, the right ones, I paused to think, which was exactly why he wouldn't have wanted me out on this patrol with him. Real embedded journalists were one thing; some guy with a camera who'd been doing your job a year ago and probably still thought he could was an absolute nightmare. My hands felt itchy, useless, and then I remembered the guy next to me, breathing at a rate of knots and cradling the Minimi like a safety blanket; he'd just arrived from home, this was his first tour, his first patrol. I grabbed him by the helmet.

'You all right?' I screamed, surprised by the noise and how loudly I needed to shout to be heard. He'd looked up, as if out of a reverie, and nodded. 'Good,' I'd bellowed redundantly. 'Can you see the flash?' He shook his head, and I steered us round so we could see the corner. Now he nodded, and even through the thick, damp osprey armour you could feel something stiffen in the young man, something grow, something straighten in the spine. Still, ever so slightly he paused, my hands itched nervously. 'Well, get some fucking rounds down then,' and the weapon burst to life, and a glow surged through the both of us. I forgot my nakedness and redundancy, living the ambush through the young private like a Small Arms School Corps instructor in a horrible, pale-olive utility waistcoat. We burrowed our way up towards the firing point where the ANA platoon leading the patrol was pausing to launch the final assault, and I looked up to see Sergeant Jimmy in a black beanie, grinning like a lunatic and giving me a big thumbs-up, and, perched on a roof with a pair of binos like Will Ferrell playing Monty, Toran Lalaka, Qiam's right-hand man, who also looked down and gave me a hearty wave just as the rate of fire went up, and someone shouted 'GO!' and everyone broke the cover of the ditch and charged headlong for the door.

Hazrat had been right when we had said our goodbyes up in Sangin, the Grenadiers had been right at Daz Chant's funeral, Qiam was right as he had looked through me last night. I had missed them. I had missed this.

Sergeant Jimmy

Sergeant Jimmy was the first ANA soldier I interviewed rather than just chatted to: the first guy I asked if I could record our conversation with a view to actually sitting down and writing about the *kandak*, the first guy who shrugged and thought: sure, why not, posterity will be proud. He was commanding a small group of ANA, only half a platoon, sharing a run-down roadside shack with a handful of 2 Yorks mentors up on the northern edge of where the Nad-e Ali security bubble gave way to more contested land. Little more than some covered sleeping rooms around a Hesco checkpoint, Blue 17, its map designation, made it sound more permanent than it was. Looking out from the sangar over the flat no-man's land, the wooden struts marked by bored sentry doodles and hastily scribbled references of incoming fire, I realized it was exactly like the first PB we had shared, presumably exactly like all the other PBs he had more or less been living in since.

Jimmy had heard on the radio from someone in Shawqat that one of the old mentors was back so was half expecting me. I told him about my surprise reunion with Qiam and Syed the day before and about Qiam's suggestion that I should write about the *kandak* as he welcomed me into the checkpoint with a broad smile and a cup of *chai*. We were only there to launch the patrol forward, but we had twenty minutes or so while the guys got their kit ready. He had paused, thoughtfully. I wanted to check he didn't mind having his words recorded so I asked the 'terp to explain again. Jimmy sat on the edge of a camp-cot, staring impassively at the teapot before looking up at me and nodding, not smiling, but determined as if to say, 'Well, get on with it then.'

Sergeant Jimmy had first come to our attention back in 2007 thanks to his insistence on his nickname. It had been during those chaotic early Shorabak days when we couldn't tell most of the *kandak* apart let alone knew any of their names, and we couldn't have been more relieved than when a thin, hard-looking soldier suddenly introduced himself as 'Jimmy' and we gratefully seized on it, glad to be able to put any sort of name to a face. I never did find out if it was a pure nickname or just a version of an actual Afghan name which the months of working with thick-tongued Brits and give-a-shit Americans had taught him we'd find much easier to remember and pronounce. It stuck

Sergeant Jimmy in 2009, smart as a carrot in the new ANA digicam and proudly wearing the UK 11 Brigade Tactical Recognition Flash on his right arm.

like 'Smiler' and 'Tree Frog' and 'Mr Bumblebee' and was hope-fully less offensive.* He was a loudmouth around camp and had picked up just enough English, we assumed from his previous mentors as it was mostly military jargon and filth, to make him-self heard and obvious. It seemed at first like he might be trouble; he attended all the early training we tried to conduct with the *kandak* but refused to take part in any of it. He admitted to being, or was claiming to be, a non-commissioned officer, which was more than some of his peers were doing, but like them on the rare occasions he was wearing uniform he certainly wasn't wearing his rank slides.

Jimmy was from Badakshan right up in the far north-east of Afghanistan, a Tajik from a province with a huge border with Tajikistan itself and even a tiny sliver up in the mountains touch-ing China. Helmand was as foreign a country to him as it was to the Fijians and Brummies getting ready outside. His family had stayed put during the years that the Taliban were in power, rela-tively remote and relatively untroubled. Nonetheless he spoke with feeling about the 'many problems' of Taliban rule, Tajik and Uzbek and Turkmen all 'divided', was the interesting word he used, with only the Pashtuns well looked after. This was familiar enough and almost what seemed to be taught to all Afghan recruits undergoing training, but I was struck by it com-ing from Jimmy, who was too much of a cynic to parrot lines. He hadn't fought during the tumultuous early nineties, perhaps he was too young, though he never told me his actual age, and had done what little work he could on building sites during the years of Taliban rule. After 2001 he had tried to work as a driver and had moved with his family to Kunduz province but hadn't

---

* All names which by the end of the tour Ismail, Ali Ahmat, Toran Lalaka and Jamal had embraced, although Lalaka didn't know who Will Ferrell was and, for once, no one had a copy of *Anchorman* to show him.

found much work there. He had decided to join the Army, he said, 'when Karzai became president of Afghanistan'. The dates made sense: Karzai was formally elected president at the end of 2004, and there had then followed the first major recruiting and training drive for the ANA. Jimmy had arrived in Kabul and started his training in 2005, but I couldn't quite believe the hard, grinning sergeant prepping to push out on patrol from Blue 17 had rallied to the flag just for his new president. He had always seemed a natural soldier.

We had caught a glimpse of that the first time we took the *kandak* out on to the ranges. Soldiers who had been utterly uninterested when we tried to do lessons in camp were naturally more excited to be getting out with their weapons, even if it was only into the desert by the back gate, where the biggest risk was from the suicidal kids picking up the brass.* Even after we'd tried to sort out the mess that was the Kandak armoury there were still a couple of soldiers who turned up with weapons we'd never seen before. One of them was Jimmy's. He'd been keeping it under his bed, he explained with a shrug, as if to say, no big deal. What was encouraging was that it seemed to be immaculately clean, oiled and maintained. What was even more impressive was that Jimmy, unlike many of his colleagues on the ranges that day, could really shoot.

Jimmy was difficult to read; neither out and out difficult to work with nor fully cooperative like Syed or Mujib. I thought he was cynical, one of those guys with a calculated laziness, but he had a passionate streak and had nearly flown off the handle when patrolling with Will Harries' OMLT and 1 Tolay during the confusing early phases of Op Silicon. Harries' team of six

---

* The spent casings apparently fetched a decent price at the local market. The problem was persuading the kids not to try and come on to the range to pick them up while people were still firing.

Grenadiers and an ANA platoon had been driving back from what passed for the front line in a creaking convoy, his one working WMIK towing the one that didn't, the ANA's Rangers showing their age. A decent-sized IED would have done for either, but that was back in the good old days when the Taliban still thought they could have an open gun battle and win. The Green Zone north of Gereshk in spring was a muddle of villages and fields, sprawling stone compounds and acres and acres of poppy where mostly the locals had seemed pleased to see us and everything was open and friendly.

Friendly until Jimmy, patrolling ahead of the front wagon, had turned the corner into a hail of fire, accurate and sustained and deadly fire, not some haphazard insurgent chancer with a rusty PKM,* which turned out to be another British platoon who had misunderstood the concept of battle-space management. After some pretty heated exchanges over the net, the guys had said, fairly enough, that the lead ANA scout wasn't really wearing any uniform so had looked just like a raggedy guy coming towards them with a gun. Jimmy, who had been that scout, said equally fairly enough, though I suspect the interpreter had watered some of it down for us, that seeing as he was patrolling next to a bunch of British soldiers who were not only wearing uniform but carrying expensive radios which he thought we fucking talked to each other on, he was hardly likely to be Taliban. Perhaps the whole thing could have been laughed off, the kind of thing that happens all the time in that strange, thick gloop they call the fog of war, but some locals had been caught in the crossfire, and, as if that wasn't bad enough, a couple of girls had even been hurt. Will and the mentors who'd been there

* The PKM was not dissimilar to the British Army's universally unpopular (and by now pretty obsolete) LSW, the light support weapon (or 'long shit weapon', as it was affectionately known).

came in looking haunted, the unit that had been fired on even more so, obviously, but the ANA had been more angry than sad, and none more so than Jimmy.

I saw that seriousness again when I asked him about his family. He had got married quite soon after being shot at by the British – nothing like a near-death experience to stiffen the resolve. By the time I sat down with him again more than two years had passed and he had had a daughter but, as it turned out, hadn't seen her or his wife for over a year and was still waiting for his leave. The grin vanished, and he stared at the floor. 'I can't describe home,' he said, 'I cannot talk about my family, because then I will have to think about them, and they are not here.' We changed the subject, but he returned to it when talking about the challenges of being an Afghan soldier. 'I have not seen them for years. This is why it is hard.'

Gloomy thoughts of home permeated the cold and muddy outpost, hung like everywhere else with slightly sad-looking Christmas decorations. I changed tack and asked him what his happiest memories of being in the Army were. I soon learned not to ask this question, or to try and phrase it more subtly in order not to get the sweetly polite but surely not true reply 'All the time we spend working with our British partners.' This was Hassan and his cheesy chips all over again, and I had particular difficulty accepting the stock answer from a guy who had been shot at by his 'British partners'. Even more embarrassingly, with that same polite insincerity which is a frustrating *lingua franca* in Afghanistan but not as inherently dishonest as exasperated ISAF troops tend to think, Jimmy began fondly remembering the 'missions' we had done together, me and him and Toran Will as if the three of us had taken Helmand alone (while I quietly wondered why Will had been given an unmerited historical promotion and I hadn't). Later, as I sat listening to the others reminiscing, I realized again that this sense that the time we had spent with the *kandak* in 2007 was some sort of golden era probably was true, but it had very little to do with us. Before the summer of 2007 the *kandak* was still finding its feet; by 2008 it was starting to tire and getting more challenging postings. By the end of 2009, as I sat listening to Jimmy, they were all knackered. He hadn't lost the mischievous spark though.

What was the funniest, stupidest thing that had happened to him in the Army? I asked. A smile. 'When you took us on a mission up in Sangin and wouldn't give us any water.' I smiled too. On one of the few operations we did without Qiam or Syed or Mujib, Toran Lalaka and I had taken a hand-picked squad on a long fighting patrol with the Royal Anglians: MOGging with the Vikings in the Vikings.* It had been a tough few days, and we had been hammered as we limped into Sangin, but the ANA had been most upset about running out of water in the middle of the desert. Apparently all my fault, although I got no thanks for swallowing my pride and begging some off the Brits after I'd spent most of the patrol arguing with the commander that he wasn't using the ANA enough, that he should give us more responsibility. I couldn't be bothered to reignite a two-year-old argument and could tell from the chuckling that there was an element of teasing going on. Jimmy had been given plenty of water like everyone else on the patrol and, like most of the others, he had wasted it instead of saving it for the long op like we'd told him to.

With Jimmy you suspected he might even have sold some of it down at the market in Gereshk. He had that canny cynicism and, after all, he had known then as I harangued him just as he

---

* A MOG was a mobile operations group, a bigger-than-usual, longer-than-usual fighting patrol. 1 Royal Anglians, nicknamed the Vikings, were, confusingly enough, often ferried around Helmand by the Armoured Squadron of Royal Marines driving the tracked Viking vehicles, hence the silliness.

knew now that ultimately I would go and fetch him some more. If people know that you'll give them something for free whether they waste it or not, they will waste it, and if Jimmy or another sharp sergeant had made a few cents on water it was at least better than flogging it to the Taliban, who always seemed to have a few too many bits and pieces of kit that had previously been lent or given in good faith to the ANA. There would be the usual hypocritical over-reaction, as if the lads never put their own unwanted kit on eBay,* and then everyone would remember we had more important things to worry about than where the unwanted rations ended up. I reminded him that he never seemed thirsty himself, always seemed to have a can of soda to hand when everyone else was on rations. He laughed again: that was because, unlike me, he said, he was brave enough to go to the shops.

In that way Jimmy encapsulated many of the frustrating paradoxes of the ANA. A good shot who couldn't be bothered to make sure his squad looked after their weapons. Too lazy to carry enough water for a short patrol, but brave enough to dash out into the centre of Sangin with fire-fights raging just up the road to pick up some Mirinda, which he'd then share with you. He missed his wife and baby girl, but he enjoyed soldiering and knew he was good at it. I had last seen him in 2007, ramshackle and dirty at the end of a too-long operation and off for leave, maybe his most recent. In the *kandak*'s smart new digicam combats, having traded in their AK47s for M16s, Jimmy and his squad looked the part. He was wearing his rank now, and Velcro badges galore after the current fashion, and looked a more complete soldier. What was more, he had survived four years on the front line. We had had only the briefest of chats over *chai* while

---

* Or even, like a wonderfully dim Irish Guardsman once in Wellington Barracks, an actual rifle.

the vehicles were made ready, and the next thing we knew the patrol commander was shouting for everyone to mount up. I apologized as I headed out, and we agreed to meet again later, but when we came bouncing back in to the checkpoint two hours later, buzzing on the adrenalin of the fight and all of us covered in cold sludge from the crawl up the ditch, me still pinching myself to be back like that, Jimmy had already disappeared on a resupply.

Two days later the *kandak* was providing a security cordon for a *shurah* in Shin Khalay, north of Nad-e Ali. It was the first public event in Shin Khalay since the ferocious fighting summer of Op Panther's Claw and the first chance for what passed as Afghan civil society to stamp its authority on what had been a wild west village only a few weeks back, a chance to offer the bored-looking farmers an alternative to being scared of both Taliban and ISAF depending on who was rampaging through their fields at the time. It was a big deal. The patrol we'd done together two days earlier had been to probe the insurgent positions around the village, see which compounds they were fighting from and where they didn't want us to go. For the past forty-eight hours elements from the Grenadier Guards battle-group had been engaging those targets, fighting the insurgents if they were there and occupying the strongholds. That morning the entire *kandak* had been out in force, providing the security for the soft stuff to follow, even Qiam strutting around importantly with a new radio, preparing the ground for the first time that Habibullah, the larger-than-life and twice-as-bearded governor of Nad-e Ali, would speak openly to the villagers. The *shurah* was better attended than the civilian advisors had hoped it would be. The elders listened while the governor and police chief explained what the hell it was we were all doing there and seemed reasonably impressed when the local British commander said his piece. Some of the grey beards nodded, others remained impassive and some narrowed eyes shot fire and daggers at the infidels throughout the whole thing, but at least they were all there. In nearly every respect it was the model little operation for what we were supposed to be doing in Helmand, a million miles from platoon houses and mowing the grass.

Sergeant Jimmy was on a perimeter security task. As the *shurah* was drawing to a close his patrol disturbed a man trying to arm an IED on the route the governor was likely to take out. In the panic the guy decided better to blow something up than nothing. His squad captured the bomber, but Jimmy lost both his legs in the blast. When I asked around, none of the guys had seen or heard from him since he disappeared in the back of the medevac.

Snapshot

Spend even the briefest amount of time in the Army and you'll
have more group photos than you know what to do with: pre-
tour, mid-tour, post-tour, course, team, unit, parade and every
other faint justification. On the walls of thousands of down-
stairs loos hundreds of tiny faces, virtually indistinguishable,
stare out under ever so slightly different identical hats. If you
look carefully you'll see a couple of tragic jokers looking off-
camera into the distance;* at least one goon, First XV veteran
no doubt, pulling a 'war face'; inevitably an earnest-looking
foreign cadet looking straight ahead with an enormous beret;
and, usually, a subtle grouping together of certain regiments
and corps. Within the constraints of the tallest in the middle,
shortest to the flank, you'll see the Guardsmen vaguely together
at the back, the Cavalry boys all sat together. What you may or
may not see, but I promise you it's there somewhere, is a rogue
cock or ball.†

I got back off patrol from Blue 17, fresh from talking with
Sergeant Jimmy and keen to try and do the same with Qiam and
all the others. I had promised Syed I would bring my laptop
with me to supper so that while we talked the guys could pick
photos for me to burn on to CD-ROMs for them, and while I

---

* Guilty: Second Lieutenants P. R. Hennessey and J. A. R. Quarrie, PCBC
051, Brecon 2005.

† I was delighted to see that while this book was being edited, the *Radio Times*
had fallen for this oldest of gags by including a photo of 42 Commando,
Royal Marines, relaxing during their decompression in Cyprus, with a very
casual but very obvious johnson hanging out in the front row.

was waiting to head over I started flicking through the digital albums from 2007, looking for good shots of us all together. Sure enough, we must have summoned the battalion photographer because there's a nicely framed shot of the whole Queen's Company, in front of our vehicles in full war kit on the morning before Silicon. Of course, you can't tell who anyone is in the photo; I only know which one of the tiny pink heads is mine because I can remember where I was standing, but that's not the point. Disappointingly, we didn't do a joint photo with the ANA, so the closest thing I have to a group photo of the *kandak* is a series of unstaged shots which someone must have taken when we did the big joint O-Group for Op Silicon. Up until that point the powers that be had wanted to keep as much of the detail of the plan secret from the ANA as possible. It was a ludicrous measure not only because nothing made soldiers more

1st Kandak O-group for Op Silicon, Camp Shorabak, 27 April 2007.

resentful than not being provided with up-to-date information no matter which language they speak, but also because the 'terps just told the ANA everything anyway. Officially I was only able to plan around vague dates with Mujib and Qiam; in practice they already knew as much if not more than I did, so it was a huge relief when we were finally given the nod to get the whole *kandak* together and run through the plan in front of all the soldiers.

It's not entirely clear what is going on, and when I say 'the whole *kandak*' I obviously only mean 'all those who were there at the time', but these snapshots are the closest I have, and they tell their own story: there are no balls on display. The best photo shows young and old, bored and interested, all squatting around a hollow square, ten foot by ten foot in the desert criss-crossed with little dug trenches, coloured ribbons and dotted with upturned ammo boxes which were supposed to represent the series of fields and compounds the *kandak* would be assaulting through within the next couple of days.

The *kandak* on its haunches must have been boiling in body armour and helmets, and we had insisted every soldier parade in his full kit so that we could check they all had it. Stood in the near left corner is 2 Tolay; Hazrat with his head neatly shaved leans slightly forward in his body armour, hands clasped behind his back, staring intently at the model. To the rear, in the 1 Tolay corner, Lieutenant Harries and his 'terp, faintly ridiculous in a white linen shirt tucked into combats and a schemagh wrapped around his head, point something out to the greying, fidgety commander. To their right Marouf and Mujib are talking to the 3 Tolay soldiers, relaxed with their back to the camera. Qiam is also looking hard at the model, while Nawroz and I look bored in the far right corner: Nawroz out of place but at least cool in flowing white *shalwar kameez*, me, pretty silly in a cut-down desert hat, wielding the long VHF radio antenna as my mighty three-foot pointer. Stood in the middle of the chaotic scene, Guardsman Lloyd looks straight back into the lens, hot and bemused. Later, General Mohaiyadin added his personal touch to the orders. Nothing we were taught at Sandhurst or Brecon about the rousing delivery of a 'Summary of Execution' to stir the troops compared to the old warrior whipping his bags into a frenzy. Major David later recalled that one of his greatest regrets was not getting a photograph of the *kandak* roaring 'Allah-u-akbar' out across the desert.

Back with the ANA, sipping super-sweet Mirinda which Syed had brought specially from the stores and flipping open the laptop while everyone huddles round to point and laugh at the old photos and zoom in on who looks scared and who doesn't, the first photo I bring up is that same one of the *kandak* O-group. There are nods of recognition around the room, Qiam points to himself with satisfaction, but what strikes me as we go through, first that photo and then the subsequent snaps, is that, although it has only been two and a half years, there's virtually no one left. Every time I zoom in on a half-remembered face, or wonder about this soldier or that soldier, the replies are the same: the lucky ones have left, the unlucky ones, injured or worse. I looked again at the photo of the *kandak* sat around before Silicon, and contemplate the waste.

The next few hours passed in blissful recollection. It's difficult to explain how torrid months of fighting can be remembered as a halcyon period, salad days when we were green in uniform as well as in judgement. There was quite a gaggle in the room that night, so I started off by throwing it open to the floor, asking the soldiers about their most striking memories of being with the *kandak*. I looked to Qiam and to Mujib, who had stuck his head in just as we had finished playing with the laptop and was now making himself comfortable on a rolled-up sleeping bag, but to my surprise it was one of the soldiers I barely knew at all, Younes, the logistics sergeant, who spoke up first.

He too remembered Op Silicon as the 'best story', remembered Mohaiyadin visiting the patrol bases up on the front line by Kakaran, full of fulsome praise of his heroes, who had been first to the finish line, but he also remembered the three days we spent protecting the Engineers while they built the bases: 'There was no food, no water, only fighting.' A slight exaggeration, but I let it go; a good story to impress the younger soldiers on a cold night in Shawqat just like we all did at home. He also remembered the *kandak* up in Sangin, his least-favourite memories of his whole time in the Army. 'There were others who ran away, but then came back,' he said, shaking his head and, perhaps it is just my imagination, perhaps not, darting a glance at some of the jokers in the corner. He talks of Musa Qala, after my time, capturing the District Centre, and the frustration of having meat and supplies, 'but not a single moment to cook it. We spent months in Musa Qala district doing nothing but fighting. Then another *kandak* came and we went back to Shorabak.'

'The best time I have spent in the Army,' he said, without a hint of a smile, 'is on leave.'

Younes, someone said, was the oldest soldier in the *kandak*. I'd looked over to him at the time for confirmation, and he had shrugged and nodded, not absolutely certain. The problem with such a statement is it's relatively meaningless. It was our own brigade commander in 2007 who observed that trying to get sensible numbers out of the Afghans was impossible: there was just 'one', 'two' and 'lots'. Khoja Wakil, another of the older soldiers in the *kandak*, had once tried to explain to me that the reason he was now a mere sergeant when he had formerly been a colonel was because the ANA was too small; back in the day, he insisted, the Afghan army had been 10 million strong. A lot was said about the problems of building a civil society out of an illiterate one, the difficulty of training recruits who couldn't read or write, but in pure military terms innumeracy was as great a problem, maybe even more dangerous. The British Army, after all, had a long and pretty recent tradition of functionally illiterate soldiers, countless devices and traditions from different-coloured chits* to soldiers counting off on parade supposedly harked back to an illiterate army, but you always needed to know how many rounds you had left and how many enemy there were. It used to worry us when we first heard that 100 Taliban were approaching until we discovered it usually meant more than whoever had seen them could count on his fingers.

When it came to ages it was the same: you were basically either young, old or over forty, so Younes was ancient. On the other hand, whether he was 'TV' old, 'Army' old or 'Bus Pass' old, there was no doubt Younes had been around the *kandak* for ever, one of the originals. Qiam and Syed confirmed as much. The fact that I'd never met him, or more pertinently the fact that he'd survived so long, was down to the fact that he'd been a true rear-party bod, one of the guys who had made it to Shorabak and never left, melted into the background somewhere between the unattended roll call and the empty storeroom. No one seemed to begrudge him, though, and he was pretty far forward that night in Nad-e Ali.

I asked him if he missed his family. 'Yes,' he said, and then paused. 'I am a widower. My wife was sick and she died. I have a son, he is eight years old. His grandparents look after him. My father has a shop, but he is an old man, he can't work any more

* A pink one being the commanding officer's permission to leave camp, hence the favourite expression of a married man going crazy on a night out with the lads that he was on a 'pink chit'.

but he has a shop. My brother is still at school so when he is not studying he helps in the shop. I am a soldier so I leave the problems at home to them.'

I expressed regret, didn't want to ask if he had missed his wife dying while he had been stuck up in Camp Shit Hole in Sangin, but couldn't help thinking again of the uncomfortable contrast between how we looked after ourselves and how the ANA were left to their own devices. In a random stroke of cruelty, one of my sergeants lost his mum while we were living in the PBs north of Gereshk. We had just come in from a patrol and were glugging water and tending to knocks and scratches when an urgent message came for me to get in touch with HQ in Shorabak. We'd had a couple of similar messages in the past few weeks, and they usually meant someone had died somewhere else in Helmand, so my heart sank as I went to the radio, but the sad news was actually that I had to tell this poor guy his mother was dead and whisk him back to camp so he could be sent home for the funeral. He'd been numb, I think, when I called him over and sat him down in the shade behind the wagon, the last thing he'd been expecting. There was no silver lining to that, but at least he was back in the UK with his family in forty-eight hours. Younes had just carried on scrapping. I asked how he was able to carry on, more generally to the room, how any of us were able to just carry on. Younes shrugged stoically: 'Everyone has their problems.'

Finding Qiam

As Younes had been speaking I had been faintly aware of fidgeting at the back, some whispered words and meaningful glances. Now, at the pause, a few short words and a flurry of activity as the room emptied of most of the unfamiliar soldiers and it was then Qiam and the old guard. With the extra space he leaned forward, almost rubbing his hands. Everything else had been prologue, this was Qiam's story after all, but he clearly had a few questions of his own.

'How was Japan?' he began. Astonishing. I had wanted to ask him about his rank, whether he was actually a major or whether he had been bluffing all along, but how could you ask such a suspicious, almost accusatory question of a man who after two and half years remembered our last discussion, daydream planning of where I would go for my end-of-tour leave. What could I say? It was an impossibly exotic concept to the average ANA soldier, a holiday in Japan, which itself might as well have been Narnia as a real country, although one they all recognized because of the masses of kit all around Afghanistan donated by 'The People of Japan' – which some would have said was a more sensible and cost-effective contribution from a country which didn't deploy troops because in theory, if not in practice, it didn't have any.

Qiam moved straight on before I had answered: 'What about Iraq?' I paused again. I was obviously a terrible interviewer; Qiam was completely in control. I wanted to ask him about the gaps in my understanding of who he was and what he did, to find out if my fit of pique on his behalf had been misguided, to find out if he'd ever been a captain, let alone a major. Had he really been demoted because of intrigue or had his boastfulness just got the better of him one too many times? I wanted to tell him that the answer didn't matter, that I'd seen him fight like a lion time and time again, and that was surely all that was important, but he seemed to sense the atmosphere in the warm stone hut and was warding me off with compliments of his own. Two years earlier he'd veered between interest and petulant annoyance that I'd served in Iraq, had resented that we had fought other wars in lands he'd never visited. Now he seemed to regard it as an achievement to be applauded and discussed lest the conversation move on to what he had been doing over the last two years. 'Japan was good,' I said and paused and pulled a pantomime sad face, 'Iraq, not so good.' Taj was a good 'terp and obviously managed to convey the sarcastic understatement, Qiam laughed and clapped his hands. 'Too many BOOM,' he said, and I agreed, 'too many IEDs, like here, like Helmand now.' The room went quiet again, Qiam did not want to talk about Helmand now.

'What about money?' he asked. This was a final diversion tactic. 'Before, when you were a soldier, you said you had no money. Now you are a writer, do you have more money?' Qiam had often put me on the spot about money, forced me into an uncomfortable position of feeling simultaneously honest and insincere. By Afghan standards we were all wealthy beyond belief: we dripped flash digital cameras and stereos and expensive boots, a seemingly inexhaustible supply of dollars for trips to the NAAFI, for pop and even ice. Some ANA made a tidy profit selling cans of soft drinks at vastly inflated prices to British soldiers who didn't mind paying because we wouldn't have known where to buy them in foreign and dangerous towns: only the ANA would go on patrol in order to do the shopping – you can't fight the market.

Qiam was more direct and made me more uncomfortable. He saw us handing out dollars to local elders for what the Americans called QUIPs, Quick Impact Projects, and he had heard the rumours, like all the ANA, that low-level insurgents would be brought back into the fold with jobs and money. He would ask me directly for money. You are rich, I am poor, we are friends, you give me money – that was his logic, and it put me in a difficult place. 'I am not rich,' I would laugh awkwardly and explain that my overdraft and my outstanding student loan were vast by Afghan standards, that on payday that month Qiam's most junior soldier would be cash-richer than I was, but it was all nonsense. Qiam's most junior soldier then was probably on between $150 and $170 a month. A senior soldier like Syed was probably on twice as much, Qiam himself a little bit more. When we'd both been soldiers together I had been earning more every day than any of the ANA had been a month. If the propaganda was to be believed, you could have earned twice as much working for the Taliban.[15]

You couldn't actually compare the wealth and living standards of an ISAF soldier and his ANA counterpart, let alone a horribly privileged former officer like me. The denominations were the same – US dollars, pounds and Afghanis – but the numbers were so different as to be meaningless, like the abstract bail-out sums of the credit crunch, you couldn't comprehend what endless zeroes actually meant. Qiam would shake his head, unsure if I was telling the truth, uneasy with the concept that his mentor would owe so much money to someone else, could owe so much money to someone else. I think he knew it was bullshit as much as I did, but it was a convenient way of getting out of a problematic situation of his own making. 'You should never borrow money,' he would tell me sternly and without a hint of irony seconds after asking me for cash so he could buy a new phone. I gave him the benefit of the doubt; after all, it was not as though he ever made any suggestion that if I gave him cash he'd ever pay it back.

Two and a half years later and we were back here. Qiam was playing up for the young soldiers who were now crowding back into the room, had heard that one of the old mentors was back from London and was going to interview Toran, or was it actually Biridman, Qiam and wanted to watch, to hear about Qiam in the bad old days. I pointed at my ripped, muddy trousers, I had only taken one pair out with me, forgetting that this time round, a civilian, the pay sergeant wouldn't have a nice new pair waiting for me every time I trashed mine crawling around in an ambush. Qiam understood and laughed; two and half years later we were back here again.

How to describe Qiam? With all the benefit of hindsight it should be easier. To the extent that every story must have a hero, maybe he is this story's hero, but only in an older, darker sense of the word: heroic in an ancient, martial sense, laced with pathos and dangerously volatile.

Qiam is from Ghazni. It's where he grew up and went to school and even apparently worked while studying, before becoming a soldier. 'I liked it there,' he said, matter-of-factly; it was one of the most genuine things I think I ever heard him say. He studied up to ninth grade, which would have made him about fourteen or fifteen, a serious education by modern Afghan standards, and then, which was news to me, was sent to military high school near Kabul and even more surprising, after three years there, went on the military university and commissioned as an artillery lieutenant.

Qiam is sat on a camp-cot, 'acquired' somehow from one of the British units that has lived in Shawqat in the last year but now unmistakably Afghan, built up with a foam mattress and draped in cheap, soft blankets and an oddly camouflaged sleeping bag that looks more like it came from Toys'R'Us than the quartermaster's stores. He used to lounge flamboyantly like a victorious centurion on a chaise-longue, but his retainers have all gone and there's less of the showman about him than there was two years ago. I suspect out in whichever forward patrol base he's currently in charge of he would be more demonstrative, but while we wait for someone to bring fresh *chai* and as he finally stops side-tracking, there's a sense he's aware that more senior and more serious soldiers are near by. Khoja Wakil sits on the other side of the room, pinching the cigarettes he's already been offered as if he's worried the offer will be rescinded and looking for all the world like an elderly Dickens character, stooped and slight with a shuffling gait and a greying beard and something in the eyes that you're not quite sure whether he's harmless or not. He could be sixty but then again he could be in his mid-thirties. 'Who has been in the Army the longest?' I ask no one in particular.

'I am forty-nine,' says Qiam. It's the first time I've ever heard him categorically state his age, I don't know why but I would have put him down as being younger. 'I joined the Army when I was seventeen, so . . .' he laughs rather than finish the sentence and do the maths. Thirty-two years is a decent military career. He changes his mind. 'I've been a soldier for thirty years.' Khoja Wakil chips in before I can ask whether that means he started at nineteen or is actually only forty-seven, odds on the latter, there's no way Qiam waited that long to start fighting. He'd always previously told me he started at fourteen, but maybe there's a fine Afghan distinction I don't get between firing your first rifle and joining the Army properly.

'I've been in the Army fifteen years,' says Khoja Wakil proudly. This is even more confusing, I'd have thought Khoja Wakil well into his fifties, and he even used to boast about having been a colonel back in the good old days. Fifteen years doesn't seem like a very long time in that context – maybe he means fifty. I've often seen British and American soldiers get stick for stereotyping – all Iraqis are lazy, all Afghans are liars. It's ugly, but you can see why they do it. I have lived and fought with these guys for months on end, have pulled them out of ditches and had the favour returned the next day, we've called each other 'brother', and still there's no getting a straight answer from anyone. I had thought I'd have a built-in advantage – I wasn't some random foreign journalist, I was a former comrade in arms – but the *askar* were wary of my civvie clothes and even more so of the Dictaphone, and quite rightly. Greying, clownish Khoja Wakil, the *kandak*'s bumbling dirty uncle, leering over photos of girls on laptops and in wallets, probably doesn't know exactly how long he's been in the Army and although he might remember the year he joined and knows exactly what year it is now, it wouldn't occur to do the maths, so he's just thinking up a number which accurately conveys 'a long time, but maybe not as long as Qiam'.

I remember seeing this time and time again when we'd get intelligence or casualty reports. Half a dozen Taliban on the back of an old Toyota would be described as a 'platoon', which would be about thirty, which would sound unimpressive, so the reporting *askar* would round it up to fifty for good measure. Anything more would be airily described as 100, which is to say, more than usual, but would invariably only end up being ten at the most. By the end of the tour we would divide any numbers under ten by three and any numbers over ten by five before we even started thinking about things. It seemed funny when it was enemy sightings, when the only ones who suffered breathless, uncomfortable, calm-before-the-storm nights were the foolish mentors. Somehow it was all more serious and depressing when it was casualties. The six ANA soldiers who had been killed by a blue-on-blue with an Apache hellfire missile in the heat of the battle for Adin Zai turned out to be a rather sheepish sergeant with an impressively bleeding but otherwise harmless cut on his head and a couple of warriors with burst ear drums and a head-ache. It seemed callous, but when villagers came to us with horror reports of dead civilians, the nightmare 500-pounder on the wedding party scenarios, there would only be five victims where fifty had been reported, one or two no less tragically injured people whose only misfortune was where they hap-pened to live in the middle of all this mess, but somehow it seemed like a result when the angry police chiefs had been shouting at you an hour earlier that your idiot colleagues had fired on the wrong house and killed ten children. ISAF could be equally guilty, happily accepting the exaggerated estimates of their ANA counterparts when it came to totting-up the num-bers of enemy killed in certain actions. For an often inefficient and pragmatic foe, if British and American reporting was to be believed, the Taliban were incredibly conscientious about clear-ing away their dead, and far too many blood trails were reported back up the chain as 'possible EF KIA', which would somehow slip to 'confirmed' via a dusty ops room laptop. Like everything else in Helmand, even usually solid numbers were uncomfort-ably fluid. Qiam was old by the standards of an Afghan soldier and had been in the Army his whole adult life. Khoja Wakil was older, but not quite as experienced. They were both proud of how long they had served, and that mattered more than the pre-cise number of days and months.

Qiam finally warms to his subject and dismisses Khoja Wak-il's years as a private with a flick of his wrist.

'He was a radio operator, I was in Artillery, in Ghazni province and Paktia,' he grins as Taj translates and sweeps artillery projectile arcs across the room with his arms: *'pheeeew . . . diouf diouf'*.

Everyone laughs as he wafts a cigarette to mimic the smoke from his imaginary rounds. The hardest fighting he saw was with the Northern Alliance against the Taliban.

'Now there is no fighting in Afghanistan' – this is a more eloquent translation than I think at first as I look quizzically at Taj and he looks back at me and we both look around the room, full of soldiers and uniforms and guns. 'Before, it was very dangerous, real fighting. Now they are just playing, it is very easy, they just sit and wait for the helicopter. Before, it was very hard, more than twenty *kandaks* were fighting in one place. I killed many Taliban then.'

Pitched battles of twenty *kandak*s sounds far-fetched, but there's no doubting the contempt with which he views the soldiering he's been doing since ISAF arrived. 'Bullshit' was how he described it when I tried to explain why, even with all our air-power, the plan was not just to carpet bomb Helmand. Qiam has always had a strange antipathy to helicopters, which he thinks are somehow more cowardly than planes. He was the agitator in chief when a hapless Apache pilot targeted the compound we were in, rather than the one the enemy were in about 100 metres north. I was pretty upset myself, but no one was hurt, and it was an easy enough mistake to make on a long, hard day of half-chances and near-misses. Qiam practically had to be restrained from grabbing a PKM off the nearest soldier and shooting the chopper down. Even after we showed him that everyone was fine he was ranting and raving about fucking helicopters – although he cheered along with everyone else once the lad got the target right and neutralized the machine-gunner who'd been causing us the real problems that morning. I never asked, always hoping it might come out in one of his stories, why he had such a problem with helicopters in particular. Soviet Hinds and Hips had been the scourge of the Mujahideen and civilians alike during the war in the eighties, and I wondered if there wasn't something personal in Qiam's dislike of rotary assets, but he never told me if there was.

'As soon as I started, in those days, every province was at war.'

The other soldiers in the room stop their quiet, side conversations as Qiam continues, sensing he's about to reveal some new and fascinating detail, to add another chapter to his own myth.

'From Kabul up to Logar, in Paktia, from Gardez all up to the border with Pakistan, the Panjshir Valley, all like this . . .' his voice drifts off into a sigh and a wave of his hand either recalls some unknown element of the fighting or sadly takes in Helmand and the mess it's easy to forget but that lies just outside the camp gates. 'I remember my first fight, I was shot in my first fight, injured in my stomach. It took me about three months to recover, it was very painful, the wound in the stomach and, somewhere else . . .' Qiam has pulled up his top now and is pointing towards an old but ugly scar on his gut, wincing and tracing the path of the bullet up through his abdomen while Taj struggles to think of the medical translation. Qiam collapses dramatically back on to the bed and continues his monologue Kurtz-like, staring up at the ceiling with a perfect sense of theatre. 'In my next big fight, I was injured in the head' – he pulls his fringe aside to reveal a neat little scar by the temple – 'not so bad but there was blood everywhere. That was in Garji Mangal, near Paktia province in the year 1363.'*

Stop. 1363? I frantically try and do the calculations in my head. If Qiam is forty-seven and he's been in the Army for thirty years then he must have joined at seventeen, in 1980. And if he got injured for the second time, a lucky grazing gunshot wound to the head which a fraction left or right or up or down would surely have killed him, back in 1363, then that must have been 1984. But he didn't just pick up a rifle at fourteen, like we always thought, like his demeanour and attitude had always suggested. He went to military school at fourteen, then university, then officer training. He's watching me as I work this all out and finally get there. 'You

* By the Persian or Jalali calendar in use in Afghanistan.

weren't Mujahideen' – even as I say it I don't know whether it's a question or an accusation – 'you were Russian trained. You were fighting on the Russian side.' Qiam senses what I'm saying before Taj translates it and gives me a grinning half-look. Khoja Wakil also seems to be grinning; the younger soldiers in the room look mystified, as if the conversation has taken a turn they don't really undertsand, which I suppose it has. Qiam's grin is not guilty, it's almost condescending: how stupid of you lot to waltz in and assume that everyone with experience had fought against the Russians – not that simple. Qiam chuckles in a way that seems to say 'of course', but he doesn't want to be distracted from the grand catalogue of his wounds, regardless of who inflicted them and in what cause they were sustained.

Qiam is quite proud of the fact that he has been injured no less than five times. I'm reminded that back in Vietnam American soldiers who sustained three battle injuries were allowed to go home. Qiam's got five, none of them Mickey Mouse; problem is, he sustained them all at home. The stomach wound he got while riding a tank, perched on the side catching a lift as foot soldiers will do when working with armour. He nonchalantly under-states: 'I didn't drop off quickly enough when it attracted fire.' I'm seeing everything in a whole new light. Not Qiam with a rabid hate of helicopters from futile nights spent cowering behind rocks, pinned down by seemingly invincible Hinds and praying for a charity stinger from Charlie Wilson, but Qiam propped up on the back of a T72, riding through a rocky pass as the column is suddenly sprayed with RPGs and hesitating just a second too long before dropping off the false safety of the tank and on to the hard ground, feeling wet first rather than pain and probably as a young, fresh officer in his first contact relieved to look down and see blood, relieved that he hadn't pissed himself with fear, and then pain coming in an overwhelming wave.

When he describes the second time he got injured it sends a shiver down my spine, familiar but through a crucial filter, same-same but different.

'There was a dark cold night. The second night we were given a brief to go and attack the enemy positions from out of a tree-line. Suddenly I was shot in the helmet.'

His hand goes up towards his head of its own accord, brushing his fringe to one side in a nervous, subconscious gesture, ghosting over the scar he showed us minutes earlier but now seems to have forgotten, absorbed in the memory. In training I once attacked an enemy through a treeline. FIWAF, they call it, Fighting in Woods and Forest, which always seemed either a tautology or an unnecessary distinction, as if there might be some difference in tactics between fighting in mere Hockeridge Woods as opposed to the mighty New Forest. An enemy in pre-pared defensive positions in a wood has all the advantages: he can see you coming, you can't see him; he has channelled your routes of approach into his most devastating arcs of fire, you are stumbling through the half dark and eerie quiet, cursing the branches that snap back in your eyes and each noisy snapping twig which trumpets your arrival to the waiting gunners. When I did it my battalion were on TESEX, wearing our Quasar Laser kit on Salisbury Plain and terrified to see how quickly the 'casualties' stacked up. Within five minutes of entering the woodblock, my own platoon the lead element of the big assault, my own vest starting to buzz and beep and the little screen flashed 'Casualty! Casualty! You have gunshot wound to the spine. You can no longer use or feel your legs': by the time I'd realized I was 'hit', we'd lost half the platoon. The guys were sat propped up against the trees, grinning to be out of the battle and jeering at the platoons echeloning through us. I got a cheerful thumbs-up from one of the section commanders: 'Gunshot wound to head, sir. I'm dead. Time for a kip.' It's not as if we were ever going to do it for real.

Qiam had done it for real, at the same age I was when we were training in the woodblocks. Gunshot wound to head. Shot in the helmet. He never wore a helmet on patrol – getting the ANA to wear helmets and body armour had been one of the big things on our tour and every tour since, patronizingly explaining that, yes, they were heavy and uncomfortable and constricted movement but they saved your life. We'd spent one afternoon trying to get the officers to support us; I'd put it to Mujib that we couldn't expect the warriors to wear helmets if he and Qiam never bothered. He had shrugged as he did and said that he'd wear a helmet if we wanted him to but we'd never get Qiam to. All along he'd known the value of a helmet better than any of us. The last time I saw him before coming home we were both out on a security cordon, a high-profile ANA-led operation with a lot of international media snapping away, and the ANA had responded by putting on a good demonstration of efficiency and uniformity: the battered Rangers had been left in camp and the new Humvees were parked smartly around, soldiers were brandishing the new M16s, and everyone was wearing the new digicam body armour correctly fitted and a helmet. Everyone except Qiam.

Qiam has a good scar for each of the five times he's been injured: through the shin by a PKM round in Urgan in Paktika, during a 'normal contact'; in the arm, just grazing the shoulder, though he can't remember whether that was in Paktika or Paktia; and, finally, with much hilarity when he pulls down his trousers to show the room, just below the hip on his upper left thigh. Is he lucky or unlucky, I wonder aloud. To be shot five times seems pretty unlucky, but to be shot five times and sat here casually showing off the scars suggests a certain amount of fortune. He shrugs off the more philosophical aspect of the question with a simple 'I'm alive', but acknowledges that he spends some of his time in great pain and gets terrible headaches. Perhaps this is where his temper comes from, maybe even his unpredictability; I don't voice this possibility. He continues, trying a serious face, 'This is why I cannot wear a helmet.' There is a pause while we look at each other, and for half a second I think I'm about to feel once again the guilt of lazy misjudgement, but he can't hold it and bursts out laughing – wah.*

The 'wah' relaxed me considerably, made me feel less like the foreigner in the room – the standard, international language of the military wind-up, the joke of jokes for bored soldiers everywhere. The probing money chat, the playing with my expensive camera and phone, the confusion of dates and years and then the relentless litany of Qiam's injuries had been alienating me bit by bit, making me feel out of place, intrusive, wondering whether I shouldn't just make my excuses and push off back to the other side of the Hesco to where the joking in the ops room was all in English and the lads who weren't working or sleeping were watching *Match of the Day* in the cookhouse. There's something reassuringly universal about a 'wah', so thoroughly military, and I once again felt like someone who had fought alongside these men even if we were strangers in so many other ways.

If there had been uncertainty over which side Qiam fought on in the eighties, there was no doubt which side he'd been on since. His hatred of the Taliban was always one of the most consistent things about him, and he'd fought against them in the

---

* Wind-up, taken to deadpan extremes usually by convincing junior officers that on their first Buckingham Palace Guard they had to send flowers to the Duke of Edinburgh or something silly. It was usually fun, but it could back-fire, like the time we phoned Seb up on the first day of the Lords' Test to tell him he needed to get his arse back to barracks because someone had bombed the underground: 7/7 wah.

long years of civil war that had followed the Russian withdrawal and for the Northern Alliance when Operation Enduring Freedom kicked off in 2001. Part of the myth that had grown up around him was that his father had been killed by the Taliban. The way some people told it was that he had been an outspoken and heroic opponent, brutally silenced; others that he had been a pretty suspect figure himself and that he had got on the wrong side of the justice system, albeit the pretty dodgy justice system that barely deserved the name while the Taliban were in charge. Qiam allowed the different rumours to linger but didn't seem to talk about it himself, which made me wonder whether it was something more prosaic: perhaps his father had been killed fighting the Taliban like any other soldier on the other side; maybe the seemingly invincible, five-times-wounded Qiam didn't like the idea of so mortal a father. Worse, what if his father had not been fighting the Taliban, had been the unhappy but distinctly unheroic civilian victim of the endless war?

'Yes, yes,' he began with resignation when I asked him if it was true members of his family had been killed by the Taliban. He said it with a sadness, looking down and playing with a stick in the dust on the floor, not boastful or dismissive like on previous occasions. 'My father.' The records compiled by the enterprising Marines, mostly redundant with the ebb and flow of soldiers through the *kandak* and the improvement in the ANA's own record-keeping ability, listed Qiam's father's name – Mia Khan – as the only known information about him. Apparently he had been a general, which sounded suspiciously senior but would have accounted for Qiam's upbringing – only patronage would have been sufficient to get him to a military school and straight to officer training in a specialist branch like the Artillery. He had never mentioned this before, never name-dropped his own military ancestry when arguing tactics with his bemused mentors, which made me think that with a pinch of salt it probably was true. Syed later said he had heard it was, which was as close as anything to cast-iron confirmation. Everyone seemed to know that the next bit of the story was absolutely true.

'Nothing was in that time,' was how Taj translated Qiam's words. We spoke about it later. Was Qiam referring to the existential crisis of Afghanistan, mirrored in his own family's loss? Was there some poetry in his personal anguish and Audenesque cry? Was Taj knackered after a long week with an annoying Englishman who wanted to sit up long into the night talking nonsense to the soldiers instead of just translating patrol orders? Taj thought he meant that there was no reason for it, that the fighting had stopped, that his father wasn't agitating in some way, wasn't in the middle of a battle or a public dispute, was up to no mischief. Whatever his father had been he had fought with the government and the Russians, for Najibullah and against the Mujahideen, so was hardly an ally of the Taliban, but, we reckoned Qiam was trying to say, neither was he deserving of what came next. 'Nothing was in that time.'

'The Taliban came, they told him he was in the Army and, with no trial, they hanged him.'

Just when you think there's a connection, there isn't; when you think you understand you don't. Qiam's father was hanged, like that. There was a silence in the room; it had got late quite suddenly and was colder. Qiam seemed to have shrunk, to have said too much, it was amazing how much he appeared to change in stature depending on his mood. He was fidgeting now, scratching the snake on his arm. I asked him, again, about his tattoos.

'The tattoos are my enemies which I keep in myself all the time. The snake killed my family. These are my memories, how I keep them safe. When I have killed all my enemies, I will have them removed with plastic surgery.'

He had dragged us deliberately back to now, when just briefly we could have been brooding on blood feuds in the mountains thousands of years ago. I pointed to his arm.

'This is a boat on a river with water trying to capsize it.' The boat was the crudest of all his tattoos, by his hand; it looked painful, self-administered and not very well. Looking at it before, down by the canal in Gereshk, I had always wondered if it was a prison tatt'.

'Everyone in my life tries to capsize me, but I am still afloat. This is the moon and stars which come out during the night, when I fight. This . . .' he shuffled round and pulled his shirt down at the neck to show his shoulder '. . . is a passion tree because I am passionate.'

I pointed to the dagger on his other hand.

'I won't tell you that.'

He stared at me, hard again, defiant.

'These are my secrets. I have a long life, like Afghanistan, my homeland. Go away from me. You have broken my heart. The soil of the bone, but I am still on the bone. A girl picture on my arm, an eagle which is freedom obviously . . .'

He was doing that strange thing of chopping and changing theme mid-sentence, probably difficult enough for Taj to understand in his own language, let alone for me through the valiant 'terp. I only really noticed it later, listening back on my headphones through hours and hours of fuzzy recordings of distant voices, ever such a slight pause, half a question, half a challenge.

'You have a lot of interest in us Afghans.'

And then.

'The eagle has captured a small mouse and flies all the time with the mouse in its mouth.'

He was inviting the question, gently. For some reason the normal etiquette of talking straight through the 'terp seemed inappropriate; this particular question needed distance: 'Is he the eagle or the mouse?' I asked Taj.

'I am the mouse.'

Only connect. But what if you couldn't? He changed the subject, as if he noticed the others in the room also listening, started playing up again, joking crudely about whoring down in Lashkar Gah, teasing me about how he'd used to say he was going on a resupply patrol when actually 'I jiggy jiggy a couple of hours every day.' I'm not sure I believed him, it was too crass even for Qiam, and he was watching me too intently while he said it. It was a throw-away for the young warriors, who all giggled obligingly and repeated it to each other with much amusement: *jiggy jiggy*. Qiam grabbed his phone: 'I have missed calls on my mobile from a girl.' Possibly true, possibly banter. That was just the thing with Qiam, you never knew, but when he was driving troops forward, bellowing at the top of his lungs, impervious to the rounds and the chaos, it didn't really matter.

One of the things that troubles me when I think of the Afghans is that, unlike with British Army friends, I'm never sure if they're OK. Their many casualties go unreported and unnoticed. With the mingled sadness and relief which would come with each MoD announcement, sadness for the loss and relief if it wasn't someone you knew, I was struck by the possibility that Syed or Mujib could have been shot or killed in the same incident, and I'd be sat back in London, snoozing in the back of a cab or wringing the faintest dregs of adrenalin out of the cycle to work, absolutely clueless. With Qiam, it somehow wasn't a worry, he was one of the immortals.

Syed told me once about a big operation the *kandak* had done in 2008, somewhere around Dagyan and Yatimchay, which he described as 'very riskful . . . hard areas', and I suddenly remembered an incident recorded by a journalist who'd been around

Qiam (centre) telling his tale with Lalaka (left) and Syed (right), Shawqat, Christmas 2009.

that area at around that time, the appearance out of nowhere of a familiar, colourful figure. ' "I kill Taleban. I fuck kill fuck Taleban," yells the Afghan army officer who had jumped in at the DC with a backpack full of his own RPG warheads. Short and powerfully built with a body pockmarked by the battle scars of past campaigns . . .' There was Qiam. The irrepressible life-force of the *kandak*. An Afghan officer of forty 'who looked fifty-five', complaining of missing his wife and daughters, reaching for the RPGs with a sooty grin in the midst of the ambush, firing, giggling, swearing and yelling. No doubt. As one of the watching Jocks had apparently shouted 'Quality mate. Fucking Quality!'[16]

Qiam, like Evelyn Waugh's similarly primitive and vital Captain Grimes, was a life force: sentenced to death in the Panjsher, he popped up in Kabul; disappeared in Kabul, he emerged in Helmand; engulfed in the dark mystery of Afghanistan, he would rise again somewhere at some time, cracking a crude joking, laughing, inspiring, *kharkus*.

Building Cathedrals

I remember once trying to explain the difficulty of working with the Afghans, of finding a common thread which linked guys as different as Qiam and Syed and Mujib and the rest with guys as different again as ourselves. My friend had paused and said it reminded her of the Parable of the Three Stonecutters, which I had never heard of so went away and looked up. A staple of overpriced MBA courses apparently, the sort of thing they lapped up for $200,000 a year at Harvard, which ultimately meant bugger all, but, as it turned out, she was absolutely right. The story went something like this.

A traveller comes by three stonecutters on the side of the road and stops to ask them what they are doing. The first stops and looks up as if at an idiot and says, 'I am cutting stones.' The second, without pausing, tongue between his teeth, replies, 'I am doing my job.' The third grabs the traveller by the arm with zeal in his eyes and says 'I am building a cathedral.'

A lot of the ANA are just cutting stones. They have rifles and wear green and get blown up, they are *askar*, soldiers. It is hard, unglamorous, not badly but not well enough paid. It is what it is. Qiam? Maybe Qiam was building a cathedral; most of the British certainly thought they were. Syed Meraj, however, Syed was a professional, Syed was doing a job, his job, and he was doing it as well as he could.

Syed had seemed utterly unsurprised to see me when I showed up, sheepish in Shawqat. He had made no comment on my strange, civilian attire, no grand pronouncements about what it was that had drawn me irrevocably back to Helmand or the fates which had landed me back with 1/3/205, he had simply recognized me about to set out on patrol, smiled and shaken my hand before promising to come and talk to me when he had dealt with something else. If I'm honest, it felt a little anti-climactic after Qiam's histrionics. About three times over the next couple of days we made plans to sit and catch up, but every time something intervened – a resupply patrol to Lashkar Gah, a sick soldier at one of the patrol bases, dinner. Each time Syed apologized profusely, as if he shouldn't have been doing his job instead of talking to some freeloading tourist. Each time I tried to assure him that I was bottom of his priority ladder and had plenty of people to talk to, and he would smile, and his mobile phone would begin to chirp, and he'd stroll off again with an apologetic wave. When we finally did sit down, late, late at night before I was due to fly out, long after Qiam's excitable acolytes had gone to bed and the *chai* was getting cold, he looked more worn out than I had previously realized.

'Big problems, very big problems. Some of the guys have 'flu, some of the guys say they do not want to go on the mission, they want to stay here.'

It was ever thus, except, of course, now Syed had ultimate responsibility for it all. There was a long deliberate operation coming up (How long? Seven days, 'possibly ten'), and the usual shirkers had heard about the couple of guys in the Shawqat sick room with pretty violent 'flu so had put the two together and were trying to get out of the hard work. The average warrior was rarely a coward, but he was often idle and would rather stay as close as possible to a steady supply of fresh rations and a camp-cot than not. In that respect at least he was no different from most soldiers who've got over the first flush of excitement of their early battles. I could remember perfectly well what Syed was up against. I offered him a cigarette, and he immediately refused and looked a little hurt; I was sure I remembered him smoking, but the memory was false. 'I have never smoked,' he said. 'You don't remember?' I shrugged; for some reason in my memory he had. There was genuine indignation in his tone, and it occurred to me that perhaps it wasn't all one way after all, perhaps the Afghans wanted us to remember them just as much as we wanted them to remember us. 'Quite right, it's bad for you,' I said, taking a drag, and we both laughed, more at Taj, giggling disproportionately as he translated, than at the lame joke, but it helped clear the air (so to speak).

I said that things didn't seem to have changed: when I first met him he had been organizing the warriors, trying to get them back off leave, find out who was on the sick. Back then he'd just been a sergeant, now he was officially doing it for the whole *kandak*. Syed responded with a self-deprecating chuckle. He was being keen by any standards because he'd just been promoted. He'd been with the *kandak* as a squad leader right from the beginning, but the Marines up in Sangin had seen his potential and somehow ensured that he was promoted to platoon sergeant before disappearing up to see his family for the first time in eighteen months. He was late coming back from his leave, like most of the *kandak*, because getting across the country had been so difficult and slow, and had started keen as mustard because he had assumed otherwise he would have been in trouble, maybe even stripped of his promotion for having been missing for the last few weeks. Now it's my turn to chuckle self-deprecatingly; we wouldn't have known either way, we were just relieved that with his return things started to actually get done. Syed recalls being a platoon sergeant with great affection, always speaks of 'his' platoon in a way most British sergeants would instantly recognize, but you didn't hear as much from the Afghans, they weren't just some thirty guys he had to keep alive, they were his boys. It's a measure of what the *kandak* has done in its short existence as he reels off the different places he served: 'I became a platoon sergeant in Gereshk, that was when you were there. My own platoon. I took that platoon everywhere – Kajaki, Now Zad, Garmsir, Babji, Lashkar Gah, Nad-e Ali – and we had lots of different, hard jobs.'

Different, hard jobs was something of an understatement, and that was coming from a man who'd joined General Dostum's* army aged fourteen and at the end of the nineties been in the brutal fighting around Mazar-i-Sharif, the last city to fall to the Taliban, with no quarter given on either side, at exactly the same time that the hardest thing I'd ever done was GCSE revision.[†] In 2010 Syed was promoted again to become company sergeant major of the *kandak*'s HQ Company. Given that in the ANA the regimental sergeant majors don't tend to deploy, this meant that Syed was effectively the *kandak* sergeant major, which is no more than he deserves to be and no more than recognition of what he always was in all but name. Even three years ago in his first months as a platoon sergeant he was effectively the senior non-commissioned officer in his company and given that, as our tour wore on, his company was invariably the lead company, Syed has basically been the senior NCO in the *kandak* for the last three years. Different, hard jobs indeed.

Syed put on his serious face. 'I am sorry that I gave you a time to come and see me and I was not able to be here. I have been very busy with the mission. I am sorry that I cannot give you an interview because the XO has said there is no permission from Corps HQ to talk to anyone, even though we know you.'

---

* General Abdul Rashid Dostum had fought on pretty much every side over the long course of Afghanistan's disintegration but he was a survivor, still senior in the ANA, still respected by most of the country's significant Uzbek minority and still remembered as the man who liberated Mazar in 2001.

[†] Reports vary, but as the city changed hands between May 1997 and August 1998 atrocities were committed by both sides, culminating in the systematic execution by the ultimately victorious Taliban of thousands of Hazaras. I got 7 A*s but didn't do as well as my teachers had hoped in Latin.

My heart sank. Syed was the one I knew would give straight answers to straight questions, was the one who might actually make sense, a character, not a caricature. The one there was and could be a connection with, for me. Of course he was also the one who, on hearing that I was around and wanting to 'interview' all the old gang, would have taken the sensible and necessary precaution of checking with his chain of command, and the ANA chain of command had predictably enough said 'no'. Syed must have sensed my disappointment because he suggested the alternative himself: he couldn't talk about missions and the *kandak*, anything operational, but surely there was no harm in reminiscing, in talking about the old times and small personal details.

The ANA has an odd relationship with the media, at times sophisticated, at others reminiscent of the worst sort of controlling, suspicious, bureaucratic nonsense the senior officers must have learned from the Soviets. There was a valid concern about revealing too much biographical information. The family of a *kandak* commander who had been featured in an American magazine piece had been targeted by the Taliban, and when TV cameras were around it was not uncommon to see soldiers copying the 'terps in wrapping their faces in shemaghs and shuttering themselves off behind dark glasses. It wasn't exactly the ideal look for reassuring the locals whose hearts and minds we were all supposed to be winning, but you couldn't blame them. In fact, coalition forces all over the place were indulging in similar behaviour, as if by copying the special forces and demanding anonymity certain soldiers were declaring themselves more special than the rest. Snipers, pilots, apparently even helicopter ground crew, any excuse to black out eyes and pixelate heads was being taken, and the ANA, despite it making them look more like tragic student protesters than the professional national army ISAF was supposed to be fashioning, were just joining in. Syed's concern was not that someone would recognize him from *Panorama* – he'd been delighted when I had told him that his excellent marksmanship featured prominently in the BBC documentary. His concern had more to do with pissing off his senior officers, who were probably caught between being miffed that they weren't being interviewed themselves and terrified that he might stray off-message. Both were absurd worries, but the latter more so, as it was far from clear what constituted 'on-message'. Syed was the closest thing to a living, breathing, fighting and smiling personification of 'the message' as I'd ever come across, but never mind. Syed warmed to the idea of the personal.

'I will tell you all the stories,' he said with the emphasis on the 'I', and so he did.

Syed drew a distinction between being in the Army and being a soldier. He joined the Army in 2005, the *kandak* is all he has known in a regular uniform (which is as much as I knew from other people), but he'd been fighting for many years before he turned up in Kabul and signed on to serve in Karzai's brave new force, that much was also obvious, not from the stories but from the way he fought from the start. Syed was Northern Alliance through and through, had been fighting since the flow of roubles dried up in 1992 and the country had started to go to hell and had never really stopped. He says matter-of-factly that he first started fighting at fourteen. The myth of the warrior Afghan with an AK in his hands before he can walk and RPG on his shoulder while he's still at primary school is, like most things about Afghanistan, grossly exaggerated. Asking various soldiers what they did before they joined the Army, I'm invariably looked at slightly quizzically and met with a response along the lines of 'I was at school. Why? What do kids in England do?' Syed is proud of his education and his English, which I tell him I know full well is better than he lets on in front of most of the British soldiers he works alongside. He shakes his head and claims that it is always easy to understand what people are saying, even if you don't know the words they are using. I think back to Qiam's grand gestures and the giggling young warriors watching him in the corner and whispering to each other; this much is true. Syed knows that even though he was young when he started fighting, he owes his education and the relative safety and stability of his family to where he comes from. Home is Jamzi Jan, just north of Mazar-i-Sharif, where, as Syed says with great understatement, the Taliban aren't exactly welcome.

So unwelcome, in fact, that under General Dostum and his militia the city and region were relatively peaceful throughout the otherwise tumultuous mid-nineties. Syed's sister was married to one of General Dostum's senior staff. The rumour we had heard from the other soldiers in the *kandak* was that Syed was related by marriage to Dostum himself, but he dismisses this with a laugh. He was a driver for his sister's husband, who must have been relatively senior to have a driver at all, but had only just started when, in the summer of 1997, the Taliban fought ferociously to take the city, the last in Afghanistan holding out against them. They were unsuccessful that year, which Syed notes with grim approval; various other accounts suggest thousands of Taliban soldiers were massacred in the aftermath, which was why, when they returned the following year, there were brutal reprisal killings of thousands of Hazaras. It was only after this that the city fell and the Taliban could be said to control Afghanistan. Syed remembers a week of constant fighting, three days' scrapping neither behind nor in front of enemy lines as the city and area around it descended into chaos. Like Qiam's memories of fighting with the Northern Alliance, these are Syed's worst memories compared to which the fighting the Brits have done alongside him and the *kandak* over the last four years, fighting routinely described as the most ferocious since this or that, since Korea or whenever, is easy.

'The units had to go forward with no air support. When General Dostum's soldiers were pushing back they were getting killed; the general was forcing them forward, the only way was forward.'

Syed paused, and I wondered if these things had been going through his mind when we used to complain about our own lack of air support to take on a couple of Taliban on a roof, or whinge when we pushed back out to our 'forward' Patrol Bases. It was worse for him, he concludes with brilliant simplicity, because he was so young.

Recalling the fighting around his home is one of the only times Syed slips into ethnic partisanship. Sharaf Udin and Qiam would regularly express their anger in the broadest terms against all Pashtuns, even those handful fighting gamely alongside them. Syed rarely spoke disparagingly of, or acted dismissively towards, the Helmandis, who, when you patrolled out and stood them side by side, you really realized were as foreign to him as we were: different language, different culture, different skin, hair, eyes. Maybe memories of bitter fighting in his teens, the dark years of moving and hiding and worrying and no more English lessons for the ambitious engineer's son or perhaps even darker memories of the capture and recapture of his home town. Brutal killings in 1998 gave way to more of the same in November 2001, the beginning of the end for the Taliban and the triumph of the Northern Alliance, but tainted by the accusation of further massacres on prisoners of war, scores of Taliban left to die in freight containers.

'The problem,' he suddenly exclaimed, 'is with education. In the north and west the literacy rates are higher, about 80 per cent.*

* I checked afterwards with Taj if 80 per cent was the right translation – it seemed high – but Taj was sure and backed it up (perhaps not surprisingly, a fellow northerner). Syed's stat, not mine, so maybe we should divide it by five, but I think the point is the same regardless of the actual numbers.

The people in the north like to have knowledge, they want to get education and go to school and university.'

He paused and jerked his head towards the window, out in the direction of the dark night, the faint glow of torches in the ANA sangars and out beyond, the jumbled compounds and fields and ditches of the south.

'These people, they only want to look after opium. Our people were great traders, they went out to European countries, Arabic countries, they have been all around. These people, they have never been out of their homes.'

'So what's the answer?' I asked.

'There is one thing which it is possible to do, is it possible to bring the peace? Take all the people from the north to the west, all the people from Kabul and the west to the north, it would be peaceful. Everywhere they speak Dari, there will be peace, only where there are Pashtuns is there problem.'

He sweeps his hands expansively over the low table as if there was a map of Afghanistan lying on it, drawing the line between the Dari-speakers who get peace and the Pashtuns who get abandoned. Qiam had rejected this very idea a couple of days before, rejected angrily as if I was somehow undermining his patriotism, but Qiam loved the fight, lived for it, wouldn't know what to do with himself if it ever finished; peacetime societies can't deal with men like him. Syed was a fighter by necessity, a good one and one who enjoyed his work within those strange parameters with which men cope and thrive on combat and in adversity, but it wasn't his life. He'd got back from leave a few days earlier, a trip back up north to a family wedding, and his memories were full of the colour and laughter and taste of the feast and celebration. I could see why at that moment, contrasting memories of the worst and best of times, he was prepared to let it go.

He rolled his eyes, smiling again, with the memory of the

wedding. In truth, it turns out, organizing the *kandak* is less stressful. He hadn't wanted to go on leave in the first place, had sensed the *kandak* was vulnerable with recent high turnover of new recruits and the old hands and commanders getting tired. The new Afghan National Police chief in Nad-e Ali was a rising star and after the disaster at Blue 25 was whipping his policemen into shape faster than the *kandak* commander was bringing on his own soldiers. For the first time, it seemed, 1st Kandak's reputation was slipping, and to make matters worse the ANP, the perennial whipping boys and basket cases of the Afghan National Security Forces, were starting to look good. Syed had wanted to stay, joking that he had hoped to see the familiar faces of his old mentors from the Grenadiers, who were back out at the time, but it was his brother who was getting married, and then one of his cousins had gone to Saudi Arabia on the Haj so he had to wait for him to come back for the full family reunion: family is family.

Syed described the wedding with chaotic relish, part horror to organize, part fun to be in. Apparently the dowry, which is still customary, rarely covers the cost of the wedding, which is paid for by the groom's parents, hence his family was bearing the brunt of his brother's wedding. Syed's own wedding had apparently cost $11,000. I thought at first he meant Afghan dollars, not US, but I assumed wrong. 11,000 Afghani was barely £150; money went further in Afghanistan but not that much further, and weddings were expensive and stressful wherever you were in the world.

'I had to arrange the hotel, the food, sheep, cow, whatever. You must put up all the guests in the same hotel. Too many people.'

He shook his head, trying to think how to appropriately describe the scale of the event. 'Three movies worth of one wedding on DVD.' We both set about laughing, the new international standard measurement for a wedding: how many DVDs worth of pointless film of dancing is captured. I tell him how similar it is in England, dinner and dancing in a big hotel, except probably with a bit more booze, but Syed shook his head again.

'In Afghanistan it is just the same. There are some who drink too much, and there is always a fight.'

Good to know some things are the same the world over.

After his cousin this year, next year was to be Syed's father's turn to travel to undertake the Haj. Syed's Army salary would help pay for the trip. It was a big expense, even for a family like Syed's, who seem to be as close to successful middle-class as Afghanistan can manage. I wonder if he would like to go to Mecca himself and he sidesteps the question; he had to make his own pilgrimage back to Helmand, where another ill-disciplined rattle from one of the perimeter sentries pulled us back from thoughts of weddings and drunken brawls. Syed has four children at home in Mazar; the eldest is six and the youngest barely three months old. I wonder if he thinks he'll still be fighting when they're getting married, whether they'll be soldiers like him. He thinks the Taliban can be beaten, but not quickly, and, as for his sons, he wouldn't mind them being in an Afghan National Army with tanks and planes and helicopters but – he looks around, the stone room now bitterly cold even with the blankets and the fug of cigarette smoke, and outside the scared sentries shooting at dogs, Nad-e Ali, home of the *kandak* for the foreseeable future – not if the situation is still like this, not here.

Nad-e Ali is, in its own, limited way, a Helmand success story. The Afghan flag flies over FOB Shawqat and in the town centre. The market thrives. Such violence as there is has been pushed to the fringes and is running out of places to be pushed to. The charismatic local governor seems to be popular, not to mention cuts a pretty convincing Father Christmas dishing out turkey to the troops even if he did refuse to wear the hat. By certain measures, this is what success looks like, and it's not necessarily obvious whether this fact in itself should be depressing or cheering: the troops stationed there seem to waver between optimism and pessimism, not particularly depending on whether they have had a good or a bad day but because the balance between the two is so delicate. The stability was expensively bought. The heavy price the Welsh Guards in particular paid on Panther's Claw, coupled with the reshuffling of responsibility in Helmand which has seen US forces take responsibility for Sangin and the north, has focused such attention on Nad-e Ali that people speak of it very carefully indeed: it's precious at the moment, but very fragile.

I had returned to Helmand in late 2009 expecting only to see the Grenadiers. It had been delightful chance, but chance nonetheless, that 1/3/205 happened to be sharing Shawqat with the 1st Battalion Grenadier Guards. It had been brilliant, however briefly, to bump into Qiam and Syed and to hear their stories, but the *kandak* was dispersed through Nad-e Ali. I had seen Mujib only once to say 'Hi' and men like Hazrat and Sharaf Udin not at all. They were holding the fragile line out in the far-flung PBs, and I could no more ask them to patrol back just for a chinwag with their old mentor than I could ask the Grenadiers to divert men and resources ferrying me forwards. More urgently, it turned out that in all the excitement I had missed the last lift back to Bastion for a couple of days and was in danger of being unable to get home at all. Reality intruded, and some desperate calls were made in the ops room, where they were no doubt by now as keen to be rid of me as I was not to find myself stranded in Kandahar for an unexpected week. Someone hitched me a lift on a passing Chinook crammed with a stinking troop of rugged and scary-looking gentlemen in whatever uniform they wanted, recovering back to Bastion after getting up to God only knows what sort of mischief in the middle of nowhere. A fairly nails-looking German Shepherd spent most of the flight on my lap, but I can't tell you his name, obviously.

I had to leave when I did in order to make the first of a complex series of flight connections to get me back to the UK: to get to Bastion in time to get to Kandahar in time to get to Kabul. Even as I had lifted out of Shawqat in the dead of night, trying desperately not to stare at all the Gucci kit and avoiding the withering stare of the dog, who could clearly smell that I certainly didn't know what colour the boat house was, the whole encounter with the *kandak* was taking on a dreamlike quality. It had all been so sudden and unexpected, too perfect while it lasted, and then after ten minutes of frantic kit stuffing I was out again. Up in Kabul, surreally, it was New Year's Eve, beer and burgers and colour and noise in the embassy parties, but I couldn't shake the feeling that I had nearly, but not quite, grasped something. I didn't believe in fate, but it seemed too coincidental that our paths had crossed again like this, and I was overcome by a sense of unfinished business.

I did a lot of thinking in the back of the C-130, jammed up against the cargo nets on the slow flight from Kandahar. I did some more in the back of an up-armoured Land Cruiser weaving round Kabul traffic cops, not so much in the American embassy party tent, loads in Kabul waiting for the Afghan Border Police to let me out despite the fact that I had no entry stamp in my passport because I came in on a military flight,* and

---

* According to the guy behind the desk, he couldn't authorize me to leave because I wasn't actually in Afghanistan. '*No stamp*,' he kept on saying, pointing at my visa. 'And yet here I am,' was my exasperated reply, offering him an arm to pinch to check I was real and very much in his country.

plenty more on the almost empty Safi Airways A320,* although by the time I got to Frankfurt I was so tired I fell asleep on my bergan and missed the final connection to London. Qiam had said I should write about him and he was right: telling stories like his and Syed's was probably more worthwhile than most other stuff I'd ever done. I did a lot of thinking in the back of the Lufthansa Boeing 737, trying to work out over the Channel how to break the news to my girlfriend that, despite the promise I made about two weeks ago, I was going to have to go back to Helmand again, again.

* Worryingly enough, the cutlery seemed to have been nicked from Royal Air Morocco, and although the signs in the forward loos were in English and German, the ones in the aft were in English and Spanish.

PART IV

Retracing History

Kandak

Kandak is one of those words that the British Army will scoop up on its travels and appropriate. Right now in any barracks in the country, soldiers who've never been within a hundred miles of the Malay jungle, administered colonial India or even been posted to the relics of the British Army of the Rhine will none the less know exactly what it means to be *bashaed* up in the middle of the *ulu* passing the time with a *buckshee roik*.* Maybe hundreds of years from now the fashion among older drill sergeants will be to bawl out the non-commissioned officers to 'get the *kandak* looking sharper on parade' and fresh from Sandhurst, know-it-all young officers will remark to the sergeants (who won't give a damn) that the slang dates back to the British involvement in Afghanistan back at the beginning of the twenty-first century. Back home, as I tried to adjust, I realized that to tell the story properly I had to go all the way back to the beginning. Armed with a Dictaphone full of incoherent memories and snatches of conversations, I had to piece together what had happened before I'd ever gone to Helmand and after I'd left. I began to read every Afghanistan book I could get my hands on, scoured the indexes for any familiar Afghan name, cross-referencing the accounts of those I knew with those which were burgeoning

* Camping in the middle of nowhere with a free cigarette: *basha*, from the Bengali for house, now any temporary cover or camp; *ulu*, literally 'up-river', from the Malay for jungle and now meaning middle of nowhere; *buckshee*, from the Arabic for gift, now meaning anything freely acquired (legitimately or not); and *roik*, from the Dutch *roken*, 'to smoke', hence a cigarette.

in Current Affairs/Military History sections. I wanted to get a sense of where the *kandak* had come from, but even that was not easy without a sense of what the *kandak* was, what a *kandak* was.

An ANA *kandak* is these days as defined a military notion as a British Army battalion; the word trips knowingly and uniformly off the tongues of countless embedded reporters even as they disagree about whether they're reporting from HELmand, HelmAAAnd or HelMANd. However, beneath the confident bilingual fluency of the ISAF mission and armchair pundits, the immediacy of the derivation of *kandak*, a generic word meaning 'body of fighting men', is very obvious. Roving squads of militia and dubious quasi-official police squads refer to themselves as *kandaks*. Qiam and Mujib, recalling time spent fighting with the Northern Alliance, speak of the *kandak*s they once fought with, but they could have been referring to ad hoc groups of anything from thirty to 300 fighting men: units which bore no more relation to the *kandak* they all now serve in than they would have done to what was once my own *kandak*, 1st Battalion Grenadier Guards. But there was another, more profound, difference between our respective battalions, a difference which went beyond numbers and kit and training. The Grenadiers had deployed to Afghanistan in 2007 with 351 years of monarch-protecting, Coldstream-baiting, Waterloo-winning, tradition-upholding, standard-setting history and heroism behind them. Our new ANA partners had no smart collective noun, no famous, jaunty march, no iconic silly hats. 1/3/205 had existed for only two years; we saluted honours embroidered on our regimental colours commemorating single battles that had lasted longer than that. The *kandaks* needed a story, a reason for bonding.

I remember once catching wise-cracking 'Sergeant' Azim and some of the lazier guys in his squad whingeing about being on sandbag duty and declaring themselves on strike, lounging around in the shade listening to a cassette surrounded by spades and empty bags as if the base hadn't been mortared yesterday and they were some sort of Afghan chapter of the RMT.* Azim wasn't a proper sergeant, but he was young and ambitious and led the squad more effectively than anyone else; so long as he kept out of sight of the Royal Anglians, who didn't like his baseball cap, he was fine. The four or five dark-eyed Pashtuns in his squad were probably the least cooperative soldiers in the *kandak* at that time. Being up in Sangin got to them, being on the road with the locals passing by all day got to them, and in a way you couldn't blame them. They were closer to home than any of us and watching the town and valley get torn up every day. There was a good reason we never sent the Micks to Ireland until things had quietened down a bit.

No one likes filling sandbags in the midday heat; I sympathized up to a point and would still have rather shared a trench with any of them than Bob Crow. Ranting and raving at them wouldn't have worked, and I'd have just lost what little face I may have had, so instead of having to pretend to be cross I half-heartedly lectured them on history. Summoning Sami the 'terp from his afternoon nap, we explained that *kandak*, the military term they knew, seemed to have derived from *kandah*, which is also in Arabic – *khandaq* – meaning a ditch or trench. 'The Battle of the Trench' was another traditional name for the Siege of Medina in 627, the successful defence by Muhammad of that city against far superior numbers by the digging of defensive trenches. They were one of the lazier squads in the *kandak* but also one of the more devout, so I thought they'd like that, and

* The National Rail, Maritime and Transport Workers Union, scourge of London commuters and favourite object of scorn among soldiers who earned less than a third of a tube driver's wage, dealt every day with things a lot more stressful than the odd jumper and, of course, weren't allowed to go on strike even if they'd wanted to.

there was a good link to the job in hand: literally, *kandak* once meant 'that which has been dug'. It took a second, and then the penny dropped, and they pulled faces as I told them to get digging, but they came back with a joke of their own. Azim had worked with one of the attached Aussies who had spent weeks trying to get all the ANA to refer to each other as 'digger', the generic name for all Aussie and Kiwi troops,[*] and joked straight back that maybe the Australians should come and help.

The discussion resumed that evening. Hazrat was sure he had known all along where the word came from; Sharaf Udin scoffed dismissively: he definitely had. Qiam, never the most devout of men when I was with him, liked the story of the Siege of Medina, but he'd never heard it himself. A few others were quite taken with the idea that *kandak* had a more profound meaning than just the 600 blokes the MoD in Kabul had lumped them together with, but they still didn't fancy the idea of too much digging – no soldier ever did.[†]

The men of 1, 2 and 3/3/205 were the first ANA to be permanently based in Helmand – so incongruous when they first got down there that the locals in Gereshk didn't know what to make of them. Kabul's writ didn't run that strongly in the south, and most of the locals weren't convinced by the concept of an

[*] Anecdotally from Gallipoli, when the poor ANZAC bastards were told that they had done the hard part and all they had to do was dig, dig, dig until they were safe.

[†] Amusingly enough, although none of them knew it at the time, the lazy squad would have been supported by their boss. A few months after this particular episode, after the fall of Musa Qala, the OMLT battlegroup had complained directly to the brigade commander and Governor of Helmand that the *kandak* wasn't pulling its weight fortifying the retaken town. General Mohayadin's response had been simple, if I suspect deliberately mischievous: 'Heroes don't fill sandbags.' (Stephen Grey, *Operation Snakebite*, Penguin, 2010, p. 289)

Afghan National Army, let alone the newly trained reality which was tentatively moving in down the road. Even today those guys who had been in at the start would speak of 1/3/205 with a mixture of pride and anger: pride that they had been the first ANA living in iconic towns like Sangin and Gereshk, anger that five hard years later they were still down there. Even without an official history, without the baubles and insignia and formal tribalism of a proper regimental system, through shared experience those boys had the first stirrings of *esprit de corps*, but, thrashed for five solid years down in Helmand, barely a handful of those soldiers who had trained all together up in Kabul are still serving, let alone still in Helmand, which makes telling a coherent story all the more difficult.

Ask even an experienced *askar* about his *kandak*, however, and he has little to say. He'll remember friends, maybe squad leaders or even the odd officer and mentor, but the memories are personality driven; there's no sense of a corporate military identity, no *kandak* rivalries to match the proud brawls which used to erupt in Aldershot if too many different regiments were out drinking on the same night. Asking the Afghans about the mentors they had worked with before and after me, I could only tease out the various units they had served with by oblique reference to badges, head-dress and insignia. Syed was probably the smartest when it came to appreciating the differences between the many different mentors he'd enjoyed and endured over the years, but even his memories were of Major This and Captain That: of Jagran David or Toran Nick, not of the Grenadiers or the Yorks. The contrast with the British Army, with its strong, some would say overbearing, sense of the regiment, could not be more marked.

It's superficially easy to spin the dits* of British units by

---

* Stories, usually boastful, I guess from 'ditties', which is why, like old records, they were invariably 'spun'.

reference to regimental history: the very titles of military best-sellers like *3 Para* and *3 Commando Brigade* are testament to the pull of regimental identity. Despite the best efforts of successive amalgamations – insensitively and too hastily handled, top-down jobs in which the whole Army invariably got bunged in the wash and came out faded and shrunk – the regimental system stayed strong. Shared regional and fighting heritage screams at you from names and traditions and belt loops and cap-badges. Mine was the only regiment in the British Army to have earned its name on the battlefield, and didn't every young Guardsman being drilled up at Catterick just know it, not to mention who had won the regiments' VCs and how and when and where. The poor Jocks may have the worst of it recently – their uniforms harmonized, stripped of their colourful heckles and magnificent road-kill badgers,* and reduced to various denominations of 'Scots', but you couldn't deny them their obstinate grip on their proud history. The newly merged Rifles had gone with the flow more easily, as befitted the laid-back black mafia, but given half the chance they would still bore you for hours about Sean Bean as Sharpe, and you'd probably indulge them because, even though the rest of the Army had also been wearing green for hundreds of years, skirmishing had been a pretty good idea when they'd invented it. Likewise, the Paras didn't like to be reminded when they'd last actually had to jump out of a plane, but you'd have been wise to let it slide because, for all their tatts and the chat about hats, they were bloody good at what they did.

The Afghans had bags of history, too much history in many senses, but nothing which had been successfully forged into

* The most tragic loss resulting from the amalgamation of the various Scottish infantry regiments into five battalions of the Royal Regiment of Scotland was that the fierce badger-head sporrans of the dashing Argyll and Sutherland Highlanders were consigned to history.

shiny emblems to polish and boast of and mount in your beret. Where did a young ANA warrior go to find his corporate identity? What drunken ink would he regret long years after his initiation to the *kandak*? Some argued it didn't matter: what mattered was getting the ANA up to a decent standard. Others argued that the two were linked: you couldn't conjure the ethos and professionalism of a unit like the Paras out of nothing. Until the ANA had something to be proud of, why did we expect them to soldier with pride? More subtly, until we believed them capable, why did we expect them to perform? The only thing that could be said with any certainty was that that the ANA had a very, very long way to go.

There was no doubt that the consensus opinion of the ANA was poor, before, during and after we got back from Helmand, and in fairness to all those countries and individuals alike who were wary of their Afghan comrades, the rumours about the unreliability and general all-round shitness of the ANA hadn't come out of nowhere. Educational psychiatrists warn against preparing for failure, but hard-pressed instructors know that sometimes it's not about expectation management or fluffy, inclusive, non-judgemental training methods, sometimes you've just got a recruit who is never going to be a soldier and should just be put out of his misery and sent off to join the police sooner rather than later: far too often in its brief history the ANA had been nowhere near fit for purpose.

False Starts

The current Afghan National Army was founded not in Kabul but in Germany, by Presidential Decree by Hamid Karzai on 2 December 2002 at 1305, presumably just in time for lunch. It's hard to imagine a setting more disjointed from the reality of Afghanistan than the Hotel Petersberg, the lavish *Bundesgästhaus* favoured for international junkets over the years. Palatial and gleaming white, nestled high among lush green forest, imperiously overlooking the Rhine and the old West German capital, one can see immediately the appeal to luxury-conscious delegates knocking up constitutions before lunch, but you can't help wondering whether the various Bonn agreements and pronouncements would have been more grounded if they'd been drafted slightly more relevantly down amid the rubble in Kabul. Poetically and stirringly, the Decree concludes:

> Hoping that our endeavour will be endowed with success by the Almighty God, we are embarking on the renewal and reconstruction of the ANA as an essential step for the realization of the ideals of the Afghan Mujahideen who were martyred during the Afghan jihad, of all the people of the Afghan nation, and for the securing of national unity, peace and stability in our country. Success is from God.[17]

It was all very well hoping confidently and optimistically that the grand endeavour would be smiled upon by a benevolent deity, but battle-hardened old-timers taught us that you shouldn't mix hope and soldiering. Whenever a stuttering Sandhurst cadet, surveying the wreckage of his best-laid plans and being asked by the Directing Staff what the hell had happened, was foolish enough to suggest that he had hoped – had hoped that the fire support section wouldn't run out of ammunition, had hoped that the enemy defences were differently orientated – he invariably got the same no-nonsense response. In the Army you didn't hope. You planned, you trained, you recced, you rehearsed, you responded, you planned again, but as for hope, you only had two hopes: Bob Hope and No Fucking Hope. It may have lacked the grace of Karzai's Decree, may have not been couched in genteel language redolent of the Hotel Petersberg's five-star conference facilities, but the favourite aphorism of many a caustic colour sergeant would have injected a little realism into considerations: despite the best of diplomatic intentions, even at the start, the ANA needed more than just hope. The founding declaration had envisaged an ANA of not more than 70,000, the organization and staffing of which would 'take place on the basis of individual merit and in accordance with accepted principles of balance among different ethnic groups and establishment of trust among all citizens of this country'. Ten years later Afghanistan continues to pour its young men into an army already more than twice that size, while the 'hoped-for' national unity, peace and stability seem some way off.

Back in 2001, the initial military successes over the Taliban had been engineered in conjunction with Afghan fighters, but not an Afghan Army. The anti-Taliban militia which had swept down on Kabul from the north had heart, but little discipline and no coherence: in the words of more than one knowledgeable observer they were 'rag-tag' at best.[18] Initially grouped together as AMF (Afghan Military Forces), the coalition troops hunting down the remains of the Taliban in the south found it more effective to deal locally with what were equally euphemistically termed ASF (Afghan Security Forces). You could throw whatever letters you chose into the alphabet soup, the taste was the same: highly irregular militia loyal first and foremost to volatile warlords. Experienced scrappers, but not exactly a platform on which to build Afghanistan's new balanced, professional and centralized army.

ISAF put in place what was known as the 'lead nation' strategy by which different nations would be in charge of different aspects of what was, in effect, nation building. It's tempting to think that the detail was put in place by bored Foreign Office policy wonks having a private joke. It made sense that the USA was going to build the ANA, as that was probably going to be the first and most important thing to get right. Why the UK was going to take the lead on counter-narcotics was anyone's guess – perhaps the politicians thought it was the sort of thing that would play well at home – but at least it was poetically appropriate that we should begin by charging off down a complete blind alley. I guess the Germans taking the lead on developing the Afghan National Police made some sort of sense, evoking images of an efficient and honest law-keeping force, compassionate and stern in equal and appropriate measure and probably chasing down criminals in souped-up BMWs. Sadly, as it turned out, Teutonic efficiency was no match for the Augean stables that was the nascent police force and in a couple of years the Americans would take that over as well. Thereafter the 'lead nation' strategy took a turn for the surreal: the Japanese, the only developed nation in the world to have not had an army for the last fifty years, were somehow to oversee the disarmament, demobilization and reintegration of the anarchic warlords and their myriad *Mad Max* militia. It's when you learn that the Italians were to be responsible for judicial reform that you finally realize someone was taking the piss.[19]

As it happened, the very first ANA *kandak* was actually trained under watchful British eyes (and exhortations, no doubt, to keep the arms shoulder high, get on the heel and be the best). The 1st Battalion of the Afghan National Guard was trained in the spring of 2002 by elements of the British force that had remained in Kabul after the Taliban had been overthrown in Operation Veritas, providing security on what then became the rather more limply named Operation Fingal. In an early indication of where priorities really lay, the first new unit of the new ANA was assigned to guard the Presidential Palace, never mind that it was a fortress in the middle of the only bit of the country already crawling in foreign security forces. Karzai is still in one piece, so I suppose we can take some national pride in that first training job well done.

In keeping with the finest modern traditions, having completed our token gesture we realized we didn't have the resources and promptly handed things over to the Americans. The baton was initially passed to the presumably unimpressed and short-haired men of 1st Battalion, 3rd Special Forces Group out of Fort Bragg, who were installed at the Afghan Military Academy in Kabul, a long way from North Carolina, and began putting the hopeful recruits through a basic ten-week training package. The problems that dogged the training of the ANA's first *kandaks* have a familiar ring: misunderstandings, mismanaged expectations, misdirected efforts. Of approximately 500 individuals who arrived to undergo training more than a third would drop out: some, allegedly, when they discovered that they wouldn't be flown to the United States to undergo their training.[20] Communication with those who remained was difficult: most of the recruits were illiterate, and, more pressingly, despite the ANAs best intentions of multi-ethnicity, the Green Berets had only Dari-speaking interpreters, which somewhat left the Pashtuns behind. None the less, on 23 July 2002 the warriors of the ANA's first regular *kandak* marched off the square and into active service.

Less than a month later, the second *kandak* followed. The problem was that, while the first batch had been marching to the 'Battle Hymn of the Republic' and learning to '*huah*' with the best of them under the Americans, the second batch had been learning to '*bof*' to the strains of 'La Marseillaise' under the watchful French eyes of 27th Brigade d'Infantier de Montagne. Finer soldiers and trainers I'm sure there were few in ISAF, but it couldn't exactly be said that the French did things the same way as the Americans or as us for that matter. It says a lot for the coherence of things that in the middle of 2002 there was a point when the entire ANA was made up of three units who had all received distinct, and in some aspects fundamentally different, tactical training. Former Mujahideen who had most likely all fired more rounds in anger than their trainers, reluctant to give up their cherished family weapons, clad in ill-fitting US Marine Corps hand-me-down uniforms and armed with a Romanian Oxfam donation of a thousand AK47s, far away from their homes and families, depleted by desertions and confused as to whether they spoke French, English or American: confusion reigned.

To try and impose some order, first the Kabul Military Training Centre (KMTC) was officially opened in 2002 and then, in 2003, the US created a specific joint task force, Task Force Phoenix, initially consisting primarily of soldiers from 10th Mountain Division, to take over the ad hoc arrangements that had previously been sustaining training. Nonetheless, from 2002 to 2004 manpower and *kandak* output projections repeatedly had to be revised down while those units that did make it into service were chronically depleted by desertions and undermined by lack of discipline. In July 2003 six companies of ANA troops accompanied the US 82nd Airborne on Operation Warrior Sweep in the Zormat Valley in Paktia. Reports of Taliban and

Al-Qaeda activity in the area had prompted the ANA's first planned combat operation. Significant arms caches were discovered, and local villagers astonished to find Afghan soldiers in American uniforms, and even more so when the American troops didn't shoot them all for being Muslim.* However, as a test of the new force, it was hardly a baptism of fire: no enemy forces were encountered through the whole two months of the op. Two years after the first *kandak* had been trained, and after $500 million of investment, the ANA was still only 8,300 strong, and the AWOL rates so high that what should have been brand new *kandaks* were being eaten up entirely backfilling the existing units.[21]

Desertion rates in those first two years of the ANA have been estimated at as high as 22 per cent.[22] Repeated official and academic reviews of the ANA identified common threads behind these high rates: many ANA soldiers, even those with previous military experience, were only ever used to fighting near their homes and were reluctant to be posted far from their families in a country where a journey home of a few hundred miles can take days. It is no surprise that AWOL rates rise during Ramadan and when troops are paid – other than physically taking their couple-of-hundred-dollar monthly salaries home, most soldiers have no way of getting the cash to their families. Various reasons have been proposed for the ANA's faltering start, not least the confusion between the NATO and ISAF contributing nations supposed to be helping as to who was actually doing what. In 2004 the Americans, as usual, bit the bullet, and General Craig Weston, the US Air Force man heading what was

* Anti-Western propaganda was understandably accepted as truth by many Afghans, who would hide their Korans in case it turned out to be true – for villages with long memories, infidels of whatever shade all had form.

then known as the Office of Military Cooperation – Afghanistan (OMC-A), responsible for developing the ANA, demanded more funds for what was going to be a trickier job than had first been anticipated.

It didn't help that the desertion rates also seemed to rise as a direct result of the first operational deployments. 203 (Tandar)* Corps and 205 (Atal) Corps, deployed in what even in 2003 and 2004 was the noticeably more punchy south and south-east, were troubled by more significant desertion and, with time, casualty rates, each, of course, feeding the other in a vicious circle. One estimate puts the 205 Corps desertion rate in 2005 at 300 men,[23] another as high as 1,200 for between September 2004 and June 2005:[24] nearly a third of the whole unit. From 2004 onwards, with a combination of General Weston's increased funds and a more effective, ANA-led recruitment drive, the numbers of *kandaks* being trained started to increase, but still relatively slowly. It took the two years to 2004 for the ANA to grow to fifteen *kandaks*, of which only a handful could be sent on joint operations like Warrior Sweep. In the next two years to 2006, the ANA more than doubled in size to just under 30,000 men, notionally 40 *kandaks*: better pay conditions and more focused regional recruitment accounted for the healthy-looking numbers passing through Kabul, and, as AWOL rates began to decline, even as early as 2005, the ANA was being touted in some quarters as an emerging 'success story',[25] the Afghan solution to an Afghan problem. Compared to the lack of progress being made by the shambolic ANP and, perhaps subconsciously, also contrasting the then relative stability in Afghanistan to the conflagration in Iraq, which was reaching its nadir, this might

---

* 'Thunder', marginally less self-congratulatory than 205 ('Hero') Corps but a lot camper and, for a certain generation, too reminiscent of *Thundercats* to be taken seriously.

have seemed to be the case, but the signs were there that trouble lay ahead.

As well as requesting much-needed additional funding, the OMC-A had also started embedding training teams within the formed ANA units. What the Americans called Embedded Training Teams (ETTs), NATO called Operational Mentoring and Liaison Teams (OMLTs), but they were effectively the same thing: small groups working alongside and within the *kandaks*, in theory mentoring rather than directing or commanding but also providing the crucial fire-support, air-support and medevac which was often the difference between success and failure and life and death. The ability to call and rely upon these assets was the main difference between the Afghan troops and their still infinitely better-equipped allies. Another value the ETTs and OMLTs had was that they were confronted by the daily reality of the ANA on the ground, feeding back worrying information about combat readiness and the problems the ANA were facing even while trainers up in Kabul could boast redundantly that KMTC had never missed a recruiting target.[26] It was from these embedded trainers that the reports, which would become increasingly familiar, first began to seep. Little things at first like units being unable to march and soldiers personalizing their uniforms or not wearing them at all, but little things which hinted at the problem of a general lack of discipline, which in turn could be said to stem from the relatively short training the ANA were receiving to keep the numbers ticking over up in Kabul. From the little things stemmed the bigger things: the reports of drug taking, corrupt commanders and, most dangerously of all, ANA troops abusing civilians and alienating the local population. If the project was to work at all, was to mean anything, then the ANA could not afford to alienate the very people they were supposed to represent and protect, and early ETTs and OMLTs were perhaps most unimpressed by the fact that this most basic of all lessons did not seem to be one many of the ANA had learned.

The ETTs were the ones who invariably had to make do with the decrease in quality which seemed to be an inevitable result of the increased recruitment. 60 per cent of early ANA recruits had been illiterate, but by late 2005 that figure was nearer 80 per cent. Recruits as young as sixteen and as old as forty were slipping through a net which was supposed to be being cast at 22–28-year-olds.[27] At officer level, the original intention to draw heavily on former Mujahideen commanders gradually gave way to the practical but divisive reliance on the better-trained but less popular men who had served in the pro-Soviet Army. Gradually the ethnic balance of the *kandaks*, although still mixed, moved towards an over-representation of minority Tajiks and Hazaras and too few Pashtuns. Ominously, even throughout this expansion, the areas from which recruitment remained stubbornly low were the volatile southern provinces of Kandahar and Helmand.[28]

In May 2006, four years into the project and in the same month that the British 'investment'* in Helmand really began, retired US General Barry R. McCaffrey completed a review of the situation in Afghanistan and concluded, tellingly, that:

> The Afghan Army is miserably under-resourced. This is now a major morale factor for their soldiers . . . Afghan field commanders told me that they try to seize weapons from the Taliban who they believe are much better armed . . . These ANA units do not have mortars, few machine-guns, no Mk 19 grenade machine-guns and no artillery. They have almost no helicopter or fixed wing transport or attack aviation now or planned. They

* In both the normal sense and, as it turned out unfortunately for the Paras, also in the old military sense, meaning 'to be surrounded and besieged'.

have no armor or blast glasses. They have no Kevlar helmets . . . This situation cries out for remedy.[29]

That very same month, Qiam, Syed and the rest of the guys found themselves down in Helmand with 3 Para, miserably under-resourced, crying out for remedy.

Not Fired One Shot

If morale was a problem for the ANA, it certainly wasn't for their next wave of British partners. In early 2006, when 16 Air Assault Brigade in Colchester got the news that they were being deployed south to Helmand province, they were over the moon. It just goes to show how different perspectives can be.

After the 2,000 or so Royal Marines who had deployed on the thrusting-sounding Operation Veritas back in 2001 had gone home, the British presence in Afghanistan had been relatively muted. After 'defeating' the Taliban and smashing up the Tora Bora, the bootnecks had headed home with knickers in their webbing, leaving behind barely more than a couple of hundred engineers, trainers and HQ enablers in Kabul. When the initial British command of ISAF rotated to Turkey, public interest dwindled further, and though Op Herrick sounded slightly less wet than Op Fingal there was no doubt that by 2003, with everyone in Whitehall busting a gut to put an armoured division in the desert over on the other side of the Arabian Peninsula, Afghanistan was a sideshow.*

It wasn't that Afghanistan wasn't interesting — all that history and the whole Soviet thing still had a draw — it just wasn't combat. Between the very start of anti-Taliban operations and 2004 the British Army only lost three soldiers in Afghanistan: the first was killed by an unlucky ricochet on patrol after the GPMG

---

* In the MoD's own Performance Report for 2002–3, Operations in Afghanistan were relegated down beneath Iraq to under the 'Other Overseas Operations' heading.

gunner had a 'dizzy spell'; the second was shot by the third after an argument over a barbecue on base in Kabul; and the third shot himself in remorse. Sometimes with Afghanistan all you have to do is sit back and let the symbolism come to you. Over the next couple of years there were only a couple more fatalities – a suicide bombing in Kabul as the Taliban tried to reassert itself in a spate of similar attacks in early 2004 – and then it was almost another two years before one of the RGBWLI* lads was killed in Mazar-i-Sharif, where up until that point things had been so quiet that they were out in soft hats and the patrol commander hadn't initially recognized the sound of gunfire.

Poor old John Reid, then Secretary of State for Defence, may have made himself a hostage to fortune with the whole 'not fired one shot' line, but the infamous comment, made down in Kandahar in March 2006, has been frequently and you can only assume sometimes wilfully misquoted. What he actually said was if we'd accomplished our mission in three years 'and not fired one shot at the end of it, we would be very happy indeed'.[30] There is a nuanced difference between expecting something, hoping for something and being pleased if something happens. The excellent journalist and long-time observer of Afghanistan James Fergusson quite rightly got in with the gag early and called his account of the UK-led 'ISAF Stage 3', the insertion of 16 Air Assault Brigade into Helmand in the spring of 2006, *A Million Bullets*. In fact, by the time it was published British forces had fired comfortably in excess of a million rounds: 3 Para in its six-month stint had got through nearly half a million on its own, and you could chuck in 30,000 odd cannon rounds, not that far shy of 10,000 artillery rounds and even 7,500 mortar

---

* The Royal Gloucestershire, Berkshire and Wiltshire Light Infantry: an unwieldy, post-merger abbreviation too far even for the acronym-happy Army, which dismissively designated the new unit 'the M4 Regiment'.

rounds: well, you had to keep the 3 Para mortar platoon busy or else. Whatever the sound-bite had or hadn't been, you could safely state that the ferocity of fighting over the summer of 2006 had not been envisaged when the move to Helmand had been announced by the then Secretary of State for Defence to the House of Commons on 26 January. From the comfort and remove of the green leather benches, it had all seemed so simple.

ISAF Stage 3 was a 'planned, pre-envisaged, phased expansion' into southern Afghanistan, an 'undeniably more demanding area in which to operate' where 'the Taliban remains active' and 'the reach of the Afghan government – and its security forces – is weak'. Within a month lead elements would begin establishing a base in Helmand; you can quite easily imagine the few MPs still not headed for lunch at 1220 on a wintry Thursday mouthing across the benches to each other: 'Where?' 16 Air Assault Brigade and its main element, an airborne infantry battlegroup, 3 Para, would form the core of the 3,300-strong Helmand Task Force, a potent army, but one the Secretary of State reiterated was there to 'protect and deter. The ISAF mission is unchanged. It is focused on reconstruction.' Looking back at Hansard, you have to give credit where credit is due: it's now more than two years since the deployment should have ended and there are three times more troops in Helmand than the estimated maximum at the time. The originally proposed costs of £1 billion have been exceeded nearly twenty times,[31] too many zeroes to properly understand, and around 400 servicemen and women have died, but the Secretary of State, a good politician, covered his back. The size and structure of the force, he told the House, had been guided by 'a careful assessment of the likely tasks and threats that it will face' – try not to giggle at the back if you know what's coming next – 'I make no apology if that requires more soldiers than some people originally envisaged.'[32]

The other nuance that is sometimes overlooked, a more difficult one to process perhaps than a politician's slip of the tongue, is that while Dr Reid himself no doubt would have been delighted if the Paras had come home without a shot being fired, the Paras themselves, if they're honest (and they mostly are), would have been as gutted as hell. It's a feature of professional armies, an uncomfortable one perhaps for the vast majority whose only military experience is a paintballing stag-do and a glimpse of uniform at a local homecoming parade, but most soldiers don't want to sit around in drab barracks and march about in the rain in Wales. Neither, of course, do they want to get blown up, lose friends and alienate loved ones and find themselves sat in pubs, outsiders in their own home towns, but these are the sometimes unavoidable consequences of doing the messy hard job of a soldier. 3 Para may have been excited to be the lead battlegroup of an airborne brigade heading somewhere new, but they were not entirely sold. They knew that their expertise lay in hard combat and, as their own commanding officer observed of his men, 'they were wary of having high expectations for Afghanistan. Many were concerned that it was being billed as a peace support operation.'[33] A former Sandhurst classmate of mine, one of those very 3 Para platoon commanders poised unevenly between excitement and expectation management, pumped up but prepped in case of a peace-keeping let-down, described the jubilant feeling after the first scrap of that tour, the first real ruckus we had had in Afghanistan in five years. Getting back into base, he'd been asked what it was like: 'For the first time you felt legitimised. You felt like you had actually done it for real now and it was good, it was good.'[34] Had anyone stopped to ask them, which it doesn't seem like they did, the ANA fighting alongside might have begged to differ.

Once I started to dig around a bit, pieced together the brief but knackering history of the *kandak* itself from the more recent conversations I had, I began to understand why they were less enthusiastic about things, began to understand the state some of the longer-serving *askar* were in and why they had been so desperate for us to smuggle them out. 1/3/205 had been formed out of the bulk of the 47th Training Battalion; they had done a very basic training course in Kabul before being sent straight down to Kandahar. As Syed recalls, most of them didn't even have weapons at that stage and, although Kandahar Airfield was in the process of springing up with the coffee shops and fast food joints for which it would later become justifiably infamous as a slipper city,* it was still the Taliban's spiritual home and had only very recently been repossessed: not for nothing was the USAF Logistics HQ housed in a building known as TLS, site of the Taliban's Last Stand.

After only three weeks 1st, 2nd and 3rd Kandaks of the new 3rd Brigade accompanied the Paras into Helmand. One of the very first ANA mentors was Major Jonny Bristow, an instantly likeable, easy-going Jock officer with a slightly old-school air to him. When I happened across him in Kabul some years later he was conspicuously one of a handful of long-haired British officers in polo shirts and shorts on their day off, surrounded by a sea of close-cropped and uniformed Americans 'celebrating' the 4th of July. In 2006 it had been Bristow who had picked up the *kandak* from KMTC and escorted the nervous recruits down to Kandahar, and somehow I wasn't surprised that he remembered Syed Meraj after all that time: Syed tended to stand out. What was more impressive, given the sheer number of different British officers who have been his 'mentors' over the years, is that Syed

* In one respect 'slipper city' was a general term for anywhere more comfortable than where you happened to be, but KAF had really earned the epithet with numerous takeaways and minimal threat and had become the epitome of a cushy, rear-base area where decisions were made by those too far removed from realities on the ground.

also remembered Bristow, 'Jagran Jonny and a big red man with red hair', prepping everyone for the move south.

Another of the *kandak*'s first mentors, Tim Illingworth, remembered them up in Kabul in April 2006 as 'a decent bunch of young men who were used to a hard life, who had been brought up with automatic weapons in their homes and whose ancestors had been fighting since time immemorial'.[35] Perhaps it was an officer thing: we were graduates who'd been through Sandhurst, these days at an average age of twenty-four, but like me he was struck by the incredible youth of the bulk of the ANA recruits. Illingworth's recollection of Kandahar is that it was a bit too close to home for the more locally recruited soldiers in the *kandak*, who were jumping the already flimsy fence, so the onward move into Helmand was brought forwards. In good, old-fashioned style the *kandaks* had been brought together for some drill and a mind-numbing speech from a random general. The mentors watched with amusement as the size of the *kandak* on parade dwindled as the bored, squatting troops furthest from the general shuffled quietly away and did a runner back to their bunks. They may have missed the key warning about deploying down to Helmand, where they could expect 'a hard campaign'.[36] As Illingworth put it with pithy understatement: 'Helmand was a much less friendly area, and no one was likely to wander off too far down there.'[37]

Syed's memories of the same sequence of events are short and to the point: 'It was a hole in the desert. Nothing was there, just two or three tents, and this was a very hard time. We moved into Helmand by convoy from Kandahar. There was no airport then.' One of the early mentors was scathing, noting that when one ANA company caught sight of Camp Shorabak at the end of the drive from Kandahar, they broke ranks and charged for the gates, crashing four of their vehicles.[38] 3/205 were the first permanent ANA presence in Helmand where previously only

US Navy Seals and a composite Special Forces Task Force had been operating in the area as part of the separate US Operation Enduring Freedom. Syed recalls the small ISAF presence in the region, which would have been the Canadians, Dutch and the British forward elements who had been out building Camp Bastion since the spring. When Syed had first told me that they hadn't even had enough rifles, I had wondered whether that was a bit of exaggeration, uncharacteristic on his part but understandable given the gravity of the rest of the situation: not enough water to go around, the entire *kandak* initially sleeping in one big tent together, 'the *kandak* commander, the officers, the soldiers'. I should have trusted him better; even Lieutenant-Colonel Stuart Tootal, the commanding officer of 3 Para and the man who was suddenly and dramatically in charge of the bulk of the fighting troops in Helmand, acknowledges that in those early days we were relying, perhaps unfairly, on the ANA: 'But they were still arriving from Kabul, were not fully trained and lacked much of their equipment.' So far so SNAFU; it's the next observation that's surprising, that brings home how pressed we were and how much we pressed them in turn. 'Regardless of these shortfalls, they were sent to relieve the Canadians in FOB Robinson.'[39]

One of the more surreal niceties about Op Enduring Freedom was the way the Americans interpreted the need for an Afghan presence completely and utterly literally. The marauding companies of Alabama National Guardsman and Ranger Squads who were already dotted around Helmand could only charge into villages all guns blazing and AC/DC blasting out of the speakers on the PsyOps★ Hummer if they were joint patrol-

---

★ Psychological Operations: the speakers were for taped Pashtun messages, probably cheesy stuff about coming in peace and wanting to talk, but everyone loved a bit of *Back in Black* every now and again.

ling with the Afghan National Security Forces. With the lateral thinking for which they are prized, they would simply plan an operation or patrol and grab the nearest individual ANA soldier and chuck him in the back of a wagon, give him a can of soda to keep him happy, write his name up on the patrol manifest and 'Bingo', legitimate joint patrolling.

Among other, more troubling, implications, this meant that the *kandak*'s proud claim to be the first in the province was qualified. The deployment straight up from Shorabak to Sangin was more technically a relief in place, not the invasion some histories have portrayed it as. There were ANSF elements dotted haphazardly around Helmand when the *kandak* and its mentors arrived up in Sangin, but that didn't make them any better prepared for the months to come and, arguably, crippled the *kandak* before it had even learned to walk. Wavering deserters, the undecided who had resisted the temptation to do a runner in Kabul and had fought the urge to slip out of Camp Shirzai and into the Kandahar night, guys who might have made good soldiers if they'd been allowed to consolidate in Shorabak, get some more focused training under their belts and get used to their new home, there was no way they were going to hang around to see what happened when the *kandak* crashed out up to Sangin. In May 2006 as the *kandak* deployed up to FOB Robinson, it was 60 per cent under-strength, just 200 fighting men.[40]

The Paras were, so they'd tell you probably correctly, the fittest, best-trained, most war-ready soldiers in the British Army. Since learning of their planned deployment they had trained for everything through freezing forestry blocks to purpose-built dummy compounds in Oman, put through their paces by their American airborne counterparts who'd fought through Zabol province on Enduring Freedom. You have to contrast that with the ANA training experience: ten to fourteen weeks of basic – very basic – training up in Kabul; a bit of fitness, personal weapon skills and low-level tactics. If they were lucky they'd use some vehicles; as I'd found out the hardest way myself, none of them would have been anywhere near a plane or a chopper. They were young, unsteady and unsure of what they were supposed to be doing. Contrast it and then read back Tootal's 'regardless': 'Regardless' of the lack of kit and training; 'regardless' of having just arrived, bewildered, rushed through Kandahar to stem the flow of soldiers trying to slip back home; 'regardless' of having no formal orders, no specific Helmand preparation, no introduction to the units they'd be working with.

It wasn't Tootal's fault that the ANA were being flung all over the place; that was shifting Afghan politics: Karzai appeasing Daoud;* the Afghan MoD trying to impress Karzai; ISAF too keen to show off its ANA success story. On paper in Kabul the ANA made for good propaganda: the Afghans doing it for themselves. On PowerPoint slides in KAF and Lashkar Gah they were more boots on the ground, a vital force multiplier, a friendly forces icon on the battle space. 'Regardless' of the fact that it wasn't in any state to do so, with its feet having barely touched the ground let alone got its boots on, the *kandak* was sent up to Sangin, prompting another mentor to observe that even at this early stage the ANA 'looked and felt dispiritingly like a forgotten Army'.[41]

---

*Muhammad Daoud, the governor of Helmand.

First Casualties

No plan survives contact.* All soldiers had that drilled into them at every level of training, and all of them who ever actually encountered the enemy knew it to be more or less true. Whatever the plan had been at the beginning of 2006 it certainly didn't survive contact. As far as the *kandak* had been concerned they were hoping just to move into their new home at Shorabak and perhaps start receiving some much-needed field training from their new ISAF mentors: it didn't quite work out that way.

By late April 2006 elements of the 3 Para battlegroup were in place across central Helmand, and things were starting to hot up. The *kandak* took the first casualties of tour, ambushed in convoy with a French patrol on the 611, the dangerous road which ran north from Highway 1 near Gereshk up to Sangin. Four warriors were killed and brought back to into camp in body bags, limp in the back of a pick-up.

On 1 May 2006 the Stars and Stripes was lowered and the Union Flag raised in Lashkar Gah, Helmand's provincial capital. Since the beginning of Op Enduring Freedom the Americans had lost five soldiers in the province: five soldiers in five years. The ANA had lost five in the first couple of attacks. We would lose five in the next five weeks, and that was just the beginning. On the lazy Sunday morning of 2 July, in beds and cafes and on

---

* A maxim of Helmuth von Moltke the Elder, a German Field Marshal and military theorist who was also known, ironically in retrospect given how many times we had his maxim barked into us, as 'the great silent one'.

Ikea tables back home in England, people unfolded *The Sunday Times* and were plunged by Christina Lamb into the thick of an ambush in Zumberlay. From the moment Company Sergeant Major Mick Bolton of C Company, 3 Para offered his Browning 9mm pistol to the experienced foreign correspondent who, in the ditch north of Gereshk, was having by her own admission the worst day of a pretty eventful life, we realized Helmand was going to be something different. Theories swirl as to what went wrong. The 3 Para battlegroup, as much by the demands of local politics and a convoluted command structure as by Taliban pressure, found themselves forced into a reactive crouch. A mini-crisis here in Now Zad was followed by a mini-crisis there in Sangin, and before anyone really knew how or why, the units were spread too thinly across the large area and fighting from defensive positions, vulnerable to an enemy which knew the terrain and had freedom of movement, stuck in the infamous 'platoon houses'. There has been much written about the battles fought over that summer – the honours and awards bestowed upon the brigade some months later, and the sad casualties it sustained, tell their own story.

The first British troops to come under fire in Helmand were probably the Pathfinder Platoon, shot up outside Now Zad as they were recceing the province ahead of the arrival of the rest of the incoming brigade. Their encounter probably shouldn't count, although it set a precedent which would become an interesting sub-plot of the conflict, because the guys shooting at them were technically on their side. Up in FOB ROB, quickly and aptly named 'Camp Shit Hole' by the detachment of Royal Irish who were up there,[42] the *kandak* was undergoing its own baptism of fire. The 'big red man' Syed remembered as one of his first mentors was Captain Jim Philippson, the first British soldier killed in Helmand. Syed recalled FOB ROB with a phlegmatic half-laugh and the noise of a mortar 'all the time, boom down on our heads'. The situation was far from ideal for either the *kandak* or their mentors; the OMLTs were ad hoc and at times as small as four men and they frequently found themselves a long way from the support of other British units and low down the brigade's priority list.

Leo Docherty, another of the Helmand campaign's early mentors, but more tellingly one of the first men to return from the province disillusioned and angry, recalls the first mission to Sangin, the *kandak*'s first 'mission', as almost laughable in its naive simplicity: 'Seize Sangin and re-establish governance.'[43] General Napier might have been able to get away with that sort of brevity back in the day, but he won.* Sangin wasn't the Sindh and, more obviously, the 7 RHA OMLT was not the 22nd Regiment of Foot, and the *kandak* was not a sepoy army. Fergusson had grasped the Achilles heel of the OMLT project: you could be a Team for the T and Mentor and Liaise all you wanted for the M and L, but it was the O which was a problem because the ANA 'was far from what the British Army would consider "operational"'.[44]

Philippson was shot in the head in an ambush. It's difficult to tell from speaking to various guys from the *kandak* who were there at the time whether this was in fact the first occasion they'd properly been in contact, but a number of different soldiers can and do recall the first 'big fight' the *kandak* had was in Sangin – the big fight in which a mentor got killed. More nods and even a muttered *bale*, ah yes. The ambush in which Jim Philippson got killed. Questions were asked over the chaotic circumstances of the ambush: was the patrol adequately prepared and equipped? Less remarked upon was the thin glimmer of something more

---

* General Sir Charles James Napier, who conquered Sindh province in modern Pakistan in 1842 and reported it back to his commanders in the form of a one-word quip: *peccavi* (Latin for 'I have sinned').

positive to be gleaned from the way the ANA responded to the death of their mentor. The response Tim Illingworth remembers, the response of the *kandak* to losing their first, but sadly by no means their last, mentor, was absolutely typical and belied the poor regard in which many held them:

The Afghans who worked with Jim . . . they see death differently to us, but they were clearly very sorry that he'd died, and they consoled us, but they also saw it as a matter of pride, that he had died for their country. Mixed in with that, I think, there was some guilt, the sense that it should have been one of them.[45]

Heroes and Cowards

Of all the ANA stories from 2006 the one which was retold the most back home, the one that captured the imagination of all future mentors and excited and scared us in equal measure, was that of Captain Tim Illingworth. When I returned from Afghanistan the second time, I instinctively turned to accounts of his formative 'mentoring' experience. Possibly unfairly it had become shorthand for what working with the ANA was like, but it turned out to have lost a lot in the retelling, filtered through mess chat and gobby OPTAG sergeants until it became a searing indictment of how bad the ANA were. When he tells it in his own words, Illingworth paints a subtly but importantly different picture. What we all knew was that as an acting captain commanding an OMLT down in Garmsir, Illingworth was awarded the Conspicuous Gallantry Cross. The seemingly relevant bit of his citation read 'The Afghan force abandoned him, but in spite of his isolation he attempted to assault the enemy position, expending seven magazines of ammunition in the process . . .' Flying in to Helmand three months after Illingworth was gazetted, it was difficult to know what was on our minds more: the bit where the ANA had abandoned him or the fact that he had got through seven magazines.*

* Each magazine carried thirty rounds so this was potentially 210 rounds. Old pros used to say you should stick a tracer round about two or three up from the bottom of the magazine to warn you that you'd nearly run out and needed to change, which sounded preferable to the dead man's click of an empty mag but might have meant you wasted a couple in the change. Either way, the boy had fired a hell of a lot bullets.

In that context, you'd think he'd have had more cause than most to regard the ANA askance, but it doesn't come across that way. It is the editor of his recollections, not Illingworth himself, who refers to the 'frightened and uncommitted Afghan soldiers';[46] Illingworth is more forgiving of the 'inexperience and youth' of the few ANA who let him down. In the fierce battle of 13 September 2006 in which he won his medal Illingworth's ANA partner Toran Daoud Sherzad, Captain Daoud, was killed. Illingworth described him as 'the sort of man the Afghan Army needed for the future of their country, a born leader, with tactical nous and a lot of balls',[47] *kharkus*. Other than his citation, I had never read any of Illingworth's reflections until I had also come back from Helmand and I'm not sure whether that's a good or a bad thing. Part of me wishes I had because a lot would have made more sense, a lot would have felt less surreal, but another part of me thinks that there were so many similarities that it would have been unnerving, and no one likes to feel unoriginal, especially when the first guy clearly did it all significantly better. One thing that was inescapable was the unerring sense of recognition in how Illingworth had felt about the soldiers he mentored. Talking about Toran Daoud, the officer to whom he had grown close and who had been killed in battle, Illingworth said:

There's a feeling of helplessness. I had a close bond with him. He was awesome. For a long time I felt . . . in fact, I still do feel responsible for him being where he is and me being where I am . . . Two millimetres – the difference between me dying and me sitting here now, talking to you and planning to go to the pub later. That's how it goes.[48]

No one who'd lost anyone didn't recognize that feeling, but there was something different, not better or worse but different somehow, when it was 'your' ANA.

The clear implication of Illingworth's citation was that the ANA had lost their bottle when their commander had been killed, and this was mostly where people stopped hearing the story, but the ensuing argument was about whether or not a rescue mission should be launched to recover Daoud's body. Captain Doug Beattie, a twenty-year veteran, Royal Irish, late-entry officer who was also down in Garmsir, could see with more seasoned eyes and dismissed the idea as a suicide mission, but in a potent demonstration of their capacity to confound expectations the same *askar* who had run away charged back into the fray: foolish and dangerous, but far, far from cowardly.

In their desperate bid to recover the body themselves the ANA and ANP lost five men badly wounded. Illingworth thought it was by an enemy SPG-9 rocket, but Beattie discovered the more prosaic truth: that having almost pulled off the audacious assault and broken clean of the enemy, one of the warriors had let off an RPG in the back of the truck they were riding in. Perhaps the all-or-nothing thing was just the Afghan way, zero to hero, and then snatching calamity from the jaws of unlikely victory and screaming back into the base a pitiful mess of mangled limbs. As Beattie wondered poignantly, regarding with disgust the calm way in which the ANP commander considered the horrific injuries to have been worth it: 'Where was the humanity then? I wanted to stick my fist in his face and mark time on his head.'[49]

I met Doug Beattie, surreally enough for two soldiers, at a posh literary festival, sharing a platform way out of our respective comfort zones. He's the sort of hugely impressive man the very presence of whom shamed me for having left the Army. He was robust in his assessment of the Afghans he worked with and damn near died with one too many times, but you don't have a career like his without more insight than the old RSM in him sometimes hid. He grasped the shortcomings of the ANA as quickly as anyone – lunatics who couldn't read a map – and, like everyone else at times, had no idea what they were trying to achieve.[50] But like Illingworth, like many of us, having been through so much with them, he couldn't not also see the achievement when, as his ANP did under his brave command (Beattie won an MC while Illingworth was winning his CGC, which as much as anything gives a flavour of what life was like down in Garmsir at the time), 'a disparate band of men, seriously outnumbered, almost fatally under-trained, embarrassingly low on resources, yet they had achieved their goal'.[51] No surprise that within a few months of sharing that slightly odd stage with me, Beattie, a proper soldier in a way I never was, had un-retired and was back out in Helmand.

As Illingworth was the first, but not the last, to observe, the Afghans were different about death. It's telling that, talking to me three years later, Syed remembered Philippson, but couldn't recall all the names of his own comrades who had died that first summer. Time and time again we'd see how much more the ANA seemed to value us than we realized. Neither Syed nor Mujib, who I thought might know because he tended to have a good sense of what was going on elsewhere in the brigade, could recall Daoud beyond the stories that had inevitably filtered up to Shorabak and through to Sangin and the rest of the FOBs, just as, sat in tedious classrooms in Warminster, Illingworth's and Beattie's exploits distracted us even further from our lessons. Strictly speaking, the units down in Garmsir weren't part of the *kandak*, not my *kandak* anyway, but there was something so unerringly familiar in what Tim Illingworth said about Daoud that it's best to leave it in his words. Illingworth was interviewed for a book about British medal winners, and rightly so, but, instead of justifiably banging on about his CGC, he said:

But then Daoud – if he had been in the British Army – would have won a Victoria Cross, because he was leading his men from the front, taking them to enemy positions in the face of very heavy fire. But because he is an Afghan he gets little or no recognition.[52]

Sex, Drugs and Shades of Grey

The more I pieced together where the ANA had come from and what the *kandak* had been through, the more I listened to the new stories of freshly returning units and kept an eye on the regular trickle of news from Helmand, the more I saw the same things cropping up again and again and the more I began to wonder if there wasn't something more profoundly impossible about what we were trying to do with the ANA. The nature of the tours that preceded my own was that the OMLT commanders were largely volunteers: young but reasonably experienced officers with brains on them and bright prospects. Perhaps invariably, therefore, they were more romantic and reflective and inclined to synch with their ANA charges and relish the mission in a way most of the rest of the Army would not. The likes of Illingworth and Docherty might have been impressed, might have stitched ANA badges on to their uniforms with a sense of exhilaration, but others weren't and didn't. I knew very well the look they probably got when they tried to defend the Afghans, tried to explain their inconsistencies and the shades of grey in which they operated to tired and unresponsive comrades who trained by the book and lived by the British Army's clear demarcation of black and white. T. E. Lawrence said about training indigenous armies: 'It is better to let them do it themselves imperfectly than to do it yourself perfectly. It is their country, their way and our time is short.'[53] Plenty of well-read and well-intentioned officers had briefed their deploying units and sub-units with those same wise words; in one pretentious

HQ in Kandahar they had even gone so far as to put it up on a wall, but that seemed to be as far as they got.

It was easy to quote Lawrence to yourself and your troops, but much harder to live by his maxim. It's no particular indictment of the Paras who were the main element of that first summer in Helmand that they had formed an early low opinion of their Afghan comrades. Even the usually good-natured Canadians they were taking over from seemed to have had enough of the Afghans, one remarking to Leo Docherty: 'I just wanna get away from these people. You never know what they're thinking . . .'[54] The instinctive first reaction to the ANA seemed to be at best mistrust and at worst revulsion. Was it a form of racism, I wondered? Possibly on some level it was. Not the spiteful hatred of EDL wankers and the cancerous old Combat 18 crap that the Army had long got rid of, thank God, but something more instinctive, an inability to understand the different and a lazy reluctance to engage with the unfamiliar, the counterpoint to the comfort that people seem to draw from being surrounded by other people that look and think like them. Hugo Farmer, about as far from the caricature of an airborne meathead as you could imagine (which didn't stop him also winning a Conspicuous Gallantry Cross for his balls-out leadership of his Toms in 2006), observed of the *kandak* up in Sangin that they had learned little from their ISAF training and 'were going feral'.[55] Farmer's chain of command shared his concerns, noting the performance of some of the *kandak* up in Sangin was 'little better' than that of the ANP, who had mostly defected to the Taliban or fled. One of the platoons had to have its corrupt commander removed leading to 'a complete breakdown in discipline'.[56]

The context was key, but as the fighting season began in earnest and the troops in Helmand began to realize the scale of the task facing them, no one was that interested in context.

Interviewed by James Fergusson, Captain Will Libby, another of the early OMLT officers, could see exactly what the problem was and also knew that the *kandak*'s general lack of *esprit de corps* was hardly its fault. The familiar fault lines from the mixed training the ANA undertook in Kabul were dangerously exposed and exaggerated on the battlefield:

> The officers were trained by the French, but the junior NCOs and the rest were trained by the Canadians, so they didn't know their officers from Adam. And that's reckoned to be an essential part of training in Western armies . . . we focussed on the importance of bonding, teaching NCOs to teach their blokes. But the officers got selected on nepotistic lines . . . there was a huge disparity between the best and the worst of them in terms of experience and quality. The lack of kit and preparation led to units hastily being bolted together, which led to a lack of trust between the men and the officers.'[57]

What might have come as something of a rude shock, however, to those passing judgement and unfavourable comment on the ANA was that the Afghans also took a pretty dim view of the way we did things from time to time. The Pathfinder Platoon engaged by the nervous ANP had, after all, returned fire; these things cut both ways. We might have thought we were bestowing the gift of training and professionalism, but it was clear from the outset that others didn't necessarily agree. An interview with one of the *kandak*'s new recruits appeared in the *Guardian* at the beginning of our tour, complaining about how harsh the training regime was and comparing KMTC to Guantanamo Bay. The soldier, Ahmed Jawad, said he'd been shot at trying to escape through an icy river, which I didn't bother to write in and explain was bullshit when I realized that Jawad had been one of the 475 new recruits I'd escorted down from Kabul the week before and had had ample time to escape if he'd really wanted to. It sounded like classic ANA exaggeration to me when I read it but it raised a smile and probably had a germ of truth in it, especially the harshness of the training. No matter how many times we repeated Lawrence, we still couldn't relax to an 'Afghan way', which must have been just as infuriating for them as it was for us. The *kandak* may have been making a more or less unwitting bad impression on their new mentors, but neither was it a given the Paras were doing any better.

It never ceases to amuse me that one of the things thousands of British troops rotating through Helmand have struggled with the most is the relative intimacy of their Afghan counterparts. One officer observed diplomatically that '[t]he exact role performed by the tea-boy doting on every ANA officer is consequently a source of endless banter amongst the Brits',[58] but it was the Tom who said of the ANA, with the eloquence of a true Para, that 'they were all bender boys'[59] who was more representative. The more intelligent critics, the 'I'm not racist but . . .' brigade, would dress up their disapproval in paternal concern for the catamites one occasionally found in ANA squads (and, a little more frequently, amongst the ANP), but there was something broader than that at work, and I wondered if it was a shudder of self-awareness which was too difficult for most of us to work out: a clash between the necessarily testosterone-heavy macho culture on which front-line soldiers survived and its knee-jerk reaction to the intimacy that very culture bred. At a pre-deployment party before the *kandak* set off for Sangin for the first time the DJ had played Electric Six's 'Gay Bar' on the PA; the Brits had all laughed, and the Afghans, not knowing the difference, had just jiggled along. 'Let's start a war,' the lyrics went, perhaps the DJ was funnier than he thought, 'start a nuclear war / At the gay bar, gay bar, gay bar'. The immediate irony confronting the intolerant Toms was, of course, that the Paras were exponents *par excellence* of the strange balance between the macho and the homo-erotic. The military shorthand which equated a lack of robustness and even cowardice with effeminacy took a curious turn in more experienced front-line units where such close bonds grew up between comrades that the gay taboo was somehow bypassed. The preening in gyms in rear bases had more to do with vanity and boredom than anything else, and the handlebar moustaches and other camp icons might just as easily have been appropriated from the military as by them. Either way, by the mid-noughties it was difficult to tell the difference, and it seemed hypocritical that lads who spent their days pumping iron and sculpting their sideburns found it difficult when the ANA rocked up to patrol in eye-liner. More profoundly disjointed was the overplayed horror with which the common Afghan practice of men holding hands was greeted, especially when contrasted with the ever more bizarrely sexual banter which characterized isolated fighting platoons. 3 Para mortar platoon might have had the original reputation and the rumours, but the rest of the infantry had caught on, and even when I was an innocent young second-lieutenant, fresh on Platoon Commanders' Battle Course in the notorious Brecon boozer the Welly, rumours abounded of the lads on the Section Commanders' Battle Course who delighted in shocking their new officers by noshing each other off at the bar. Most counter-intuitively of all, as one of the cheering onlookers said at the time, 'to prove that he's not gay, sir'.

It shocked us closeted officers at the time, as it was meant to do, and in Brecon among the sheep and the hikers we could dismiss it as braggadocio and banter, the unpleasant but unavoidable co-opting of a prison mentality that came with the isolation and the forced company. But out on operations, the constant gags that this young Guardsman or that young Gunner was looking prettier the longer the tour went on, that it was only gay if you pushed back, were too oft repeated to be merely an extension of the default lad's mag humour. Even those of us who considered ourselves above the crude jokes weren't immune to something cultural that was happening which manifested itself in how we placed our comrades above our friends, the appropriation of 'brother' for comrade, which carried more meaning than fake Hip-Hop gangstas could have imagined. I later found out that even girlfriends and wives felt ever so slightly uncomfortably displaced by the way we were noticeably more tactile with Army mates than others, how especially the difficult invariably drunken first months after a tour were punctuated with long and curiously intense bear-hugs and uneasy, rugby-tour homo-eroticism.

On the one hand that sort of blokey togetherness was a million miles away from forced *liwat*★ and some of the abuses which undoubtedly went on. According to certain Afghan traditions, keeping a catamite was a sort of military status symbol, power reflected in the youth and attractiveness of the kept boy. It was difficult and upsetting to most of those who came across it, and you felt especially for senior men with young kids themselves, but I suspect far more soldiers knew someone who'd 'definitely' seen it than had seen it themselves. There was also the sense that perhaps we had a conveniently short corporate memory. I didn't doubt the sincerity of the general repugnance, but you had to wonder whether the harrumphing old warrant officers had forgotten where the notion of 'the Guardsman's defence' ('the Portsmouth defence' if you were in the Navy) had come from. The Marines taking over on Herrick V might have listened aghast to tales of the hand-holding, khol-wearing, Thursday-night 'man-love' Afghans they'd be sharing the FOBs with, but

★ Homosexual sex, literally people who perform the sins of *Lut* or Lot in the Bible (of wife, salt and pillar fame).

Just the sort of thing that used to get the sergeants in a flap: silly hat, non-regulation kit, holding hands; never mind that this pair had just spent a successful six hours patrolling through the Green Zone. May 2007.

they all had pink lacy thongs hidden in their kit somewhere, and the stories one heard from down on Union Street* would have caused seasoned Afghan dancing boys to faint.

Like frustrated rock stars, when we weren't obsessed with sex we were obsessed with drugs, and again I'm unsure quite how righteously we sat in judgement on the ANA, even allowing for the particularly confused relationship militaries have with intoxicants. Soldiers who wore their paralytic drunkenness back home as a badge of pride dismissed the entire *kandak* as dangerous and incompetent addicts the moment a soldier somewhere or other was found smoking dope. Docherty was more honest

* In Plymouth, traditionally not a place to be out on the piss if you weren't 'Royal'.

than most, admitting to chewing 'brown' in Shorabak with Toran Hamid Ullah, the Kandak HQ Tolay commander. The 'rush of tingling'[60] sounds fun enough, but the heaviness and nausea which apparently followed less so, although not that much worse than the dreadful chewing tobacco to which the entire US military seems to currently be addicted. Booze was banned in Helmand, unlike in Kandahar or Kabul, but you'd have had to be a pretty hardened drinker to have wanted to wake up in Sangin with a hangover. I'm still not sure that either the rules or the situation quite justified the inevitable knee-jerk response to the odd Afghan toker and a reasonably small minority of smokers of cannabis casting a stink over the entire *kandak*.

There are various reasons given by the Ministry of Defence for a policy which barely notices and tacitly supports an oftentimes dangerous institutional drunkenness but operates zero tolerance in respect of substances coming under the woefully ill-conceived, poorly drafted and outdated Misuse of Drugs Act 1971. In keeping with higher national policy on drugs they are mostly incoherent and certainly not evidence based. I can only wonder what Aldershot was like back when mephedrone was still legal:* early-morning PT must have been a struggle, but I bet there were fewer fights in town. In my time I saw good soldiers kicked out having had their drinks spiked in nightclubs and told that, even if it wasn't their fault, they'd brought it on themselves simply by being in a club where that sort of thing was going on. I saw naive and foolish young men back off six weeks' post-deployment leave booted out for an error of judgement by functioning alcoholic officers who were still cadging lifts from everyone else in the mess while they served out their drunk-driving bans. The most frequent reason given was that

---

* Or 'Meow Meow' as the British media, falling for a brilliant Wikipedia hoax, woke up one morning and thought it was called 'on the street'.

booze wasn't illegal and drugs were, and soldiers had to be moral custodians of the land – this invariably by men who proudly competed over speeding fines and happily flouted the equally illiberal and badly cobbled-together Hunting With Dogs Act 2004. I guess this was a neat way of sidestepping the more pathetically outdated arguments about what effect a line on a Friday night did or didn't have on someone's ability to sit through a lecture on map-reading on Monday morning, but it didn't explain why the problem with the ANA was always expressed in terms of operational effectiveness rather than whether or not they should have been charged with possession with intent.

The Army's Compulsory Drug Testing (CDT) regime had been introduced, so it was once explained to me, in the eighties to combat two distinct but related problems. At the height of the Troubles during the era of long and tense and difficult, but often also quite boring, residential tours in Northern Ireland, random drug tests weren't really an Army thing. Quite a few soldiers, however, were alleviating the boredom smoking something a little more exotic than your average *roik* (tradition dictated Lambert and Butlers for the lads, Camels for the officers, although by my day it was Marlboro Lights). Rumour had it this was most popular among Close Observation Platoons, guys who were already bloody good soldiers and were rightly trusted and, more importantly, trusted themselves. No doubt that if they were passing 48 hours in an OP overlooking some god-forsaken farmhouse down on the border they weren't going to let themselves get in trouble, but they had to pass the hours. Those sorts of stories were apocryphal, but there must have been enough of a problem that the Army decided to take steps. The other more serious problem was the much smaller minority who were apparently so bored in high metal guard towers that they had started taking smack. Granted, no one wanted to sleep, or rather not sleep, in a base supposedly guarded by a lunatic who'd been injecting heroin in between his toes,* but I suspect those cases were even rarer than the tiny number alleged. Either way, it sounded pretty similar to the Afghan situation: what was Helmand if not Afghanistan's Northern Ireland? An exaggerated handful of bored and tired and scared soldiers smoking weed and a tiny, tiny minority availing themselves of something stronger that happened to be cheap and easy to get hold of. Of course it was a problem, still is a problem, but the way you read it in the papers the ANA were shooting up before stepping out on every patrol and dropping pills every Thursday night in all the FOBs. How we squealed with righteous moral indignation, forgetting as we got all Preachey von Holier-than-thou that we had been through exactly the same thing as an army.

Context, again, was all important: the drinking thing was a good example. Michael Yon, a former Green Beret who has spent most of the last decade independently blogging from Iraq and Afghanistan, and has a decent claim to be the best war correspondent of his generation, also noted the hypocrisy, tipping out of the back of a Chinook on a night assault into a field of marijuana.

> Alcohol is forbidden here, while marijuana and opium-poppy grow by the thousands of tons. A sentence for alcohol here could be as severe as a sentence for heroin in the United States. Bar tabs in America are paid with money that says 'In God We Trust,' while Afghans are notorious drinkers and are normally

---

* The experienced warrant officer telling us the story identified the problem as having been particularly rife among the Coldstream Guards, but he was a Grenadier and so were we, so that was probably just banter.

banned from Kabul bars. And here we were, in a marijuana patch, in Kandahar Province, hypocritically calling each other hypocrites.[61]

Booze was banned for the British in Helmand, but that didn't mean that enterprising friends and parents couldn't find their way round the threatened RAF spot checks by decanting a drop of something to remind you of home into a shampoo bottle or something else which looked suitably innocent in a comfort box next to a month-old copy of *The Week* and packets of oozing, melted Haribo. I got a drop of scotch for my birthday, which happened to fall while I was up in Sangin, and, as bad luck had it, a few days before we got quite a hammering and took a couple of casualties. As I said, you'd have had to be desperate or ill to really want to go on a bender in Helmand, but there were occasions like that when everyone needed a stiff one, and as we sat that evening having the last of the frankfurters which Sergeant T had saved and fried for me as a birthday surprise, a wee dram of single malt from the Head and Shoulders bottle went down extremely well.

After dinner I tripped back down the hill to see how the ANA were doing. Sergeant Abdullah on his last day before being relieved and flown back to Shorabak had lost a leg and an arm. That was bad enough for anyone, but you knew that, if he lived, Abdullah wasn't going to get cash from Help for Heroes: did Afghanistan even have a Paralympic team? Morale was low; Hazrat, Sharaf Udin and Gholam Nabi as ever chilling out in their dimly lit HQ, cross-legged on the floor, poring over the stag rotas with a radio linked to the perilous-looking mains burbling in the background. Walking past one of the squad rooms – I could guess which – the smell was unmistakable. I raised an eyebrow and tilted my head in its direction, no more, Hazrat smiled and opened his arms as if to say, 'What harm?'

Sharaf Udin pointed to one of the lists. 'Abdullah's men are taken off patrol and guard duty tomorrow.' Well, fair enough. If they'd been drinkers I'd have offered them a sip of what we'd just had, so who the hell was I to kick up a stink? The guys had it in hand, and I'm not sure I know what the difference was. Not sure there was a difference at all.

Nuance: nuance lost on those who saw only colourful headlines, good stories in the mess and, by extension, a bigging-up of their own achievements. It wasn't malicious, I don't think, just classic military group-think exacerbated by an inability to think outside our cultural box. Everyone who fought alongside the *kandak* recognized a bravery and inherent scrapping ability. Ironically the one thing the ANA didn't need to learn from us was their core trade, it was the rest of the stuff that was the problem, and the problem which became the headline, so the stories we heard back home were ANA shooting at plucky Brits, ANA abandoning heroic Brits and general ANA naughtiness. None of the Afghans I subsequently spoke to, guys who remember their individual mentors from years back, can remember the first *kandak* officer to be sacked. Opinion is split as to which was the rotten platoon that caused A Company of 3 Para so many problems. Syed thought it must have been one of the 1 Tolay platoons, but then he was a 3 Tolay man. The corruption the Royal Marines would later encounter stemmed from a corrupt company commander who disappeared before we arrived, so it could have been either. Tootal's executive summary was typical of the image the ANA had rapidly gained; the old, salacious headlines were classic tabloid fodder: sex, drugs and crime. 'Drug taking, sexual abuse of local minors and theft of equipment from the company were common until they were eventually replaced by a more reliable ANA platoon.'[62] Like most mentors who had spent any length of time with the ANA, Captain Will Libby, who'd been up in Sangin with the *kandak* at the very start, more readily looked beyond the cheap stories about Afghans running away and addressed the causes:

> They were asked to fight alongside people they didn't know. They didn't know where they were going, or why sometimes. They were far from their homes, with minimal training, on a salary of four dollars a day – about a third of what the Taliban paid their fighters. Given those circumstances I reckon we might desert too.[63]

Boots on the Ground

Before 2007 there had been only three full *kandaks* in Helmand and only one British unit working with them, so it wasn't too difficult to trace the faint progress of the ANA and their mentors. With the increase in boots on the ground, US Marine Corps, British and most of all ever more ANA stomping all over the province, the guys were harder to keep tabs on, but there were still the odd glimpses, the flicker of a recognized face here, a familiar-sounding story there. The brigade commander enjoyed a brief moment of glory when his 'Heroes' recaptured Musa Qala at the end of 2007, Mohaiyadin splashed across Western broadsheets waving the black-green-red Afghan tricolour like *la Liberté* herself, but the spin of an 'ANA-led' success story quickly unravelled, and the *kandak*'s memories of the northern fort town were less photogenic and more ambiguous.

Musa Qala had been an itch for the British since the Paras had negotiated an exit from / retreated from / tactically redeployed from / abandoned it (delete as applicable, depending on who you asked) back in 2006. No matter whether that particular tactical move had made sense at the time, the town had been retaken by the Taliban and had become a serious problem, a secure rearops holiday base where they could regroup and plan in safety and at leisure. Up in Sangin, the nearest town with an ISAF presence, you could sense the proximity of a major enemy HQ; we'd spend long nights listening to the intercepted radio messages of the fresh fighters coming down the valley, the exhausted and the injured passing them on the way back up for a bit of R&R. You didn't have to be a general to know that it was bad strategy to allow the enemy to sit unchallenged just a few miles behind your front line, but our worry in 2007 was that we'd be the ones asked to go and recapture the town. We were as up for a scrap as anyone, but all the intelligence indicated that the Taliban had turned the town into a fortress, dug in, built up, booby trapped and wired all to hell, an Afghan Verdun they would all fight to the death rather than relinquish. When the orders came out for 12 Brigade's last deliberate op and they left Musa Qala well alone, very few of us weren't secretly a little bit relieved. It was a problem, but we'd had a long tour, and it could be someone else's problem, 52 Brigade's problem.

Of course, the ANA didn't have the luxury of leaving it to someone else, and within months of our leaving them, all three of the fighting *kandaks* in Helmand were committed to the huge operation to retake the town, Operation Mar Karadad,* which meant 'snakebite', or did it? I've seen it translated as 'snake pit', which would be more appropriate. Musa Qala was a snake pit, but in the end the vast coordinated op to retake the town found that its defenders did not bite as hard as had been feared. The *kandak* went over the top first, literally as it happened, out of the riverbed and into the town with their mentors, only to find it deserted. A British officer mentoring the 2nd Kandak recalled that it looked like the enemy had 'well and truly fled'.[64] Jah Muhammad, a soldier who'd been with 2nd Kandak for the op, remembered that same officer, 'Captain Nick who got injured'. Captain Nick Mantell of B Company, 2 Yorks certainly did get injured, took a knock in the blast that killed Sergeant Johnson:

* We'd transitioned from the Silvers and Silicons of the periodic table to gung-ho Pashtu midway through our tour, starting a trend that would last through Oqab Tsuka (Eagles' Summit), Sond Chara (Red Dagger) and Panchai Palang (Panther's Claw), until the US presence swung the vibe back to anodyne cheesy, and the blokes headed out on Moshtarak (Together), presumably holding hands.

somehow, miraculously, the only British fatality of the main assault on the town. Jah Muhammad described the whole operation, with understatement, as 'difficult'; some of his 1st Kandak comrades were less diplomatic.

Old Younes was one of the ANA who had been right there 'with the brigadier when the district centre was captured', which made it sound more glamorous than it actually was. As the journalist Stephen Grey rather quaintly but accurately observed, the notion that the ANA had done the 'heavy lifting' to take the town was 'poppycock'.[65] Mohaiyadin himself had made it clear to the Americans, who, as ever, were the ones really doing the 'heavy lifting', that they would make sure Musa Qala was clear before he marched in. Syed reckons that in all some elements of the *kandak* spent eight months in Musa Qala, having been moved straight there from Sangin, where we'd left them. None of the ANA reckon it was the worst posting the *kandak* had; their predominant memories are of the mines rather than the Taliban. Lieutenant Gholam Nabi, who I had left commanding one of Hazrat's platoons up in Sangin, remembered being blown up in a Mastiff and emerging unscathed, delighted by the protection of the impressive truck: 'No one injured, no damage, just change the tyre.' Perhaps it was a mark of how inured the ANA had become to violence that their memories of Herrick VII were so good: 'Never the British or the ANA had any injured,' was Gholam Nabi's recollection, but the records showed that the ANA still lost fifteen men over the 'quiet' winter months before the Paras returned in spring 2008. As Grey recorded in his detailed account of the huge Musa Qala operation and that tour, whatever you may have thought of the phoney, flag-raising gesturism, the ANA 'had no shortage of bottle'.[66]

Snakebite may not have been the moment the ANA showed they could do it all themselves, but some progress was obviously being made, and by 2008 reports of the *kandak*, media glimpses and the snapshots recorded in the ever-growing library of 'Afghanistan' books were less clichéd and pot-smokingly chaotic. The incoming Royal Irish mentors were pleasantly surprised at the *kandak*'s capability. Having been led to believe that they were just 'people running about with guns', one Royal Irish sergeant remembered that '[t]hey do have an idea. More than a bit,' and, most importantly, 'when it comes to trusting them out on the ground, I would'.[67] As the returning Paras struggled through the summer with the slow, hard, Sisyphean main effort of dragging the 220-tonne third turbine up from Kandahar to the Kajaki dam, one could even sense a grudging respect emerging for the way the ANA operated, not least their agility. In Sangin Lieutenant Patrick Bury, commanding a platoon from Ranger Company, 1 Royal Irish, noted admiringly the arrival of the ANA, 'their new OMLT commander skidding his open-top jeep to a halt in a cloud of dust and, with a nod of his cowboy hat, beginning the sweep-through. The villagers comply and those light, nimble ANA search the entire village in a couple of hours, far quicker than we could.'[68] Reading back at home, I felt a surge of pride: my boys, my boys.

One of the only ANA soldiers I caught up with who hadn't been to Musa Qala was Sharaf Udin. He'd been sent from Sangin straight up to Kajaki instead where, he later told me: 'The situation was good, our mentor was Captain Doug, and he was also writing a book about us. About the Afghanistan condition.' Good old Doug Beattie must have been a perfect match for the fierce platoon commander who'd taught me to fire the Dragunov. Trying to piece together what the *kandak* had done, trying to flesh out and verify the piecemeal recollections and stories the ANA had told me down in Shawqat, I turned again to books like Doug Beattie's and realized with a jolt that I was suddenly nervous and protective. Other soldiers and writers had also met, worked with and formed opinions of Qiam and Sharaf Udin. What if we disagreed or worse? What if connections which we all thought had been ours and ours alone were simply the ANA playing the game? Beattie reckoned the Irish had a particular affinity with the Afghans: a disparate group from a variety of backgrounds, a 'chaotic, violent federation of clans and families'.[69] Sounded about right.

I had been asked to do an assessment of Sharaf Udin while working with him up in Sangin as part of our preparation for the handover. I found the notes in the still-dusty folder which I'd dumped in the bottom of a box when I got home and had been challenging myself not to look at ever since. Apart from the worrying few slips of paper which by their markings should probably not have come home with me, it's a pretty faithful paper-between-waterproof-A4-pockets record of a tour: meticulously cut-out, impossibly airbrushed shots of officer-suitable fitties,* ORBATs and ZAP numbers you probably still knew by heart, sketch maps and J2 snippets and, which marked it out, the sheets of incomprehensible Dari. I'd written the following about Sharaf Udin:

SU is the most hands on of the platoon commanders, putting himself forward in defence and deploying on patrols. An astute commander who observes and learns quickly, something of a technical guru in the company (largely by virtue of owning an MP3 player and a real digital camera) and the closest to a British platoon commander. A qualified Dragunov sniper and SPG-9 operator and generally very useful commander. Sharaf Udin can, however, be headstrong and stubborn and occasionally resistant to mentoring, arguing that his practical experience outweighs our theoretical bullshit (possibly quite

* Kate Moss in an Agent Provocateur campaign as it happened.

true!). Respected by the men rather than liked (particularly by the Pashtuns in the company) but leads by example and has often been the only ANA soldier still putting himself in harm's way in the defensive battle.

Beattie's 'Sherafadin' was my Sharaf Udin all right, carrying an old polaroid picture of himself 'resplendent in traditional Afghan dress, sitting aside the still-smouldering Russian armoured personnel carrier, with corpses strewn all around'.[70]

'We were only one platoon in Kajaki and I was responsible,' he told me proudly later, 'Our tasks were going well in Kajaki, and Captain Doug and his sergeants helped us, and we had patrols in northern Kajaki, it was good.' He had paused, and we had both looked down involuntarily at his useless arm, clad up to the shoulder in white plaster. Sharaf Udin was not a man for the rear. A full year after I had done the same in Sangin, Beattie and his OMLT were messing in with 2 Tolay lads, Sharaf Udin was still strutting around bare-chested when in camp, still quite the disciplinarian, beating one of his soldiers caught trying to steal one of the Para's cot-beds (which was likely far less a punishment than the Paras would have meted out) and doing a pretty good job. In his own words, it was good.

Beattie saw more of the good and bad of the Afghans on his two tours than most would if they spent twice that long in Helmand. Switched to mentoring another *kandak*, counter-narcotics guys, he even witnessed the cold-blooded murder of a Taliban detainee. The narco *kandak* had been recruited locally, had received less training than their regular ANA counterparts and were prey to local pressures and tribal feuding; it was a worrying glimpse of what happened when the focus was on quantity, not quality. When I'd first heard about the incident, the sense of anger, deflation and even betrayal was palpable. It was easy to be glib, to note that it hadn't been the *kandak*, hadn't been troops

270

who'd been mentored by us, that there are rotten apples in every barrel, but it was the sort of thing that crushed you: two steps forward and a giant leap back. On a more reflective level, perhaps there was a pertinent contrast to be drawn with our own recent performances. While talking heads and armchair generals frothed with righteous indignation at the barbarity of the ANA, we should surely have been slower to judge and quicker to recall how we'd disgraced ourselves in Iraq and Baha Mousa's sickening injuries. As ever, a double standard was being applied: our own shortcomings were invariably blips and regrettable anomalies, the ANA's symptoms of endemic corruption or crisis. The question should have been how do we make sure these terrible things never happen again, but all we heard was Beattie's heartfelt: 'What was the fucking point of being here?'[71]

Stalemate

There are various measures of progress – 'metrics' the Yanks liked to call them, which meant pretty soon everyone else did too. Helmand became a political football: not enough helicopters, not enough troops. The situation on the ground was constantly fluid and always the same. When 3 Commando Brigade handed over to 19 Light Brigade in the spring of 2009 the incoming troops found themselves into double figures on Op Herrick X. If you looked at the photos of Task Force Jacana, 45 Commando bunker-busting through eastern Afghanistan way, way back in 2001, they were the same Marines, but they might as well have belonged to a different army fighting a different war. The days of flimsy black Hi-Tec boots and ragged cotton Combat 95s, six SA80s in a section and one GPMG per platoon were practically as distant as red tunics and muskets. A lot had changed in a short space of time. When I left the Army in 2009 the kit and capability of a basic infantry platoon had advanced more in the brief five years I had served than it had in the previous twenty-two between the Falklands War and when I'd joined up. More than being arguably better tactically equipped than any previous expeditionary force the British Army had ever put in the field,* the brigades deploying to Afghanistan in 2008, 2009 and 2010 were stronger and larger than ever before. Thousands and thousands of British soldiers,

---

* Not the same thing, of course, as being as well equipped as you could or should have been, but something that was often overlooked in the general clamour.

sailors and airmen accompanied by the enormous surge in US troops levels announced at the end of 2009* and newly trained Afghan National Army soldiers were being concentrated into ever more focused, localized areas of operation. The problem was that as 'big' was not always 'beautiful', so 'more' wasn't necessarily 'better'.

Officially, the 'capabilities of the ANA [were] improving steadily'.[72] Beyond the 50,000 strength envisaged by the Bonn Agreements at the start of the decade, by the end of 2008 the government of the Islamic Republic of Afghanistan (GIRoA to ISAF, which made it sound like something you bought in a hardware store) had an army of nearly 80,000 warriors and an ambitious plan to expand to grow it to 134,000 by 2012,[73] attracting envious glances no doubt from Glasgow:[†] you had to go back to before Options for Change[‡] for when the British Army was last that size. We couldn't afford a big army, of course, but neither could the Afghans. As the world crashed into recession, where was the cash going to come from? The United States had increased funding for the ANA from $1.9 billion in 2007 to $2.7 billion the following year,[74] but by one estimate that still left a massive $6.7 billion dollar shortfall through to 2010.[75] Good thing the ANA weren't supplied with the £70,000 Javelin missiles we all so loved to fire. Sustainability was a problem in the medium and long term, but the real looming crisis for the ANA,

---

* In an address to the West Point Military Academy on 1 December 2009, President Obama confirmed that a further 30,000 troops would be sent to Afghanistan, this in addition to the deployment of an extra 21,000 following the announcement of the new administration's 'comprehensive' strategy on 27 March, just nine months previously.
† Home of the Army Personnel Centre, in charge of everyone's careers and, for as long as anyone could remember, how to manage a shrinking army.
‡ The 1994 Defence Review, in which the Cold War Army was consigned to history.

what none of the personnel projections in Kabul or policy documents in Washington considered, was not the warriors of tomorrow it didn't yet have and couldn't afford, but the ones it already did, neglected and knackered on the ground. As Stephen Grey observed, returning to Musa Qala two years after he'd been the first journalist into the town as the *kandak* 're-took' it, the ANA was 'better armed, better trained and more able to lead its own operations. But, after three years of fighting in Helmand without relief, many were also exhausted.'[76]

In 2009, the Welsh Guards may have been in Afghanistan for the first time, but it was obvious to them that their Afghan counterparts were 'battle-weary'.[77] The same bad first impressions were being made all over again. One company commander remarked of the ANA with disgust: 'I have no idea what they actually did apart from loot the compound and eat the livestock left behind. They really are animals and next to useless as soldiers.'[78] The unquestioned fighting spirit of the ANA which had won it so many admirers in the past was of less value in the softly-softly-catchy-monkey world of counter-insurgency, where it was all about winning the population, not the fire-fight. General McChrystal's mantra of 'courageous restraint' was difficult enough for some of the more experienced ISAF troops to get their heads around – a far cry from proud regimental mottoes like '*Nemo me impune lacessit*'* or the wonderfully to-the-point 'Death or Glory' – but it was a complete anathema to the ANA, and an unforeseen consequence was that the difference in approach began to come between the British and their Afghan partners.

---

* 'No one harms me with impunity', or, as the Jock Guards, whose motto it was, brilliantly managed to get edited on to Wikipedia, 'No one fucks wi' me and gets away wi' it.'

The defining operation of 2009 was the celebrated, lamented Operation Panchai Palang, Panther's Claw. Pressure on the provincial capital Lashkar Gah had prompted the governor of Helmand, Gulab Mangal, to push for more troops in central Helmand. From Musa Qala the *kandak* was bounced straight down to Nad-e Ali and into the mess which was to consume the Welsh Guards battlegroup and dominate the summer: bogged down by IEDs, the shortest of drives between checkpoints and PBs becoming painstaking, lethal, inch-by-inch ordeals. Mujib reckoned 3 Tolay alone had lost two killed and twenty-five injured since the *kandak* deployed to Nad-e Ali, two dead and twenty-five injured out of less than a hundred. The IEDs, referred to universally by the ANA as 'mines', were a factor, but the guys were also deeply unhappy about the subtle changes in the way operations were conducted, were convinced that 'courageous restraint' was costing lives. Syed was typically coy, only saying, disjointedly, that since 2008 'there have been some changes, now not any more helping, less friendship, a bit different'. Stretched to the limit by Panther's Claw, losing the initiative to endless IEDs, the *kandak*'s perspective was that, through 2009, their relationship with the British deteriorated. The ANA command structure asserted itself as much by what it refused to do as what it did, withdrawing its men from key points within the area when the British failed to deliver resupply. In one particularly damaging incident the bodies of two soldiers killed by an IED in the process of trying to recover the body of the popular Sergeant Ohlab were simply left behind as the British refused to deploy helicopter support from Bastion to reclaim them. You could imagine all manner of good reasons not to bring in the vital medical helicopter for guys who were already dead, but the message to the ANA was that 'their dead would not be afforded the same respect as that given to the British dead'.[79] The ANA were furious. When I asked him why there was, in his own words, less friendship than before, Syed pointedly drew a comparison with the 'good old days': 'we had a good relationship with our mentors; when we got casualties they were carried by helicopter, so Helmand was not a problem.'

It was stretching it to say that Helmand had not been a problem in 2007, but Syed had a point, and it was noticeable that the Grenadiers, coming full circle and heading back out to take over from the Welsh Guards, were in a far more sombre mood than when we had deployed two years previously. It wasn't just that subtle difference between going and going back – half the Battalion were heading out for the first time in any event – the difference was in a greater expectation of grittiness, a diminished sense of adventure, a mental clenching against the coming slog. It was all very well flooding the key areas with troops and pointing excitedly to the growing numbers of new warriors passing off the square in Kabul, 3/205 was only 7 per cent of the ANA's combat power and down in Helmand it was facing 35 per cent of all the enemy activity.[80] Those of us who retained a sense that the mission in Afghanistan was worthwhile, that something positive was achievable, were starting to sound as tired as each set of battered, returning brigade. The metrics said one thing, but you could say anything with metrics. The ANA themselves said another: they felt they were regressing, and that was worrying.

Close Shaves and Bad Omens

Throughout 2007 the *kandak* had been good, but it had also been lucky; maybe it was impossible to divorce the two. Qiam had been shot five times in his life and had nearly had his head blown off on the first day of our first op together, but he'd been fine and survived to drive the *kandak* forward for the next two months. Poor old Abdul Marouf had shot himself in the foot on day two of that same first op, clambering in through the window of a compound, but he was back on the front line with us two weeks later, foot in a bandage and a new-found respect for his safety-catch. On the dicey drive to Sangin somehow our only casualty had been a negligent discharge which even more fortunately had only nipped the tip off Muhammad Raza's ear. The squad leader of the vehicle in front looked a bloody mess, and we had to bandage up his head like an eighties tennis player, but somehow, improbably, he'd been fine. When we'd watched *Any Given Sunday* to hype ourselves up before Op Silicon, we hadn't realized how right Pacino was: life was a game of inches. Even the fearsomely bearded, shaven-headed, scowling Pashtun Sergeant Zadiq Ullah, the first casualty of our tour, was lucky in the sense that very few people get shot in the eye and live to tell the tale. No wonder the commanding officer of one of the other battlegroups once called us the luckiest call-sign in Helmand. To an extent you made your own luck, realized what Mr Leyland had been on about in fourth-form Latin teaching you *fortuna fortis favet*, but it couldn't go on for ever, and it didn't.

Before heading back out to Helmand, again, I was assigned a press liaison officer. Doing it properly this time round, through official channels and with letters of introduction and contracts and insurance policies, I was able to actually ask specific questions, pinpoint who it was I wanted to see and where and for how long. Mindful that everything had been quite haphazard the last time round, I phoned ahead and mentioned some names to the charming late-entry officer, crackly over the sat-phone, politely disguising his bemusement and finding himself coordinating an official visit from the sort of pup he'd quite rightly have been thrashing around the square barely a couple of years ago. As battlegroup press officer, Captain Paul Green had grown used to dealing with a variety of bone requests from real journalists and proper visitors – the classics like 'Couldn't we just drive down to Marjah?' and 'Do I really need to bring my helmet?' – but no one had ever asked him to find the commander of 3 Tolay, 1/3/205, or which patrol base Sergeant Syed Meraj was in. Even over the phone, pondering the strangeness of being sat at home in London, talking to someone in the same ops room tent in Helmand from which I had once phoned home in the other direction, I could tell that there was something in his tone which suggested that all was not well. There was a questioning lilt in his pauses; the whispered repetition of the names of Qiam and Hazrat was uncertain; he'd have to get back to me to let me know who it would and wouldn't be possible for me to see.

Just before I set off we had another distant, expensive call. Amazingly, Captain Green had found my needles in his Helmand haystack. The *kandak* was still in Nad-e Ali with a new commanding officer and a new XO; Syed was down there, very well regarded by his mentors and by the sound of it still holding things together, but the news was not all good. The *kandak* was taking a battering. A number of officers and sergeants had recently been injured, some even discharged. Sharaf Udin, so far as Captain Green could ascertain, had been injured in an operation somewhere in north Helmand; there was a rumour he was out of the ANA altogether. No one seemed to know where Qiam was: he'd disappeared, possibly on leave, but some said maybe he'd gone AWOL. Perhaps most upsettingly of all, just a few days earlier it seemed like Mujib had also been injured. Injured seriously or something minor? No one was sure. In contact or an accident? Again, to my frustration, no one knew. Shorabak thought he might be up in Kabul, Kabul thought more likely Kandahar, Kandahar said he was still down in Helmand. It wasn't Task Force Helmand's fault particularly, but I lost my temper nonetheless, unfairly shot the messenger. What sort of fucking duty of care was this? Could you imagine us not knowing where one of our boys was? 'A Ministry of Defence spokesman confirmed that Captain X had been shot, or maybe blown up, anyway he'd definitely hurt his leg, no, arm, one of the two. It's OK now, though, because he's been evacuated to Selly Oak, or, wait, maybe was still in Bastion? Actually we don't really know, but we're sure he's fine wherever he is. At least, we hope so.'

At least they knew where Hazrat was. Still commanding 2 Tolay, still bollocking his blokes and taking the fight to the enemy, his reputation undiminished. At least I'd finally get to tell him how chillingly right he'd been, to laugh with him about how much I'd missed it, how much fun it had been wading down a ditch with the heart pumping in a way it just hadn't since we'd last scrapped together. Back when Hazrat had shaken me by the hand, made me that gift of a uniform and warned me I'd miss it, I hadn't believed him. But he'd been right. I wanted to ask him if he ever wanted to get away from it, if he didn't want to escape home to Takhar or further afield, at least to test his own proposition. I had spoken to him on the radio from

Shawqat at Christmas, but I had had to leave before he could patrol in on a resupply, so we missed out on seeing each other in person. He had confidently predicted I'd be back, and I'd promised that, if and when I was, I'd come and find him and we'd catch up properly, forgetting one of the golden rules we had learned about working with the ANA: never make a promise you can't keep.

PART V

One More Summer

Military Tourism

The Grenadiers had a proud tradition of eccentric officers. As young second-lieutenants we were brought up on the story of the legendary captain who had left just before Gulf War 1 kicked off and, determined not to miss out on the show, had flown himself out there with all his old uniform and blagged his way into the conflict with the Yanks by pretending to be a liaison officer. I hadn't been a soldier for over a year and I certainly wasn't a proper journalist, but I was heading back out to Afghanistan one more time.

I needed a visa, which was a novelty for someone who had found authority for previous excursions in UN resolutions, but that was easily obtained from a helpful lady in the embassy in Knightsbridge. Opposite the adventurers and unashamed orientalists of the Royal Geographical Society, the embassy of the Islamic Republic of Afghanistan was surely a throwback to the days of the Shah. Its prime Royal Borough location and dilapidated, peeling, stuccoed grandeur was rather sad, and the wary glances I got on the stairs in the shabby visa annex were all from Afghans wanting to stay in Britain, curious as to who would want to be going the other way.

The ease with which my adventurous aunt had travelled across Asia in the seventies, the old hippy route from Goa up through the Afghan fields like a flower-power Robert Byron through Oxyana and on to Turkey, is a thing of the past. In theory every civilian needs a sponsor to visit Afghanistan: 'tourism' does not feature prominently among reasons for visiting. The rules on working and multiple-entry visas have recently been tightened, partly in a half-hearted attempt to stem the flow of military consultants into Kabul but as much, I suspect, to increase revenues from the steady stream of mostly journalists making the trip. A slightly neglected photo of President Karzai in his trademark Karakul cap is propped on top of a faux-mahogany chest in the visa waiting room. There are no Ferrero Rochers among the plastic stacking chairs and institutional paraphernalia in the decaying embassy, and I wonder what went on here during the years of Taliban control. The pleasantly efficient lady on duty when I last visited, bored but helpful under a headscarf that appropriately enough for SW7 looked more like it was from Harrods than Herat, would not have been there: neither, I imagine, would I. My theoretical sponsor was a ghost, a kindly provided point of contact down in Lashkar Gah who had no more intention of hosting me than I had of visiting him. I paused as I filled out the form and contemplated that 'reason for visit' space: couldn't quite bring myself to write glibly 'pleasure' so settled instead, not untruthfully, for 'visiting friends' and hurried, as advised, past the questioning pause and straight to the issue of payment. Would it be best, I asked a touch obsequiously, to opt for the £100 fast-track visa rather than the £50 standard one? The smile and the rubber stamp suggested it would.

I emerged blinking into the sun and the swarming museum crowds making for the park up Princess Gate with my passport stamped and ready to go. Buying tickets had been as easy as half an hour online and a credit card. In uniform, departing for Afghanistan had been the culmination of months of training and careful preparation, a delicately choreographed build-up each step of which felt as though it brought us closer to Helmand and further from home. Now it was simply a case of sending out a few emails, calling in a few favours and hoping the customs guys in Dubai didn't ask too many questions about the body armour in my luggage. It was all so straightforward I was almost nostalgic for the way we used to do it in the Army: frustratingly slow and uncomfortable, but with a certain charm and sense of occasion.

I recalled chatting once to some of the younger bods in my new company, sat in the unsettlingly civilian departure longue in RAF Brize Norton, waiting for the aged VC-10 or creaking TriStar, bought reassuringly at knock-off from Pan Am in the eighties, which would carry us off on the first leg of the long trip to whichever desert it was that time. A certain nervousness was to be expected of those who had never been on operations, which was most of us, but I was startled to learn that one of the Guardsmen was far more worried about flying for the first time. We were the cheap-flight generation, pampered, Easyjet-setters who forced their friends out to ever more far-flung destinations at the merest hint of significant rite of passage. Even as recently as the Second World War, the vast majority of young soldiers had never been abroad before they were sent across the world in queasy troop containers; these days a young guy who had never been on a foreign holiday seemed a curious throwback.

It was difficult to imagine how this young man's impression of the act of travelling itself would be formed by the military experience. 'Abroad', for most of us sat there in Brize, was what was first discovered on early language exchange trips, beyond the drab ferries from Dover. How many first impressions have been formed in Normandy's service stations: an exotic and beguiling land of zippo lighters, flick combs and dirty magazines on the low shelves? Once we'd outgrown the watch of harassed language assistants and overcome the inferiority complexes bred of those early and invariably humiliating interactions with impossibly sophisticated continental teenagers, travel would be summer group holidays, cheap and beery flights more about escaping parents than discovering foreign cultures.

But the way the military travels has little in common with the way the rest of us do. It is far less about going somewhere new and far more about extending the reach of the familiar into foreign lands. The moulded-plastic benches in Brize Norton might have shared with those in airports the world over the fact that they seemed to have been designed to make comfort impossible, but once you stepped out of the terminal building and on to your flight, the similarities with going on holiday ended. Embedded journalists deploying for the first time remark upon the fact that only on RAF flights do you don helmet and body armour when the 'Fasten Seatbelt' light illuminates. The real differences, however, begin when you reach your destination.

The young Guardsman boarding his first ever flight was leaving his homeland for the first time not for nearby northern France or the foreign but familiar package Med', but for alien and hostile Afghanistan. Once there he would quite possibly spend the next six months speaking only English, eating only British food, listening to familiar music and reading familiar papers and magazines: perhaps it was just like a trip to the Costa del Sol after all. If lucky (if lucky is the right word) the camp-bound young soldier would even spend his hours watching British TV: Sky Sports highlights packages, the *Eastenders* omnibus and *Hollyoaks* for the really bored and frustrated. His first experience of a foreign land would be trudging through deserted villages and watching the nervous world from scrim-netted sangars. For some in Afghanistan the most exciting variation in the daily routine might be a trip to an American dining facility for burgers instead of a roast; for the real travellers, the gap-year casualties who in a different life would have been writing for *Lonely Planet* not the *British Army Review*, the cultural highlight of a trip to Kandahar might have been a kebab on the board-walk – the closest many would get to local cuisine.

As if in a further subconscious snub to whichever nation was our more or less welcoming host at the time, deploying British troops never even officially entered the country. Haunted by memories of the inadequacy of my own pristine passport compared to the splendidly battered testaments to university friends' expensive gap-years, I was quietly disappointed that my passport would remain forever silent on deployments; as far as impassive border guards were concerned I had never been to Iraq or Afghanistan. The young Guardsman on his first trip overseas would experience only a militarized reflection of travel, an approximation of being abroad but not quite the real thing. Six quite possibly life-changing months later, as he came back from the obligatory survivors tour to Ibiza through paranoid, dystopic Stansted passport control, a bored young girl from Enfield would glance-up, flick through the pristine pages of the passport he only got because the Army told him he had to, and it would be as if he had never been further than San Antonio. Afghanistan wouldn't even exist.

I'd done the journey in and out of Afghanistan a number of times and, for all the convenience and speed and comfort of the civilian option, I'm not sure I'd choose it of the two. Most people flying RAF have one goal and one goal only, to get home as soon as possible. In a straight race against the clock from Camp Bastion to the sofa, the civvie option probably wins, but there's a quality to the journey which goes beyond how long it takes and how good, or existent, the in-flight food and entertainment. There is a commonality of purpose on those creaking RAF TriStars, a palpable sense of shared nerves out and a thirsty impatience to get home. And you avoid Dubai.

I'd far rather pass the hours waiting for a transfer with a six-month-old copy of *Nuts* and a free brew in a tent in Kandahar, stepping out into the night for a piss in the diesel air, than among the mercenaries and the exiles and the sheiks and the shops in

Dubai International. If you push your face up to the glass you can almost make out the palm trees and the Emirate beyond, but under the incessant garish display lights, in the chilled, recycled air, you might as well be in any shopping mall. Sit for long enough on the uncomfortable wooden benches in Kandahar or lounge on the warm floor of a hangar in Akrotiri* and you'll hear some bad war stories and some rubbish jokes, but sit too long in Dubai International Airport and you'll begin to spot too many unattractive little vignettes – the meaningless spending; the strange nods of semi-recognition from the muscular, conspicuously desert-boot wearing Westerners transiting through dubious regional 'consulting' jobs; spoiled package-holiday-makers and the occasional glimpse of the exploited and exhausted migratory herds of Indians and Bangladeshis that sustain the place – nasty little demons on a shallow, twenty-first century Breughel canvas.

The Afghans wouldn't have agreed. Dubai, or at least some travel brochure ideal of it, held a special place in the aspirations of the more cosmopolitan warriors in the *kandak*. Above and beyond the usual jokes about being smuggled back to London, the handful or so of ANA soldiers who didn't just want to go home wanted to go to Dubai. I think part of it was a yearning for the perceived modernity. A society had to have great ugly glass malls with long escalators, tacky fountains and bad food courts before it could choose to reject them. On patrol in Helmand, on the walls of deserted compounds you would often come across strange posters, garish and brightly coloured scenes of an urban Islamotopia, cities such as Mecca and Karachi rendered like the digitized artist's impression of new-build Surrey

---

* The Western Sovereign Base Area and airfield on Cyprus that is the British military staging post into the Middle and Far East and home to the lucky and sun-tanned soldiers of 2 Battalion, the Duke of Lancaster's Regiment.

mansions awaiting planning permission in the front of *Country Life*, oddly coloured, smooth cars and sparkling tower blocks and mosques against garish turquoise skies. They seemed an uneasy combination of Saudi and Western propaganda: if the kids were going to grow up visiting the mosque, someone seemed to have decided, we might as well make sure they want to drive to it in a massive shiny car. But, like the fakely freckled gingers in 1950s Coke adverts, the kids were too pristine, the images ghoulishly lacking in humanity and all the more weird for being tacked up on a mud compound wall like a poster of a favourite football team. The London that Qiam imagined and used to ask me to take him back to seemed to have as much to do with what he gathered from his reading of *Nuts* and *Zoo* as any burning desire to see for himself the splendour of St Pauls from Parliament Hill. Mujib's regularly expressed desire for the relative urban sophistication of Kabul always translated into a curiosity about what London was like, what sort of streets we lived on, how we shopped. In context the glittering appeal of Dubai was obvious, and the regular conversations we had amongst ourselves about where we were going for R&R must have been as confusing as they were insensitive to the ANA and 'terps listening in, but perhaps that was appropriate – an eloquent demonstration of a cultural gap that even six months of fighting side by side couldn't bridge. Either way, and I never thought I'd say it, flying in as a civvie made me pine for the delays and discomfort of the RAF, when it was all a bit of an adventure and Afghanistan was the great unknown, sat waiting nervously at the start of a tour when 'window or aisle?' was the least of your worries.

Urban Warriors

I returned to Afghanistan like a prima donna to the curtain for a third and positively final time in the summer of 2010 and was sent immediately to the Afghan Ministry of Defence in Kabul: the price of doing business. Six months previously I had been a slight joker, a former officer being indulged by the powers that be because my old unit were looking after me and I gave good interview. This time it was different, I had an actual assignment and proper interviews to complete, and that meant protocol.

The funny thing was, step back from the heat, the slightly sweet smell and the immaculate gardens which could be any south Asian capital and what strikes you about the Afghan MoD is its similarity to the institutional Portland Stone of our own Main Building, thousands of miles away on Whitehall. Not architecturally, of course. Pevsner called the 1950s government offices, originally home to the Board of Trade, a 'monument of tiredness'.[81] It was a sentiment with which the SO2s pounding keyboards in its open-plan hubs working twenty-hour days in fast-track MA posts would no doubt have concurred. There's a lot less bustle in Kabul and no grand atria; the Afghan MoD seems perhaps a monument more to sleepiness than to tiredness, lethargy rather than fatigue, but there is the unmistakeable aura of bureaucracy: clean, brightly lit and full of somewhat gaudy, fake-marbled offices in which political and personal agendas are played out too often in ignorance, and at the expense, of the *kandaks* and warriors on the ground. Kabul had taken a beating in its time, but now, well, it felt a long way from Helmand.

I had fascinating chats with charming, sparkling erudite

generals and watched neatly uniformed colonels striding around, and experienced, pen-pushing sergeants walking the corridors confidently with clipboard shields.* Perhaps lethargy is unfair; there was activity, streams of whispered messages flowing in and out of strange offices and ante-offices. A constant trilling of mobiles which interrupted all conversation, *chai* and sweets going back and forth and plenty of evidence of staff work: maps, folders, the detritus of planning. It was all there, it just wasn't clear what difference any of it made to the guys on the ground in Gereshk. Herrick XI had, inexorably, become Herrick XII, 11 Light Brigade had been replaced by 4 Mechanized Brigade, Lamborghini bulls by Black Rats. The Grenadiers in Nad-e Ali had been replaced by the 2nd Battalion Duke of Lancaster's Regiment (2 Lancs) and the 2 Yorks by the 1 Scots. The *kandak*, of course, remained out in the same patrol bases it had been manning for the previous game of Task Force Helmand musical chairs, and the previous six before that. That went some way to explaining why the warriors in the south were ragged, but to really understand the *kandak*, why it was, how it was and what it was becoming, you had to see where it had come from, and the Kabul Military Training Centre was possibly the one institution the whole ANA had in common.

The MoD in the centre of town may have been where they thought they were calling the shots, but the heavy lifting was being done down the road at the Kabul Military Training Centre. A couple of minutes through KMTC's front gate are accommodation blocks that look like propaganda pictures of rubbish, crumbling Soviet-era towns from eighties textbooks,

* The tactic favoured by juniors working in rank-heavy HQ was to always walk around carrying something in each hand, so as to avoid having to salute the inevitable senior officer round every corner. A clipboard was particularly useful because by clutching it to your chest you could also conceal your own rank for added ambiguity.

but are actually pretty nice up close. Dotted with absurdly care-fully tended gardens and delicately hung with drying PT kit is the hulking cookhouse. Approaching the building on foot, you can smell it before you turn the corner and see the long lines of platoons waiting to go in, squatting back patiently on their heels behind a troop leader with pennant or catching up with friends from other training companies. In one door stream the hungry recruits and out another in a constant snake march the freshly fed. Twice a day the kitchen serves up rice and bread and lamb stew to 15,000 hungry ANA recruits. It may be one of the busi-est single kitchens in the world.

When Hazrat and Syed and Mujib and the rest of the guys in 1st Kandak underwent their training here, there were barely 15,000 soldiers in the whole ANA, let alone going through an accelerated training programme. It must have been an odd course, a curious mishmash of ISAF training personnel deliver-ing basic lessons to an even more curious mishmash of wide-eyed teenagers handling weapons for the first time and veterans of both sides of the previous war, grinning at the back every time the instructors said something which bitter experience had already taught them was complete nonsense and eyeing each other warily. Military training establishments will always go through waves in which recent experience gained by a few sits uneasily alongside the received but maybe now outdated cor-porate wisdom. What could the sergeant instructors who'd never fired their rifles say to the young Para lance-corporals and corporals who turned up to do their promotion courses at the Infantry Battle School in the months after they'd retaken the Falkland Islands with such brutal efficiency? I can still remem-ber the foreign cadet at Sandhurst, a Ukrainian ex-ranker who sat patiently through all the theory and practical lessons on 'the ambush' and was then on the verge of failing his command appointment because he'd set the whole thing up completely wrong. The directing staff monitoring him had assumed there had been a lost-in-translation moment and had stepped in to rescue the situation and wonder if he hadn't misunderstood what he'd been taught before the exercise. He had shaken his head and looked back at the instructor with just the right mix of deference and exasperation before explaining that he was simply doing it the way he'd always done it in Chechnya, when it had worked just fine.

Qiam never talked about training in Kabul, only his glory days at the military university. The others suggested he had been there; maybe he thought it was beneath him to retrain with a bunch of former Mujahideen and, probably worse, complete novices. Syed and Mujib were both pretty coy on the subject, which made me think that they didn't think a lot of it either. They'd probably done more fighting when they arrived than any of their Afghan instructors and had almost certainly done more than their ISAF ones; the course was something to be endured, but it had still been hard in places and, what is more, by the sound of it, had also been thorough. Syed recalled being formed up in Kabul for a full seven months. Mujib described the training as 'very good' up to the point where he felt relaxed coming down to Helmand afterwards, although that soon changed. Seven months is the same amount of training that it was narrowly possible a young British infantryman could go through before deploying out to Helmand, if you were trying to find the absolutely quickest way through the system. But that was back when the ANA was only expanding rapidly, when the kitchens at KMTC were only churning through thousands, not tens of thousands, of meals a day.

KMTC, out to the east of Kabul down Highway 2, sprawls across hundreds of acres and out north-west into hilly desert. The drive out is not particularly dangerous, and, despite the general tension you feel in Kabul, the complex itself seems to be almost too obvious a target to feel like it's under any threat. Presumably there's still enough of a trickle of relatively experienced recruits to be able to cause any would-be attackers a headache. There's also Camp Alamo. Camp Alamo is the ISAF training mission HQ within the complex, itself contained in a further security bubble, which is an awkward balance between a sensible precaution and a faint but obvious dividing line between the trainers and trainees – we knew the directing staff at Sandhurst lived a little better than us, but at least they didn't live behind blast walls guarded by bored American reservists and huge Mongolians.

Apart from the extra security and the unfortunate name, Alamo feels very much like any military training establishment. The corridors of its headquarters are lined with neat noticeboards pinned up with complicated programmes, exercise plans and endless photographs. Healthy rivalry is stoked up between the training *kandaks* and *tolay*, and by Afghan standards everything is run with impressive timeliness and efficiency. The elephant in the room, when talking to those charged with bringing the numbers of qualified ANA warriors up and up and up, is how one can possibly keep quality in line with quantity. Syed and Mujib trained for seven months; the current basic recruit training lasts fourteen weeks. Through a blizzard of TLAs and strategic buzz words I'm briefed that the official mission of the Combined Training Advisory Group – Afghanistan (CTAG – A, itself part of Combined Security Transition Command – Afghanistan, CSTC – A, pronounced 'see sticker') is no less than: 'To train, advise, coach and monitor the HQ of the Afghanistan National Army Training Command (ANATC) and subordinate schools in order to establish doctrine education and a training system capable of supporting the development of a professional Counter Insurgency (COIN) capable ANA in a timeframe to meet growth targets.'[82] It's quite neat in theory: you teach an army how to train itself as you train it, mentoring at every level. It boiled down to three objectives: grow the force; professionalize the force; and balance the force; but, not on a Friday.

Friday prayers mean that Friday is Afghanistan's de facto day off and, on that particular Friday at KMTC, it's also 4th of July weekend, so in Camp Alamo the Americans are kicking back in a way their fellow British trainers have rarely seen.

'They're even wearing sports kit,' observes a relaxed British

Signposts home outside the D-Fac in Camp Alamo, KMTC, show just how 'International' ISAF really is.

major, lounging in loafers and a polo shirt, 'next thing you know they'll be smiling.'

Patriotic films are being shown on a loop in the main D-Fac, but most of the guys are outside watching hotly contested games of basketball on the concrete court and soaking up the sense of a barbeque. Huge barrels are full of icy water and various flavours of Gatorade and despite the baking heat ribs and chicken drumsticks are being roasted on huge outdoor grills. A cluster of shaven-headed Mongolians, then the most recent additions to the massive coalition working in Afghanistan, stand in the corner in the shade of a doorway, barely taking in the scene before them, matching oddly in tracksuits that would pass for vintage elsewhere and haircuts that wouldn't quite, looking horribly out of place.

'They're leading the ANA mortar training,' explains another of the British officers, following my questioning gaze. Apparently the recruits don't really trust them because half of them think they're just giant Hazaras in different uniforms. It's true; the Mongolians do look similar to many of the similarly shorn Hazara recruits, except that they're all about twice their size and scowl, if possible, more ferociously. It's as if the Mongolian government, conscious that it didn't necessarily have a lot to offer in the way of hardware and expertise, had sent the national wrestling team just to make sure people were suitably impressed.

There's a ripple of wary banter round the table. It's clear the Mongolians are still something of a novelty; an unknown quantity isn't necessarily what you want when conducting live fire training exercises. A no-nonsense ISAF NCO leans in over the inedible cobb salad and wonders sarcastically how much more competent the newcomers are likely to be than the Afghan recruits – many of whom have almost certainly seen more combat, if not exactly run a safe mortar range.

I look back over at the cluster of huge Mongolians, debating whether to go back round for seconds of BBQ pork-rib or watch a bit more of the basketball. A couple of them look as though they'd be able to just pop the ball in the net so maybe the latter would be the best bet. They look strangely out of place but they seem to be enjoying themselves.

No one is sure whether I'll be able to see any of the ANA recruits. With Friday being a double day off there is a sense of disappointment that no training display can be laid on for my visit; that we can't jump into one of the vehicles and drive out on to the vast training area to see the keen young warriors crawling through the dust and polishing up their section attack drills. On one hand the training in progress was a reassuring sight, confirmation, evidence even, that there was training going on at all, that the recruits weren't just being fitted for uniforms before being sent down to make up the numbers in Helmand's patrol bases. On the other hand, however, there was something a little unnerving about the familiar sight of young uniformed men being put through their paces; if this was going on, if the training was being run by good guys we knew, why were so many of the recruits so hopeless? I didn't want to see the Afghans being marched around in their squads and sat in neat hollow squares being taught field craft I knew full well few of them practised, I wanted to chew the fat with them while they were relaxing, sip *chai* as I had done so many times with the boys from 1st Kandak and find out what it was they were actually doing in this extraordinary place.

A gaggle of young officer recruits nearing the end of their training prove that one element of building the ANA is working pretty well: they seem to be as adept as any young British second-lieutenant at saying what I suspect they think I want to hear. Kamal, a young Tajik who cannot be more than eighteen or nineteen years old, is the first member of his family to have joined the Army.

'I wanted to become an officer for patriotic reasons,' he assures me earnestly. 'I wanted to serve my country. I am young, so why not serve the country by joining the ANA?'

The British contingent has recently taken a more prominent role in officer training. Originally the British focus had been on the non-commissioned officer training, but this had proven to be one of those classic Malabar Cave moments where East and West were in no danger of meeting. The British Army has always operated with a highly competent and professional senior non-commissioned officer corps as its backbone, the sergeants' mess as the beating heart of any battalion. The assumption in putting together the ANA was that more of the same would work, and so a number of years were spent training sergeants who were then routinely ignored or disappeared in a system which, built on the old Soviet structures which predominate at the higher levels, places a far greater emphasis on officers with sergeants in a far more administrative role. The guys conducting the training won't go so far as to say that these were wasted years, but the sense of frustration is palpable and recalls our bewilderment back in 2007 with capable sergeants who wouldn't think for themselves and rubbish officers who took it as an affront when they were discouraged from often disastrous micromanagement.

Catching up the curve, the Sandhurst mentality is starting to show with the new batch of young officers. If the ANA can start churning out competent junior officers, selected in theory for stronger performances on initial courses and literacy, then it can maintain what progress is being made in advancing its standards, but my mind flashes back to the *kandak* and the competent guys who were junior officers, Qiam, Mujib, Sharaf Udin, Hazrat, who were all far more battle-hardened than these keen youngsters spouting 'duty' and 'service'. Rahul Rahman is older than the other trainees and he sports an intimidating frown for the whole time we spend chatting. He also stresses that he is a patriot, but there's an extra fervour in his voice.

'The only way we can get good development in this country, power everywhere and factories is if we all serve in some way. In my opinion, every single young man in Afghanistan should be joining the Army.'

Some of the context to Rahul's fervour becomes clear. He comes from a military family: his brother is still serving, his uncle served and even his grandfather under Daoud Khan. I notice he refers to attending 'military school', pure Soviet legacy. Rahul Rahman is clearly cut from an older cloth; the other, younger recruits are products of the ISAF machine. One of them butts in on Rahman's detailed family history:

'This is my first time away from home, my first time in Kabul. I have left my family behind. I am sad, of course I miss them, but this is service.'

Something in the poignancy with which this is said stifles my instinct to dismiss the 'Serve to Lead' platitude as propaganda. It seems genuine, but Rahul is unmoved by his classmate.

'I am not homesick. I left home four years ago, I have been training for four years. I don't find any of this hard. It is all service for my country, it is all for the good of the country.'

The six of us are sat in a cool room in one of the newer, single-storey blocks dotted around the academy. Elsewhere, the other officer cadets are snoozing in the afternoon or out in town doing a bit of shopping; later this afternoon most will go and pray, but the idea that they would use a Friday for anything other than pure down-time provokes incredulity and nearly a giggle, even from stern Rahul. The four cadets I'm talking with just happened to be moping around the corridors when I showed up with Captain Euan Sandison, who's got the distinct advantage for a trainer of having done the extended language course and speaks Dari with the sort of fluency that always makes me jealous. It's hard to work out whether the recruits are more at ease with a Dari-speaking Englishman than they would be with an English-speaking Afghan. There's less of a sense that things are being subtly modified before they emerge in English, but probably more of a sense that the speakers are watching what they say in the first place; the translator today will be the instructor tomorrow.

There are noticeably more of the colourful and dramatic ANA recruitment posters than I have seen elsewhere, and a neatly organized platoon noticeboard. Most Sandhurst colour sergeants I have ever come across would have insisted that the platoon lines needed to be more loved, to look more lived in,★ but other than the slightly Spartan feel which probably comes as much from the Afghans simply not having that many material possessions, there is no mistaking that we're in a military cadet's room. Like all cadets nearing the end of training, their thoughts are starting to turn to the future. Young Kamal, who spoke first, seems to have a sense that the end of training will actually be the beginning of the hard work: 'This is a little bit hard, but there are far worse things out there than our training. This is service, which makes it easier. We are all keen to learn to rise up through

★ The bizarre insistence at Sandhurst that your rooms should be made 'homely' was military bullshit at its finest. A neighbour of mine failed his room inspection for not having any posters or pot plants or pictures from home. He'd explained to the colour sergeant that he just wasn't like that really, he quite liked a neat, plain, tidy space. The colour sergeant had been incensed and ordered him down to the NAAFI to buy a token couple of vulgar posters. Why? I had ventured to ask. 'Because if he hasn't got anything up on his walls then when he fucks up I can't make him take anything down,' was the logical reply.

the ranks. We know corruption exists within the ANA, and one of the reasons we want to do well is so that we can get rid of that corruption, but we also know that the Army is only one small part of making the country better.'

When pushed, the quieter ones in the group admit to wanting to go into signals and logistics, but the voluble Rahul has his heart set on being in the Artillery, and again I wonder whether this is another Russian hangover, whether Artillery was the thing to do if you were from an established military family and well connected. Qiam and others I have met have all insisted on their Artillery credentials even as we wheeled out the rusting old field guns that were the sum total of the 3/205's offensive support just a few years previously. Perhaps it's something to do with gunners being perfectly positioned, right on the front if that's your cup of tea or just far enough back if you're that way inclined. Qiam seemed to alternate between lunatic forward positions and comfortably rear ones without any sense of a middle ground, and I wonder if Rahul, the stern expression but also the sense of entitlement that lurks beneath the on-message platitudes, is similar. Then he says something surprising. I ask them all what they would do if the country wasn't at war, if they hadn't felt the need to serve and were not becoming soldiers. There are shrugs all round. Keen Kamal is stumped:

'If I wasn't a soldier I can't imagine what work would I do. Maybe work in a factory. I can't imagine what I will do after this either.'

There's a look of genuine concern on his face, as if now I've dangled the possibility it might suddenly materialize. There are more recruits at soldier level who are there out of necessity, so given that the officer corps is recruited from the able and literate and willing recruits this should come as no surprise, but it still feels strange. All the more so when Rahul, after thinking long and hard on the question, looks up and announces that, if there were no problems, no requirement for him to be a soldier, he would like to be a high-school teacher, a chemistry teacher.

The conversation comes to such an abrupt halt that he thinks we haven't understood, and I realize that Rahul has more English than he has been letting on so far. He motions mixing things in test-tubes and small explosions while the younger recruits giggle, but there's a look of real satisfaction on his face, and in his imagined laboratory, his scowl briefly vanishes. The recruits all want to know what my training was like, and I tell them, not untruthfully, that in many ways it was similar to theirs. I concede that we may have watched more DVDs at Sandhurst but they're not having this and explain that they often watch films, both for lessons and also to relax on a Friday, like today. There's one of those tantalizing moments when you think you've found common ground, and I ask them excitedly which films they enjoy, wondering if we've watched the same scenes from *Band of Brothers* and all the other usual suspects, but they dismiss it, and the moment passes.

'We watch American films, war films in training,' it's clear from Rahul's tone of voice what they think of these 'American films', 'but it is the Indian films we really like, and they are not so good for training.'

I'm briefly still on the wrong page, trying to think of an iconic Indian war film while they're talking Bollywood. 'Why are they no good for training?' I ask, and there's a definite chuckle across the whole group, and one of the guys who has been virtually silent the whole time we've been talking suddenly, raucously chips in. 'Too much singing and dancing, not enough shooting.' Sounds like every Bollywood film I ever saw.

Rahul's favourite is apparently a Turkish soap opera – the others nod in violent agreement – which they watch because it teaches them social skills and good manners. I can't even imagine what sort of show they're talking about but am more generally impressed at identifiable young men, just the same as I was a few years back, growing bored of the endless war porn and prepping boots on Sunday night watching the OC and half-heartedly wishing we were all out in California when we knew deep down we'd all volunteered to be at Sandhurst. Rahul and his peers were officer cadets with six weeks of their twenty weeks of specialist training to go, the pick of the litter from the patriotically motivated volunteer ANA, but scratch the surface and they were still guys who preferred Bollywood, who deep down would rather have been chemistry teachers.

Frustratingly for all the guys working in KMTC, the solution is itself part of the problem. Camp Alamo with its generic 'international' dining facility full of enormous Americans in matching PT kit, elegant French paratroopers grumbling about the food, bemused Mongolians, laconic Brits and all the rest, cannot and should not be a permanent institution; as the ANA gets big enough, in theory, to stand on its own feet it must also get big enough and mature enough to train itself, and that is a different problem.

An ambitious non-commissioned officer in the British Army will know that in order to progress as far as he can with his career there will be some jobs he needs to do which he might not enjoy, boxes which need to be ticked. In the infantry, for example, among other requirements for advancing from platoon sergeant to company sergeant major, the hapless candidate will almost always have to do his time in the rank of colour sergeant as his company's quartermaster sergeant, the senior non-commissioned officer in charge of kitting, supplying and logistically supporting the company: one of the most tiresome, thankless and unpopular jobs in the whole Army. There are many sensible reasons for this, of course, and most take it on the chin and do the job as well as they can, and so the system goes. Similarly, successful soldiers will almost always at some point in their career progression come out of the battalions and units they initially joined and hope to return to and spend some time working in training establishments, passing on what they have learned to fresh young recruits and, in the case of some of the best non-commissioned officers, clueless young officer cadets. Being an instructor at Sandhurst with its pomp and ceremony and working effectively with officer cadets with their graduate foibles is not for everyone, but some form of instructing job certainly is. Whether it's bringing on the very newest and greenest of teenagers in Army Foundation Colleges, creating the next generation of hardened infantryman at Catterick, prepping existing soldiers for promotion on career courses or passing on expertise in specific weapons and tactics in specialist training, all good soldiers in the British Army will spend some time passing on their wit and wisdom to the next generation. The British Army equivalents of Rahul Rahman and Kamal not only undergo forty-four weeks of training, more than double their Afghan counterparts, but more importantly they are trained by the very best non-commissioned officers in the whole Army, men selected from a gruelling cadre for their relevant experience, established professionalism and innate ability to teach effectively. Rahul and Kamal are trained by men like Ahmad Shah.

It's not that Sergeant Ahmad Shah is not a model of professionalism and a dedicated instructor – it is clear that he is both – nor that he is a bad soldier or a bad role model to the various recruits under his charge – it is clear that he is neither. Ahmad Shah is as much a victim of a flawed system as everyone else; the problem is that he has never left the Kabul Military Training Centre. Over the course of what was supposed to be a quiet afternoon Sergeant Shah was still working frantically, chasing up paperwork from the previous week's training exercises, ensuring that various squads of the potential non-commissioned officers – recruits who have undergone basic training, been identified as potential NCOs and are now doing further training – are in the right place at the right time and generally buzzing with the organized chaos which hums at the heart of most training. With a slightly hectic look on his face he is unfailingly polite as we try and work out when would be most convenient to chat, and when we finally do sit down in the shade on one of the lawns outside the large block, a few of his more conscientious or obsequious cadets assiduously hovering around us tending the garden, it's clear that he loves his job, but the gaps on his CV are inescapable.

Ahmad Shah joined the ANA in 2005. I'd been excited to talk to him because I had heard the faint murmur of astounding coincidence which seems so particularly prevalent out in Afghanistan that some of the current instructors at KMTC had been in the same batch of recruits as the guys in the *kandak* down in Helmand. Ahmad Shah was one such man. At the end of his four months' training he was selected to remain in Kabul to undergo *bridmal** training, to become a sergeant, just like Syed. The quiet efficiency with which he handles the steady trickle of admin' points that come and go while we're talking shows exactly why he was identified as good potential NCO material. Lean and smart with an issue haircut and a neat moustache under a well-fitted beret, it's clear why Ahmad Shah continued to impress on his courses. At the end of his further training and on promotion to sergeant he was selected to become an instructor. At exactly the same time that some of his peers on the NCO course, some of the old crew from the 2005 training battalions, were forming up the 3rd Brigade of 205 Atal Corps and heading

* Non-commissioned officer training.

down to Helmand to put their training into practice, Ahmad Shah was asked to remain in Kabul to become an instructor, a job he had always wanted to do. Further, harder training followed and exams were sat, but by 2007, by the time I was meeting some of the guys he had gone through basic training with, guys who were already effective if unorthodox and terrifying soldiers, Ahmad Shah had completed the evolution from recruit to sergeant to sergeant instructor without ever having left the Academy. He's been teaching there ever since.

The various ISAF mentors and trainers are aware of the danger of creating a cadre of 'instructors' who have never left the schools they teach in and lack the experience essential to make the training they deliver worthwhile. The problem is not that Ahmad doesn't want to go and serve in the wider ANA, although stories abound about the better-connected reserving all the 'training' jobs for themselves, and Kabul's streets as well as the KMTC and the MoD compound seem to throng with ANA soldiers very proud of their uniforms and badges but not exactly desperate to do their time down in Sangin; the problem is that the good and experienced soldiers don't generally want to go and become teachers and, most of all, the struggling *kandak* and brigade commanders don't want to lose their best men. An officer like Mujib or a senior NCO like Syed Meraj would bring the best combination of experience and skill to a teaching post, but neither of them wants to leave their units unless it is to spend precious time on leave with their families, and the ANA is a long way from cultivating a culture in which being sent back to Kabul to be a teacher is an important step for a front-line soldier, let alone a compliment and mark of a future star.

Syed saw the logic in the British system as I explained it to him and says, as street-smart ANA soldiers invariably do, that it is not up to him anyway and he would go wherever the chain of command sent him, but even then I got the impression that, despite the comfort and safety and extra routine and leave, he would still perceive it as a slight if his orders were to leave Helmand and spend two years as an instructor. It's a moot point anyway; he and I both know that precisely those qualities which have made him an excellent soldier and would make him a brilliant instructor are those which his *tolay* and *kandak* and brigade commander cannot spare. The fighting men stay down where they are needed and the lucky, the lazy and the expendable accumulate up in Kabul doing more subtle, but perhaps more severe, damage than if they were out in the patrol bases. Ahmad Shah certainly isn't doing any damage – he's one of the best instructors in KMTC – but he acknowledges that it is difficult for someone like him to issue instructions to those who have actually put the theory he teaches into practice.

Syed Muhammad is another sergeant and friend of Ahmad whose career has followed a different, maybe more conventional, path. He joined the Army in 2007 and was also selected to do an extra few months' training and become a sergeant. On completion of that course he was posted to a *kandak* operating on the Pakistani border and distinguished himself at a time when too many of his comrades were defecting to the Taliban. He talks with a breezy openness about the porous border and about why his *kandak* didn't trust him at first: 'My whole family history is on the Pakistan border. When the border was drawn, my family were on the Pakistan side, and all my education was there, but I feel Afghan and have joined the Afghan National Army.'

I'm struck by how strange this sounds at first, how many times in pre-deployment lectures and in documentaries talking heads will repeat that the border is artificial, the Durand line a meaningless relic of empire unobserved by those who live on it, but the words are empty compared to meeting someone who wears the uniform of the ANA and his patriotism by election.

Syed Muhammad impressed his superiors despite his background, or maybe because of it, at a time when many of his scared or underpaid or ideologically unsure fellow warriors were slipping off their uniforms and quietly going home, disappearing or, worse, slipping over to the other side both literally and figuratively. He had been selected for officer training and was back in Kabul three years later, full of experience and halfway through becoming a platoon commander.

What's most interesting about talking to Syed Muhammad is how he seems to veer between praising the system he's in and knowing from the experience he has already gained where that system is flawed. He wants to talk, had heard we were wandering around interviewing cadets and had been annoyed to miss us earlier. After a quick change into civvies, he sought us out before going to prayers and couldn't look more different from his friend, colleague and instructor. Both from Kunar province on the messy non-border with Pakistan, but Ahmad Shah still in his uniform, a model of military bearing and more than a hint of his invariably Western training partners rubbing off on his style, and the other, Syed Muhammad, changed into a neat olive *shalwar kameez* and white *taqiya* with a long, straggly beard looking much older than the twenty-four he is and to me immediately more foreign, except of course that he's not: I'm foreign and have just been lulled into complacency inside the ISAF bubble. When he starts talking he almost can't stop, and Captain Sandison struggles gallantly to keep up. There's the increasingly familiar hymn to Afghan unity which KMTC and the Army are obviously promoting effectively. Syed Muhammad recalls the worst times in his career as being when he first arrived, and Tajiks and Hazaras and Uzbeks all kept themselves to themselves, but how the best time in his career was overcoming the divisions.

'Becoming one army. The training here tells us that we are all from one country, we are all brothers and we need to work together. I think this can be the model for the future, that people can learn from what we do in the Army and come together in the future.'

I'm about to point out that he didn't include the Pashtuns in the ANA group hug when, without pause, he moves on to a more pertinent point, the very flaw which Ahmad Shah, no matter how good a teacher he is, and Sandison and the ISAF training mission, no matter how dedicated they all are, cannot overcome in the current system – too many changes in direction from the top, not enough experience among the core teaching staff.

'The biggest change has been in tactics: the instructors, all the mentors change. The tactics have to keep on being developed because the enemy learn our old tactics, and we need to keep ahead of the enemy. A problem is that in OCS we have both French and British mentors so are being shown two different types of tactics. In *bridmal* we are being shown US tactics, so these are different again, and these keep changing.'

Another flurry of activity from curious recruits on their way out to the dusty sports pitches behind the cookhouse briefly distracted everyone, and I took the chance to ponder on what Syed Muhammad had just said. He was only twenty-four, had been in the Army three years and had already undergone recruit, non-commissioned officer and now officer training. He'd been taught one thing by Americans as a basic soldier, working in squads of ten in large platoons, then subtly but importantly different tactics as a non-commissioned officer by British instructors. Undergoing *bridmal* training three years earlier, he would have seen a greater emphasis placed on his role as a sergeant by well-intentioned, Brecon-perfect infantrymen than he could ever possibly have hoped to exert in his ANA unit; no wonder so many of the candidates now undergoing the officer training were those who had relatively recently undergone the British-supervised NCO courses.

Down on the Pakistani border, from his description of the fighting and the areas I can only assume working alongside hard-pushed but strong and experienced American units, Syed Muhammad had learned what did and didn't work from his earlier training and had refined constantly evolving tactics to stay that fraction ahead of a fluid and intelligent enemy. Back up in Kabul I sensed he had seen a less coherent evolution than he would have liked. There was gentle criticism in his voice as he listed the changing instructors. Where theory in training changed it did so not because hard-learned lessons were being applied but because one unit was rotating its six-month stint with another, and someone had a different way of thinking about things or, worse still, one nation was handing over lead responsibility to another. Officer training was nominally headed up by the French, who did things so differently I could remember the confusion back in Sandhurst when a ridiculously shaven-headed bunch from Saint Cyr★ turned up and tried to do joint exercises with us.

Ahmad Shah returned from dealing with whatever it was that had prompted a scuffle outside the lines and for a second in the early-evening light looked very tired. He had been the conduit for all the training and must have been as bemused by the constant changes in personnel and focus as the recruits and cadets, perhaps even more so, as he would have seen so many changes, so many handovers and takeovers and new bosses and new priorities in his three years – everything in fact except the experience that would give him a more credible voice in saying how that training ought to be done.

Ahmad Shah catches the end of Syed Muhammad's mini-rant

★ The French military academy.

and smiles as if it's water off a duck's back to him. He just loves training the recruits and would rather be a civilian teacher who could spend his mornings in the classroom and his afternoons on the cricket pitch. He is also something of an all-rounder, having recently played a prominent part in the sound thrashing of the mostly English and Australian ISAF XI that played an Afghan XI in a Twenty20 up on the dustbowl. He enjoys his day-to-day existence, which is more than can be said for many ANA warriors, but the hint of where his heart really lies is when we're talking about his family, the wife and two sons, back in Kunar province. Would he like his sons to follow in his footsteps and become soldiers? He pauses very deliberately: 'I want them to get an education first. Then, if there is still a need for soldiers, maybe they can serve but, if not,' another long pause before he looks up, smiling with the thought, 'maybe I hope they will be teachers.'

Hazrat

Never make a promise you can't keep – if only it were that simple. Helmand is as littered with broken promises as it is with IEDs. Not all deliberate lies or malicious falsehoods, not even lazily forgotten agreements, but mostly honestly made assurances and heartfelt pledges subverted by time and cruel circumstance. I'd promised Hazrat that if I ever got back out to Helmand I'd come and find him. I'd prepared properly this time, had even made notes of the questions I wanted to ask him as I sat waiting for the flight down from Kabul to Bastion. And then the day I got out to Nad-e Ali, within a couple of hours of my getting out to Shawqat, Hazrat got shot. Never make a promise you can't keep.

I wanted to tell Hazrat's story in detail, to recall the way he'd played us from time to time up Sangin with a sly grin, nonchalantly kicking at IEDs just to annoy the ATOs and pretending to be asleep when he'd had a tip-off that whatever alarm had just been raised was false. Make no mistake, when the alarm was real he was first into the fray, so I wanted to ask him about home, about Muhammad Akbar, his father, about the village of Samdai in Takhar province. I had wanted to know where he came from and what made him tick. In the end, all the information that mattered was in his nine-liner.

The 'nine-liner' is the standard format request for emergency air medical evacuation – medevac – for troops operating throughout Afghanistan. It starts with the crackle of a transmission on the net, the 'date time group' and the callsign identifying the unit making the request; then, in urgent tones, 'standby for NINE-LINER'; and the signallers and commanders and everyone else listening everywhere else in the AO will pause, almost invisibly but just a little, bracing themselves for the details in the knowledge that whatever it is they're doing, someone, somewhere is in the shit. Handy cards printed on waterproof paper for the green and forgetful summarize thus:

Line 1: LOCATION. The grid reference of the pick-up point for the medevac helicopter to come to.

Line 2: CALLSIGN & FREQ. Confirmation of the callsign of the unit involved in the incident and the frequency their broadcasting is on so they can talk the medevac in.

Line 3: NUMBER OF PATIENTS/PRECEDENCE. How many casualties in each category. A for URGENT, those who need to be in hospital within ninety minutes; B for PRIORITY, to be at hospital within four hours; C for ROUTINE, to be at hospital within twenty-four hours.

Line 4: SPECIALIST EQUIPMENT REQUIRED. A if you need NONE; B if you need a HOIST; C if you need EXTRICATION (perhaps from a minefield, in which the helicopter can't land); D if you need a VENTILATOR.

Line 5: NUMBER TO BE CARRIED LYING/SITTING. L for LITTER, those who can only be carried on a stretcher; A for AMBULATORY (which begs the question why not just w for walking); and E for ESCORTS, for when there are children or local nationals requiring an interpreter.

Line 6: SECURITY AT PICKUP ZONE. N for NO ENEMY; E for ENEMY IN AREA; P for POSSIBLE ENEMY; and x for HOT PICKUP ZONE – armed escort required.

Line 7: PICKUP ZONE MARKING METHOD.

Line 8: NUMBER OF PATIENTS BY NATIONALITY/STATUS. A for

COALITION MILITARY; B for CIVILIAN WITH COALITION FORCES; C for NON-COALITION SECURITY FORCES; D for NON-COALITION CIVILIAN; E for OPPOSING FORCES/PW/DETAINEE; and F for CHILD. Line 9: PICKUP ZONE TERRAIN/OBSTACLES.

Not the most elegant prose for those that carry them in breast pockets and webbing pouches and choke back emotion to recite them down the net, they're the most important words you'll ever learn by heart.

Hazrat had always been one of those guys who made everything into a bit of a joke. Right from the start, when he'd nearly lost his 2 Tolay, charging off on testosterone in the wrong direction towards Zumberlay to the annoyance of the Royal Anglians, the frustration of Major David, the despair of Kuku, who went after him, and the amusement of the watching combat camera crew, who recorded the whole thing for the MoD website. Even as he'd been manhandled out of danger, you knew he saw the funny side, and pretty soon everyone else did. Even with mortars raining down there has to be a funny side, and with Hazrat they frequently were, and yet somehow there usually was. There's nothing funny about a 7.62mm round fired from a nearby AK47 ricocheting off the wagon door and slicing hot through your leg. Nothing funny about being thrown in the back of a battered Ford Ranger and charging through the ambush, bouncing among the RPGs and stale bread the two kilometres down the dirt track to the shitty base at shitty Shaheed, vaguely aware of the panicking chatter of your own soldiers and the spreading numbness. Nothing funny about shivering on the stretcher, bleeding out in the dusty patrol base, waiting for the Pedros* to come in.

---

*US Air Force medevac helicopters carrying specially trained pararescue teams who extract casualties from hot combat zones.

The news came in piecemeal, uncertainly at first. 'Contact' was logged on the ANA net in the *kandak* ops room in FOB Shawqat somewhere near a map spot Check Point Quadrat, at 1750 on Monday, 5 July 2010. An unscheduled, unmentored resupply patrol forward from Shawal to Shaheed ambushed up by a village the Afghans called Nar-e Manda, right on the northern FLET* and crawling with enemy. The *kandak* ops room logged the TiC closed at 1830 and all callsigns extracting to Shaheed, but by then there was already a frantic chirruping of mobile phones across the ANA accommodation and the urgent whisper around Shawqat was that Sunray was down, the *tolay comander* himself had been shot, the indestructible Toran Hazrat was a casualty.

The first the ISAF troops up at PB Folad knew about it was the flashing headlights and too-fast approach of the ANA Ranger, kicking dust up the track towards the gate at a speed no vehicle bomber would have even tried getting away with. The first the rest of Task Force Helmand knew about it was minutes later, at 1821, when the ominous 'nine-liner' was called up over the Battle Group (Centre) net, eighteen words and thirteen numbers:

Line 1: Folad
Line 2: Advizer 12
Line 3: Alpha 1
Line 4: Alpha
Line 5: Lima 1
Line 6: Papa
Line 7: Charlie
Line 8: Charlie 1
Line 9: Nil

* Forward Line of Enemy Troops, confusingly similar to the FLOT, the Forward Line of Own Troops.

Eighteen words and thirteen numbers over the radio. The very essence of simplicity, which meant that up at Folad, by a helicopter pick-up point marked with blue smoke by A Company, 1 Scots (callsign 'Advizer 12') and with possible enemy in the area, a low-crawling teenager with an RPD and unwavering faith, one non-coalition friendly-forces soldier on a stretcher needed to be back in the hospital in Camp Bastion, URGENTLY. The optional further information which followed the 'nine-liner' told you what you really needed to know once you were already hammering low over the Green Zone with the back door open, firing off chaff to distract any speculative insurgent pot shots and prepping the team to receive the wounded man. The casualty had sustained a single gunshot wound to his right thigh, possibly damaging the femoral artery. A tourniquet had been applied but not at the point of injury. His breathing rate was ten, critically low. He was conscious.

The crucial tourniquet had actually only been applied by the Jocks when Hazrat arrived at their base. Had a dressing been applied immediately he would have stood a decent chance of survival. Even the simple application of pressure above the wound, a knee in the groin – Basic First Aid, Lesson 1, dealing with a catastrophic bleed – might have saved him. The lesson had been conducted numerous times over the past three months. A refresher lesson had been scheduled for the day before. The ANA warriors hadn't turned up. The squad had chucked their commander in the back of the wagon and sped to the nearest ISAF manned checkpoint administering crude CPR, which was probably the last thing he needed. The tough old bastard hung on until he was on the table back at Bastion, but by then it was far too late.

Night had fallen properly by the time confirmation reached FOB Shawqat that Hazrat had died. If you turned your back on the low glow of fluorescence seeping from the ops room there was nothing to spoil a dazzling clear night sky; the Milky Way a thick spray of light and the only noise the side-by-side clanging and fluttering of the Afghan flag and Scottish saltire in the welcome breeze. Three years previously – almost to the day – Hazrat and I had sat out under a similarly brilliant sky, and I'd watched while he taught his sceptical troops about the North Star and joked about the contrast between such quiet, peaceful nights and such long, bloody days. He looked older than he was, but his face wore one of those permanently amused grins; detached, knowing and even calm in the middle of the most intense fire-fights. I'd only once seen that face really clouded, contorted with an uneasy mixture of anger and grief, back in the early days of our own first real nine-liner, innocence shattered with our first casualty. The moment we loaded Kuku – his own right thigh shot through with grit and shrapnel but in safer hands and already riding the morphine, knowing he'd live to fight another day – on to the back of a Chinook, Hazrat snapped. Hazrat had lost his mentor, his young comrade, his new friend. As the chopper veered up and angled out of the Green Zone the anxious compassion disappeared, and his jaw set hard as he pushed his troops out from the cordon; the Taliban had a bad couple of weeks after that.

Two months before Hazrat got shot, 2 Tolay had captured a young man digging in an IED on a nearby route. As they searched him and his kit one of the warriors squealed with excitement and surprise and beckoned his commander over. The young insurgent had a photo of Hazrat on his phone; apparently he was an identified Taliban target. Hazrat smiled and nodded approvingly; he wouldn't have had it any other way. The day he died I asked the S2 sergeant if he thought it had been a targeted strike, and he shrugged. The signallers had intercepted communications which suggested that Hazrat was known to insurgents in the area, and the ambush bore some of the hallmarks of recent, more intelligent attacks. Perhaps Hazrat was another deliberate victim of the recent influx of out-of-area fighters eschewing IEDs for targeted shots masked with seemingly random but very deliberate bursts of automatic fire, maybe the hired Jilhazis everyone had been talking about for the last few weeks – not snipers in the sense we understood them, badged by Brecon with their own ghillie suits and covered in green tape, but dangerous enough – trained in sharpshooting as soon as they're old enough to hold an ancient Lee Enfield and, according to the legends doing the rounds among the nervous Jocks, only attaining manhood on ceremonially shooting an egg on a rock from a distance of 500 yards: 'Two thousand dollars of training / Drops to a ten dollar Dragunov', or whatever a modern Kipling would have written.

But then again, there weren't that many ANA company commanders who actually went out on dangerous resupply patrols, let alone led them. How many would have actually been in the commander's seat of the front vehicle? 31 West* was as hairy as anywhere else in Afghanistan just then, and though Hazrat was wily and a decent commander who had spent the last four years fighting and surviving anywhere punchy you cared to think of in Helmand, the word was he'd been getting sloppy of late: the most recent mentors had been less impressed than the last. Maybe his luck just ran out and he got hit by a stray round from a speculative burst from a fighter on his way home.

I wanted to sit down and commiserate with Syed and Lalaka and whoever else was around, but my host, the officer commanding the mentor company, was probably right to suggest we all leave the ANA alone for the evening. While one of the big Fijians brewed up and everyone sat around too deflated to

* The wider area in northern Nad-e Ali in which Hazrat was shot.

switch the TV over from *Coronation Street*, I pulled the little notebook out of my pocket and crossed another name off a dwindling list: Sharaf Udin, discharged from the Army with a shattered shoulder; Mujib Ulah, recovering in Kabul from a shrapnel wound to his back; Qiam, on leave; Hazrat, KIA.

I looked back through the files on my laptop for the notes I had made for the end of our 2007 tour. Recalling how the one thing we would have found really useful from the Royal Marines when we'd started would have been a thorough briefing on the key personalities in the *kandak*, I had prepared an Annex of pen pictures of the key Afghan soldiers the incoming 2 Yorks would need to deal with: strictly confidential, of course, and strictly unofficial. On the one hand you didn't want to prejudice opinions, wanted to let the incoming mentors get their own feel for the *kandak*, but on the other hand Sangin was tough enough as it was and, especially at the start, they needed to know who they could trust. At ANNEX A to PB INKM HO/TO NOTES dated 16 September 2007, this is what I had written about Toran Hazrat:

Hazrat is probably the best company commander in the Kandak, although he knows this. He leads from the front in contact and is an energetic motivator of his men. He gets on well with his platoon commanders and his senior sergeants although not always all of his men – especially the Pashtuns in the company.

In Sangin he has been briefed to remain in his Company Tac at PB INKM, which he does for most patrol actions. However, he has consistently overseen the preparation of each squad deploying and ensured they have been ready in time. He appreciates the demands of working with a UK Company and integrating the ANA, especially when the British are sceptical and suspicious of the ANA's ability. He will personally lead the

Company if everyone deploys (highly unlikely) and also leads a weekly re-supply patrol to the DC to receive any instructions from the XO.

Hazrat has a background in military engineering and is knowledgeable and useful on IEDs and Route Clearance. He is proficient on all the weapon systems the Company have and likes to fire them all himself. He has recently returned from leave so should be staying put for many months providing useful continuity within the Company. In the past he has proven himself fiercely proud of his mentors and he tries to push his company to meet our expectations. His expectations of the mentors in return are simple, he expects us to be up at the front with him, and can be highly critical of both his fellow ANA commanders and any UK mentors who he feels shirk from the fighting or try to lead from the back.

Hazrat is immensely likeable and (for an Afghan) has a healthy dose of common sense. A practising Muslim, he nonetheless puts his faith in good military practice rather than Inshallah, which is more than can be said for most of his contemporaries. He is trustworthy and has been consulted on a number of sensitive issues in the past, never without drama. He disciplines his company effectively and it might be said that his main weakness is a tendency to get caught up in the heat of a contact and lose sense of the wider tactical picture – a problem unlikely to be encountered while you are in Sangin.

Patronizing, undoubtedly; too brief to do justice to the man, of course; but seeing as Hazrat won't get the MoD website treatment, it seems like the least we can do. When Toran Hazrat died there were no tributes, no eulogies for a man who had fought alongside British troops for five years, no Op Minimize to prevent word spreading like wildfire among the ANA, no CNO to break the news gently to his family, no coverage of the unprecedented procession of his coffin from Kabul up to Takhar, of the requests made to Colonel Sheren Shah Kobandi, the ANA brigade commander, that helicopters be laid on for generals to attend the funeral, of the thousands of ANA soldiers who came out unbidden to pay silent tribute along the hundred-mile route.

Brothers in Arms

Anything encouraging I had seen up in Kabul was irrelevant; all the optimistic reports I had heard from elsewhere in Afghanistan meant nothing. Hazrat was dead, and Helmand was Helmand. Yet another brigade rotation had taken place since I'd been down there at Christmas, yet another upheaval across the province, yet another new set of foreigners for the ANA to get used to, yet another energetic HQ with new ideas and tactics. By the middle of the long, hot summer of 2010, four months tired but with two long months still to push, the normally unruffled Jocks of the oldest regiment in the British Army were at the end of their tether. It didn't matter whether you called it OMLT, Partnering or Advising, no one ever said it would be easy, but my hosts' frustration with their Afghan comrades was boiling over dangerously.

'They just lie, the whole time, lying, ungrateful little fuckers.' One disgusted corporal's assessment was a pretty common refrain. 'They just can't be trusted,' was another. Down at one of the patrol bases near Saidabad, a wasps' nest of insurgents buzzing angrily on the edge of Nad-e Ali, an Afghan family had recently been blown up by an IED. The base is on the dangerous edge of the security bubble where the handful of Jocks and platoon of ANA bear the brunt of being the current 'front line' and fight most days and nights to keep the fragile bubble from bursting. The knackered squad of mentors were low at having lost their first comrade, a young soldier who had made it through half the tour as lead man in the patrol, operating the metal detector which was their frail, broom-handled hope of finding the next pressure-plate activated booby trap before it took off everyone's legs and arms. About a week before he'd had a lucky near miss; his first slip-up of the tour when he'd stumbled on an IED which had, amazingly, failed to go off underneath him. If three months of the tension of being the lead man somehow doesn't get to a nineteen-year-old from outside Glasgow then surely lying in the dust with your eyes inches from the rusty shell, waiting for an explosion which somehow never comes, will. The lad in question had simply shaken himself down and gone straight back on patrol the next week, refusing the offer of taking a spell as the rear man, and then, of course, had been blown up a couple of days later.

As if that wasn't enough, the very next morning, while the rest of the base was snoozing just after dawn, the gate sentries had been woken by an anguished cry from a local villager coming down the road with a bloodied bundle in his arms and frantically motioning behind him: his whole family the victims of a nearby IED. The no-nonsense medic had set about her grim task with impressive calm and saved the lives of the man and child, who had only lost an arm and a leg each, but there was really nothing she could do for the young toddler who'd borne the brunt of the explosion. The family had been evacuated back to the hospital in Camp Bastion as quickly as possible, but when we arrived the following morning it was clear the whole thing was still playing over and over in everybody's minds. You had to try and find a professional space to deal with shit like that without imagining that it was your own wife screaming, your own shattered children. This particular team was coping in the circumstances, what was really pissing them all off was the attitude of their Afghan partners.

When the casualties had turned up, so the sergeant in charge explained, the ANA squad had barely stirred. The rear gate was over-watched by both a British sentry position and an Afghan one; it had been the Jocks who had raised the alarm, sprung out of bed and dashed out of the safety of the patrol base to start giving first aid. The few ANA awake had passed the message around, but the commanders had all stayed in bed, and the rest hung around suspiciously, waiting to see how the situation developed before even coming forward to speak to the distressed men who had brought the casualties in. 'Fucking lazy,' was what one of the Jocks spat out between gritted teeth as he pointed to the commanders with barely concealed contempt when we arrived the next afternoon, 'didn't even bother their arses out of bed.' These were 1st Kandak men, soldiers who last time I'd been here had been the ones waking me at four in the morning with urgent requests to go out on suicidal patrols at the faintest rumour of a civilian casualty. I remembered Hazrat yelling at me, much more scared then than I would have been of Qiam, who yelled all the time, because the response from HQ had been that the IRT would fly out for injured soldiers but not for injured civilians as we argued about military priorities and whether ISAF was an air ambulance service (which it pretty much seemed to be at that time anyway).

I left the Jocks to their brew and chat; the last thing they needed hovering around while they went through the incident with the boss was some former officer turned tourist. Taking a slow turn of the patrol base, I could see, too, what hadn't changed. The segregation which springs up between the Afghan sides and the British sides was strongly in evidence, the former an evolving ramshackle jumble of semi-permanent shelters, the latter a valiant but doomed attempt to impose some sort of order on the dusty chaos. The two British sentry positions were textbook, arcs covered by soldiers hot in helmets and body armour who smilingly waved me up the ladder, grateful for some company through the long stag, but stood sweating and attentive, radio crackling away in the corner, binos, flares and all sorts of tricks ready to go. The two ANA positions somewhat more favela-chic, three unarmed soldiers sat in one, sunbathing on the Hesco, a PKM idle in the corner and a full meal attracting flies on floor. The new, smarter uniforms I'd been impressed by were in evidence, but the further away you got from Kandak HQ, the more you saw the old-style ones, or maybe just a T-shirt, and flip-flops instead of boots, and the AK47s that many of the more experienced soldiers had been unwilling to give up for the new M16s.

The trust issue goes both ways. Qiam had slyly looked me up and down a couple of months ago and gone off at a tangent.

'Padi, we are just friends,' he had said, apropos of nothing. 'We will talk like friends, not like politicians.'

I agreed. What did he want to talk about? The new M16s – the rifles with which the ANA had been issued to replace their beloved AK47s – where did they come from and when had they been made? I had to be honest, I had no idea, I had been a soldier but never a gun nut. I knew it was American, suspected that it had entered service around Vietnam and was still used today. This did not satisfy Qiam at all, I think he thought I was talking as a politician, not as a friend. He thought for a while before pronouncing: 'It is from the Second World War?'

I could tell he wasn't certain, it had started as a statement and finished as a question, but at least I was sure this was not the case and was able to say so. Qiam's dislike of the M16 was understandable enough: he knew his way round an AK47 like the back of his hand and knew it wouldn't break down on him; the M16s, although lighter and more accurate, need far more care, and that was a problem for the ANA. Those who wanted to see their suspicions about the ANA confirmed did: as far as many were concerned the M16 was a better rifle which the ANA were rejecting because it would require a little bit more effort on their part – typical. But there was something more subtle in the two-way lack of trust. Qiam wasn't stupid, neither were many of his colleagues: they could see that what they were being given with great fanfare was still far from cutting-edge. The largesse with which the Americans were handing over thousands of Humvees couldn't hide the fact that no one other than the ANA were driving around Helmand in Humvees and no one was offering them M-RAPs or Mastiffs. Likewise, the M16 was a perfectly good rifle, but one sliding out of general service, carried slung by rear-echelon troops while those who'd be fighting alongside the ANA preferred the carbine variants: there were fashions in rifles just like everything else. It's always naive to expect gratitude for charity, especially charity which is so intrinsically linked to getting your own arse out of a bit of a mess. Qiam was wise to this. He had seen two great foreign powers in his country, he told me while we were discussing the rifles, two vast and superior armies had been in Afghanistan in his life: the Russian and the ISAF.

'You, ISAF, came here with twenty armies, and you brought nothing, you don't even have a bowl of water to drink. But the Russian, just one country, he came with water, he built a pipe.'

I was struck by that accusatory 'you', the way Qiam used ISAF, exactly how we used ANA. Were we all, on one level, equally dismissive of each other, reflexively wary of the strangers, whoever and wherever they were? Maybe we had corrupted the Afghans after all. Maybe they had they picked up that lazy, Western diffidence, watched us and learned how to look down their noses at everyone else. Or had we caught it from them? They were the ones, after all, blowing chunks out of each other and not seeming to care. Maybe it was something somewhere in between: the lack of progress, lack of effort, lack of any sense of showing willing wearing down even the most idealistic on both sides. We thought they were lazy, they didn't believe we were really in for the long haul. Everyone was right.

*

To understand why everyone was tense you only had to push out on patrol and monitor the Taliban communications. Many an entertaining hour could be spent in a ditch listening to the insurgents chatting mundane nonsense to each other on their radios, or, for an even more amusing time, find one of the *kandak* signallers who knew how to tune his radio into the Taliban frequencies and then sit back and listen while both sides chucked inventive insults (often involving donkeys) at each other: makes a nice change from blowing each other up. There can't be many small villages in Wiltshire which loom large on the insurgent radar, but you knew damned well that the Taliban knew all about the ennobled town of Royal Wootton Bassett. What for us was a touching, if at times slightly uncomfortable, symbol of public support was, for the opposition, live-streamed, twenty-four-hour-news, HD evidence that we just didn't have the stomach for the long haul. Aside from the spelling mistakes, the tedious insistence on referring to the Afghan National Security Forces as 'puppets' and the dodgy accounting which litters the website of the 'Mujahideen' of the Islamic Emirate of Afghanistan, as they call themselves, the number of articles analysing Western media trends, noting with approval that governments across NATO are belt-tightening and that fighting expensive wars in the 'graveyard of empires'™ is not popular on the home front, is highly instructive.*

In the four years since it went operational, 1st Kandak had been mentored by seven different British units, and it was only an accident that meant 2 Yorks had done it twice. Airborne brigades, commando brigades and infantry brigades had all quietly

---

* If it wasn't so serious, the Voice of Jihad website would be one of the funniest things on the internet. If the Islamic Emirate had actually killed as many British, American and other assorted infidel pig soldiers as the website claimed there wouldn't be a fighting man left in NATO. http://shahamat-english.com/.

assigned either the most under-strength or least-trained or most-unknown unit the task of looking after the ANA and had then more or less ignored them. Changes in strategy consistently sought to address this; officers and planners tried valiantly to bring the ANA to the fore, and genuine effort went in to bringing them on, but there was and remains an inescapable reality: that the ANA still lacked the capability to support themselves, let alone others, and so are forever cast in the role of the supported. The more intelligent guys in the *kandak*, probably across the whole ANA, had already worked this out and played it to their advantage, Qiam saw it as a lack of commitment. The Taliban on the radios thought the same and teased the ANA about the day when their puppet masters would go home and leave them with no helicopters to protect them.

Another unsettling aspect of eavesdropping on the insurgent radio traffic was being exposed to the mundane, the similarities between him and you; it didn't exactly put a face on him, but it certainly gave him a voice. Listening to your enemy arguing with the next guy about him being late on stag, or listening to two sentry posts whingeing about how their commander always puts them on the worst shifts, humanizes him. There is a story, possibly apocryphal, from the Second World War of a bunch of soldiers – as I've been told it Russians captured by Germans but it probably varies – who were about to be shot by their captors and dropped their trousers. Something about the gesture, the pathetic vulnerability and the obvious humanity beneath the enemy uniform meant that the captors couldn't bring themselves to carry out the execution, and the prisoners were spared. Armies evolve sophisticated systems to dehumanize those they fight, and those systems are invariably more complex when fighting a counter-insurgency. Many Afghans you spoke to, especially soldiers, blamed everything on Pakistan. They perceived the Taliban and Pakistan as interchangeable, just one big, meddling neighbour, deeply resented, bullying, unwanted. For what it was worth it seemed like many Pakistanis thought of Afghanistan as a backward, basket-case country with a victim complex, more trouble than it was worth. You couldn't help but wonder how much they could have learned from the English and the Irish. It was tribal in places, political in others, religious in others, ethnic, historical, hugely complex, which made it all the more difficult a conflict to fight. Many of the Afghan soldiers certainly 'hated' the enemy in a way I suspect most British soldiers struggled to, but with that came difficulty in dealing with the local population, who, in Helmand, shaking hands today, may or may not have been shooting at you yesterday just as we laid out rugs and set down cross-legged to lecture villagers on the peace we wished to bring, and began our *shurahs* with apologies for bombing them the day before. You couldn't just stoke up a nationalistic sentiment against an enemy as abstract as the Taliban, so he became a concept, rather than a person, 'the insurgent', a dehumanizing process which brought its own difficulties.

In 2007 we cleared a position the morning after a long night listening to the chatter of the Taliban fighters both taunting us and complaining to each other. The 'hundreds' of reinforcements in tanks they had boasted were going to come and kill us all had not, and instead we'd kicked off the morning with a Hellfire missile strike on their position and then pushed through it. One of the young soldiers in the *kandak* had given a thumbs-up as we passed the body of one of the Taliban and muttered something which the 'terp had said was the equivalent of 'night, night' and then his name. It struck me more forcefully then than at any time before or since that we'd been listening to that young man's voice the night before and were now coolly manoeuvring past his dead body. Whatever hope was his was my life also, and something about having had even the smallest of surreal connections to him almost trumped the machine-gun bullets he'd been firing at us the afternoon before. The fact that as certainly as he was dead now and we were all too painfully, hungrily and dirtily alive, if he could have had it the other way he would have done so in an instant, somehow all that was overcome by having heard his voice, and I found it much harder to cope with the concept of his death than all the others. Syed had hung back at the end of the column and covered the body with a blanket, and then stole the bread the sentries had been having for breakfast; we were all really hungry.

It was difficult enough to deal with a humanized enemy, eating his bread, shutting out his voice and soldiering on, but perhaps a greater challenge when trust broke down was the fear of an enemy within. The soldiers who were deemed most susceptible to the two-way propaganda chatter were dealt with by simply not being given a radio. The Pashtuns in the *kandak* were noticeably less trusted by the others, and ISAF mentors were wary of the horror stories we'd all heard about murderous, double-crossing Taliban sleepers. The Marines we took over from had found themselves being ambushed up in Sangin with annoying regularity and had worked out that it always happened on the patrols when the company commander didn't come out with them, and the suspicion was that he was passing intelligence on to a relative working for the other side. They never caught him red-handed, but the 'terps swore blind that he was calling his cousin on a mobile before each patrol and letting him know who was coming and when and where.

It was so far out of what you expected to face on a difficult tour that the Marines hadn't really known how to deal with it. How do you train for a deployment in which the guy you're mentoring is potentially working for the guys trying to blow you up? Understandably too sensitive to put in the formal briefings — PowerPoint slide 13 of 25, ANA treachery — but surely far too important to leave to informal Q&As over cigarettes afterwards. Whoever it was who had told us had been almost apologetic as they chucked the guilty, hospital pass in answer to the question: is there anything else we should know? Like Colombo leaving the room: oh, and *pause* just one more thing *half turn* your commander *pause* your commander is also an enemy spy *smile* hand in mackintosh pockets. They had really tried, they said, to get him sacked, but someone in the Afghan MoD wasn't budging, and staring out of the black-and-white photo in my handover notes was the mug-shot of this guy, still company commander, still a problem, now our problem. In the end it never came up. The dodgy commander must have suspected the Marines were on to him when they stopped briefing him on forthcoming patrols so he had gone on leave and never come back. For the rest of the tour we had no problems with him or anyone else, and, as far as I could tell, the whole issue of Taliban 'double agents' had been and always was grossly overplayed, until years later, when the number of ISAF casualties of 'rogue' ANA had been steadily and worryingly creeping up,* and then out of nowhere I found out about the *kandak* sergeant major.

His name had only come up because I was desperately trying to find out who was still around who I might remember, who might remember me. The more senior men were the ones most likely to still be serving, motivated career soldiers rather than the frightened recruits who had taken their money and run at the first exit point on their contract, not that anyone in Helmand could blame them. There were few more senior than the

* There is growing concern, particularly in the USA, that the upward trend in attacks on coalition forces by ANSF, whether accidental 'green on blue' or more sinister and deliberate, is being ignored. Official statistics show that only a tiny minority of the ANSF (something like 0.002 per cent) have been involved in such incidents.

kandak sergeant major, who had been one of the great hopes when we had started trying to piece the *kandak* together and work out who went where and did what.

Sergeant Major Kamal Udin cut an impressive figure among the ramshackle and scruffy soldiers he commanded. There must have been something reassuring to us Guardsmen about his height: at nearly six foot he towered above most of the *kandak* and seemed to be someone we could work with effectively. Kamal's role was slightly more administrative than a British regimental sergeant major's would have been, but the mere fact of his presence, the ease with which he filled his role and exuded a general and reassuring air of authority, was a huge boost. We'd been trying to sort the *kandak* out for about ten days when he came back from leave at about the same time as Syed. He took a good interest in planning, seemed to want the *kandak* to be involved, was pretty much critical to getting everyone out of the gate when we finally mounted up and rode off down towards Gereshk.

I only spoke with him a couple of times. I remembered a sly smile behind a neat beard and piercing dark Pashtun eyes, but that might be reconstructing. It was a good thing, we thought with our un-nuanced approach to the ethnic complexity of the ANA: a well-respected Pashtun in such a relatively senior position in a unit based down in Helmand, the perfect counterpart to the Tajik *kandak* commander. Kamal was a tall, wiry, fierce-looking soldier who did a lot of glowering but didn't seem to say much: his black eyes made of the very stuff that must have given Kipling and Newbolt nightmares. Kamal Udin, son of 'Mulajan', was from the Pachir Wa Agam district of Nangarhar province, about 30 miles south of Jalalabad next to the Tora Bora, bad country down by the porous Pakistan border, where the Kurram district of the Federally Administered Tribal Areas juts menacingly towards Kabul. Like Syed, he had a little

English, probably more than he let on, which was why I assumed he often seemed to be slightly mocking the situation, stood back listening to mentors argue the toss about something he would go off and calmly solve himself later. I wanted to know whether or not one of the soldiers in 3 Tolay was or wasn't a sergeant. This was way back when we had only just realized that the ANA had no junior non-commissioned officers, that, unlike the lance-corporals and corporals who are the crucial small gears in the engine of the British Army, in the ANA you were just a soldier, maybe a senior soldier (in the case of some of the terrifying, long-bearded lunatics who turned up the day we went on our first op, a very senior soldier) but you were just that until you were suddenly a sergeant. Zadiq Ullah had been a good example of the confusion. With his permanent scowl and the startling combination of a closely shaved head and an enormous beard he seemed to be one of the few figures the young soldiers feared. He was extremely devout and, I suspect, thought very little of us as his mentors, but out on the ranges and in training he showed himself a soldier, and we at least had the common purpose of turning a wild rabble into soldiers, so he helped out. Before Syed arrived, he had been invaluable.

Once we started getting everyone to wear their rank slides, I noticed he still wasn't. We'd always assumed he was a sergeant, but it turned out he'd just been a soldier with experience and presence in a squad with no leader. I went to Kamal to see if we could get some sort of promotion formalized without having to lose one of our best soldiers in the labyrinthine bureaucracy which seemed to swallow people who got sent up to Kabul on such administrative tasks. Kamal was polite but evasive, probably because it was all way out of his department. He recognized the problem and knew Zadiq to be a fine soldier and certainly one who we'd be relying on in the forthcoming op, but there wasn't really anything he could do. We'd smiled and chatted about other meaningless things for a few minutes before I left him, still apologizing profusely. Within a week, and without any fuss or bother, Zadiq Ullah was wearing sergeant's chevrons.

Sat with Syed, looking for new pictures to burn on to yet another CD for the guys when I left, we flicked past a photo with the *kandak* sergeant major stood at the side, watching training.

'Ah, Kamal,' said Syed, shaking his head and looking up at me as sad as he was suddenly serious, 'he is arrested.'

I couldn't believe it. Apparently six months earlier Kamal Udin had been sent up to Kabul on an administrative errand and arrested for passing crucial information about the *kandak* to the Taliban. The intelligence operation leading to his arrest had been the centrepiece of a significant joint operation between British police mentors, the Afghan National Police and the nascent Afghan Special Branch. I still couldn't believe that Kamal was the sort, or that his crimes would have warranted such a large operation. Syed just shook his head and wouldn't be drawn when I asked him whether he thought the sergeant major had been Taliban all along, had been smiling at me three years earlier and mysteriously helping me out, all the while siphoning off information to the other side. Zadiq Ullah lost an eye on D1 of Silicon, leading the squad against well-prepared enemy positions. Of course, we weren't in contact that day because of Kamal, we were in a fight because we were pushing deep into territory the Taliban had regarded as theirs for the last few months and had spent the previous week giving out leaflets telling anyone who'd care to read them that we were coming in and we were coming to stay, but the idea that Kamal, the *kandak*'s own efficient sergeant major, might have been turning his efficiency to help the guys now shooting at his soldiers, even across the space of three years, felt very strange.

Syed pulled the face he pulled when he didn't really want to talk about something, but he let some sentiment slip. When he had first muttered something about Kamal being a bad man I had misinterpreted it, assumed there had been some sort of argument between them and started going on about how Kamal had been so efficient: in many ways he reminded me of you, Syed; surely you and he are the sort of competent NCOs who will get the ANA and the country back on its feet. Syed shook his head again, not really with anger, but as ever something between sympathy and amusement at my lack of understanding. 'He was a dangerous man,' was all he would say.

The suggestion came later from Kandak HQ that the arrest had been made up in Kabul not only because that was the easiest way to get Kamal, when his guard was down, but also because of the fear that, if they'd tried to snare him down in Helmand, there would have been a leak, and someone in Shorabak like Qiam would have taken matters into his own hands and just killed him in camp. I looked at the photo again later, Kamal's neatly cropped military hair and smart bearing, stood in the middle of a complete rabble, trying to help us get the orders across correctly. It was difficult not to feel more contempt for the 'traitor' than for the young Taliban who at least grizzed it out in a ditch, waiting for an inglorious death at the hands of an inevitable air-strike. Kamal would have been a far more important asset than a foot soldier. Maybe he was frustrated by his role, like all good soldiers forced away from the action are, but re-assured about how valuable he was by higher command and gritting his teeth and sticking with it for the higher cause. When I mentioned the whole thing to Qiam he rolled his eyes far more theatrically than Syed and, predictably, started going on about how it all happened when he had been on leave, otherwise he would have killed him himself with his bare hands. I wouldn't have put it past him and, thinking back with a shiver down the spine on that cold, seemingly helpful smile, I might not have blamed him either.

Higher Rankings

I never got to meet the new *kandak* sergeant major. Whoever it was who had replaced the double-crossing Kamal Udin on paper wasn't around, and everyone knew that Syed was de facto *kandak* sergeant major anyway. I never got to meet the new *kandak* commander either although the consensus seemed to be that wasn't much of a loss. By all accounts he was not someone who particularly influenced the battle or risked being involved anywhere where the fight was raging. Whenever I asked the ANA to elaborate, they were politely reticent, one officer observing sarcastically of the new commander that the best which could be said of him was that 'He doesn't like missions.' There had been some quiet laughter, but few smiles.

Middle-ranking officers like Jah Muhammad, the new *kandak* XO, and Ataullah, his predecessor, and of course Hazrat before he had been killed, and Mujib before he had been injured, were all crucial to the future of the ANA, but they couldn't lead it. If the big operation Jagran Jah Muhammad was working so hard on was going to happen at all, direction would have to come from higher up, from the newly formed 3/215 Brigade HQ. Mohaiyadin had finally been promoted after his lengthy stint in Helmand, I thought initially to something in Media Ops, as he always seemed to crop up being quoted on the Xinhua News Agency; like all the best people he was big in Asia. He had seen enough of us come and go; as he said to Stephen Grey in 2009, 'If I learned a hundred things from each of my mentors that makes eight hundred different lessons,'[83] and in that time his Helmand counterparts, the successive brigadiers commanding the Herrick Brigade and lieutenant colonels commanding the OMLT battlegroup had garnered seven DSOs, four CBEs, two OBEs and four QCVS. The British Army, unlike others, doesn't tend to award honours to foreign soldiers and units, but it would be interesting to know what, if any, official recognition wily old Mohaiyadin got. I later learned he'd become the Chief of Staff of 207 Corps in Herat, a slightly quieter posting which he had thoroughly earned.

Mohaiyadin's replacement was the man who had been his brigade XO down in Shorabak, the impressive Colonel Sheren Shah. Sheren Shah had pretty big boots to fill replacing Mohaiyadin, but such is the 1 Scots' confidence in him that they've plastered his 'profile' all over Shorabak, another little British touch I wonder whether the ANA will retain when we leave.*
Sheren Shah Kobadi's bio would have graced the corridors of any military establishment in the world and read, as I copied it off a board in the *kandak* ops tent in Shawqat, as follows.

Colonel Sheren Shah was born in Kapisa province, Northern Afghanistan, in 1964. At the age of three he moved to Baghram province with his family, where his older brother was serving as an officer in the Afghan Air Force. After completing his

---

* In most British formations a small profile of the senior officer can be found in lobbies, guard-rooms, etc., the logic being that by the photograph everyone knows who to salute and by the profile you know a little bit about the potentially distant figure leading you. It works if the guy is good, like the officer commanding Old College when I was at Sandhurst, who had a CV like a 1970s SAS adventure book, less so when the paragraphs are littered with references to tedious postings and, most cringey of all, signed off with crap like 'in his spare time enjoys skiing, country sports and has a smallholding in Wiltshire', which made it sound like a tragic entry in the *Spectator* lonely hearts column: 'Regional brigade commander, GSOH, disappointed with modern life, seeks . . .'

education in Baghram he spent three years at the Military University in Kabul, which included a nine-month period studying in Uzbekistan.

Following graduation he served as a Recce Pl Comd in Kapisa province for twelve months before assuming command of an Infantry company for three years. During his time he became increasingly disillusioned with the Russian occupation of Afghanistan, and following two particular incidents – the murder of a child by a Russian officer and the Russian bombing of a village with the resultant death of forty-two civilians – his company revolted against the Russians, for which Col. Sheren Shah was jailed for twelve months.

On release from jail he joined a Mujahideen group operating in Kapisa, with whom he served until the Russian withdrawal from Afghanistan in 1989. Thereafter he rejoined the Government Army, serving as an Infantry *kandak* XO and *kandak* commander in the Kabul area during the civil war. He subsequently served as a regimental commander and then deputy commander of the 4th Guards Brigade in Kabul. During the Taliban era from 1996 to 2001 Colonel Sheren Shah operated with the Northern Alliance, fighting against the Taliban in Kapisa, Badakshan and across much of Northern Alliance territory in Northern Afghanistan.

Following 9/11 and the subsequent defeat of the Taliban in late 2001, Colonel Sheren Shah was appointed to the fledgling Ministry of Defence, helping to re-establish a professional Afghan National Army (ANA). He was subsequently appointed as *kandak* XO and then *kandak* commander alongside Canadian forces. His last post was XO to Commander 3/205 Brigade serving across Helmand in partnership with Task Force Helmand. In early 2010, with the establishment of 215 Corps, Colonel Sheren Shah was appointed as Commander 3/215, with boundaries coterminous to TFH.

He is married with six children, and in the little spare time that he has he enjoys hunting for duck. He is from the Pashayee tribe, a minority group (non-Pashtun) from the north of Afghanistan. He speaks Pashayee, Dari, Pashtu and a little English.

You'd make damn sure you saluted him.

Syed would always explain away poor decisions and bad strategy as 'for the higher rankings'. How could the ANA root out Taliban infiltrators like Kamal Udin? That was a problem for the 'higher rankings'. Wouldn't it make more sense for the whole ANA to rotate through the most dangerous parts of the country, rather than just leaving *kandaks* like his to get hammered in Helmand for years on end while others got fat and lazy up north? That was up to the 'higher rankings'. It was the classic soldier's stance: you didn't have to think and weren't allowed to question, so just did what you were told as best you could, and if it all went wrong, blame it on the generals. But how high up the chain did you go? Men like Colonel Sheren Shah and Brigadier Mohaiyadin clearly weren't the problem, and individual generals like Karimi didn't seem to be the problem. It wasn't the personnel so much as something institutional which permeated the ANA unavoidably, in spite of itself. Just when you thought things were coming together and the new HQ were planning operations on their own, without any ISAF input, you'd find out that the whole 3/215 HQ staff refused to work one day because some of them had apples and some of them did not. I'm pretty sure we were sometimes equally silly, but I think we saved it for when it wasn't quite as urgent; the problem with Helmand was that everything was urgent. Sheren Shah up in Brigade HQ and Jah Muhammad down here in Kandak HQ were the good, the arguments about apples were the bad, and then there were guys like Colonel Bashir who were just something else altogether.

Even though he was an officer I had never met, the Jocks were absolutely insistent that I had to talk to Bashir. He'd become more than just a source of amusement to them, had taken on a sort of iconic, mystic status, floating around Shawqat like King Lear in filthy, baggy pyjamas and with the longest, straggliest grey beard you had ever seen. Opinions differed as to his exact role or where he came from, but everyone was unanimous that he was barking mad. Bashir himself gives off a consciously ascetic vibe; I quickly think he knows more what is said about him than he lets on and milks it, playing the *kandak* druid for laughs.

'I was working with the Mujahideen since thirty years,' he explained, 'in many provinces, in the north, east, west and also here in the south: Paktia, Paktika, Jallalabad, Kunduz, Badukshan, everywhere.'

He was a missile instructor apparently, a job which would have been highly valued, highly prized, but he says he never fought and never killed, never really encountered the enemy, which seems odd in itself. I asked him about Russian prisoners, and he smiled strangely. 'Yes, we had some, but we just had very good behaviour with them as usual.' I dread to imagine.

'After our independence day, everyone let out a big cheer for the commanders. They were all called "Mullah", which is how they were able to get into Afghanistan. They pretended to be religious, and that is how it all happened.'

I'm interested in his take on the Taliban and religion; as far as the Jocks are concerned Bashir, whatever his actual rank is, is some sort of religious officer. I can't quite bring myself to think of him as a padre, he's so far removed from the easy-going, camp, quietly brave sort of dog-collar soldiers the Army is used to. The Jocks think his ideas about why Afghanistan is such a mess are hilarious. Apparently it's all to do with overpopulation: the extra weight of too many people in the world – the fault of amoral, rutting infidels – is causing the world to spin too quickly. This in turn gives everyone a headache, particularly in the middle and in mountainous areas, which, according to Bashir, is why everyone in Afghanistan is cross and fighting: brilliant.

'Look at my beard,' he said, running his fingers through the Gandalf-esque white hairs. 'This is homesickness.'

I have no idea what to say to that. I ask him what his job as *kandak* religious officer entails.

'Actually, my job was to make the people be peaceful together because we are all here together.' Well-intentioned, unrealistic; I guess he was a padre after all. Bashir had his own take on the 'higher rankings'; he'd been one himself, everyone still referred to him as colonel, even though he acknowledged that he was only a captain. 'We had an old Army and now we have a new Army. There were lots of higher commanders in the old Army, but we have a shortage of spaces in the new Army, so we have a colonel in a captain's job.' That wasn't quite correct: the ANA was actually undermanned at officer and non-commissioned officer level and still is.* That probably wouldn't have made the old colonel feel any better as he recalled how he wanted to go back 'to my previous job because that was a profession, that was my job to talk to the people. I was happier then than now.'

A mobile phone trilled an upbeat jingle and broke the moment. As if we weren't even there, Bashir shuffled off into the night to answer it and never came back. I saw him a couple of times again, wandering around camp, muttering to himself

---

* In November 2010 there were 18,191 officers where 22,646 were required and, most chronically, only 37,336 NCOs where 49,044 were required (C. J. Radin, 'Afghan National Army Update', *The Long War Journal* (9 May 2011)).

wherever he went. The Jocks would occasionally tease him, shout across the garden to ask him if the sun was too close that day or whether he thought we should slow down the moon. It was good-natured rather than cruel, and he always patiently explained as if the answers were obvious. If you boiled it down and listened carefully, his main argument seemed to be that 'because there are lots of Westerners in the country there is lots of fighting', and the logic of that was pretty irrefutable, he wasn't the fool he played. But, I couldn't get 'happier then than now' out of my head. He might have looked like Lear, but there was pathos not anger around him, the sadness of an old man which was actually the sadness of a generation and a country. Syed, Jah Muhammad, Qiam and Bashir all sat down for *chai*, and I looked from one to the other feeling that the *kandak* could have gone in any of the directions each of those men exemplified. The tension the Jocks were suffering from was more than just recent casualties, fatigue and frustration, it was living in the balance like this.

Then it's just me and Syed. The *kandak* deploy out with Delta Company on their long-planned op, and we have the camp to ourselves. It feels safer even than six months ago, the sun warming the rugged walls of the ancient fort, Afghan tricolours fluttering in all directions and the donkeys and tractors on the rebuilt sparkling white road outside the camp, through Nad-e Ali towards the market and out into bandit country. It's the perfect place to lounge on camp cots and sip *chai* through the hot afternoon.

Syed never imagined when the *kandak* arrived in Helmand that it was going to have such a tough time.

'Most of the casualties have been soldiers. It has been hard,' he reflects. I wonder how many in total. Syed is as likely to know as the *kandak* S1 sergeant back in Shorabak, if he's even there; there are no dignified plaques and carefully wrought memorials with the names of the dead warriors in Helmand.

'About eighty-three or eighty-four killed.'

There it is. That bald statistic alone told the story. I had been obsessing about Hazrat having been killed. I barely knew him. How many of those must have been much closer to Syed than Hazrat ever was to me. Even if he had only known half of them, liked half of that half and been close to half of them, I was still talking to someone who had seen at least ten of his close friends die in front of him in the last four years. I was reminded of the moment of astonishing sadness in the diary of a former Grenadier who had survived the First World War, not without some glory fought, and was celebrating his bachelor dinner at the Savoy. 'How much I missed the dead,' he wrote, simply. 'How easily could I have replaced the eleven living with eleven dead all of whom – or at least eight out of the eleven – I should have loved better.'[84]

Taj the 'terp turned up in camp the next day and came over with me to resume our down-memory-lane with Syed over a veritable Afghan feast. Syed had remembered the fish and chips and proudly flourished a plate of chips as we propped ourselves up comfortably against the outside walls of his room, a clear, mild, quiet night. Taj was playing with the Dictaphone and laughing.

'You know, the 'terp yesterday thought you were recording to check his translation,' he chuckled. No wonder he had seemed nervous, almost glad to be snatched away for an O-group.

I asked Syed about the family-run shop and restaurant and hotel up in Mazar. Why did he join the Army? Why not stay and take on the business?

'I liked the Army,' he said, simply, 'since I was a young boy.'

What did his family think?

'Yes, they were upset. Every time I go on leave they try and stop me going back to the Army.'

I thought guiltily of Jen at home. Happy memories and sad memories seemed to be quite close. Syed didn't agree.

'All of our memories are sad. All of the time we have spent with ISAF, when some of our soldiers or your soldiers were injured and you helped us, and we were happy with you guys. And when we were happy, you were happy, and when we were sad, you were sad. What I know, you also know.'

This was true, but then I went home. What of the times when I wasn't here? Missions with other mentors, other happy and sad memories? What about before I met you? Syed laughed.

'I will tell you my school memories. When I was in sixth grade, one of our classmates was the daughter of our Pashto subject teacher, and her father was the maths subject teacher. At sixth grade I was the first student in the class. When we did exams for eighth grade they took the number one from me and gave it to her. I said to her, because your mother is a Pashto teacher and your father is a maths teacher, they are helping you. There is nobody in my home to help me. At that time, the girl slapped me, and I have never forgotten it.'

Syed's father is Syed Zein Ullah Udin, an engineer with a job in 'a big gas station'. Syed has eight brothers and four sisters.

'The oldest works in the hotel, the second is a tailor, the third is a mechanic, making motorbike, the fourth one is on a course trying to learn to be a doctor. My oldest brother is married, and my second brother has just also been married.' His father has so many grandchildren Syed is not sure: 'I can't count it. Maybe thirty or thirty-two?'

'He must be proud,' I say, meaning the patriarch, but I think Syed thinks I'm asking if the children are proud of their father.

'Yes, yes. When something happens in our village, when our neighbours are talking about a wedding or a charity or something, first they ask the mosque, Mullah Moli; after that, they take advice from my father.'

Syed thinks I should come again and visit his family.

'I will call to my brother to bring the car from Mazar to Kabul to pick us up from Kabul and take you to Mazar, and there you can see the hotel and the restaurant and the shop and eat lots of big kebabs.' It sounds ideal. 'And then I give you a guarantee I will take you back to Shorabak.' Not so much. 'Bring some friends and family and come to the Mazar province. It is quiet, you will enjoy it.'

It seems plausible under the stars in the half-empty camp. I asked Syed again why we seemed to be able to talk easily, but so many of the warriors were more difficult to get straight answers from. He returned to the familiar theme of a lack of education, but perhaps something more profound, a more deeply ingrained product of such a fundamentally different way of learning that there was something insurmountable after all.

'You know, unfortunately, most Afghan people are uneducated. They came to the Army from the village. Most of the ANA are uneducated and they can't speak and they don't know how to behave with another person and because of that these guys are like animals. They were in the jungle and now they are in the town. The see the shops and the bazaars and the mentors and they don't know how to behave. They are scared. This is why they don't tell the truth, they are scared . . . It is all down to education.'

Syed's theory is that you can't understand anything about the Afghans without understanding education, or lack of it. It wasn't just that illiteracy made administering his *kandak* difficult, it was that the character of the *askar* was somehow fundamentally different because of it. If you grew up without words and numbers, then everything was in shades of grey, all stories were fluid, and memory was all you had. What little education a handful of soldiers had was as much part of the problem. The Taliban had called themselves students, of course, but their madrassas barely went beyond teaching the Koran by rote, churning out *huffaz* who knew the scriptures by heart but lacked any sort of critical thinking. For Syed that was the heart of the problem: even his soldiers with a little reading and writing had never been taught to assess or evaluate. I recalled all the uncomfortable times we'd been unable to stop ourselves thinking of the ANA as armed primary-school children; maybe we'd been unwittingly close to the mark.

I think of all the times I've been told by various Afghans about their school, about the general pride, like Syed's, in education, about the soldiers who wanted their kids to become teachers, about a general resentment at learning cut short by war, always the same phrase from the northerners: 'before the Taliban came'. Whatever misplaced hope I'd come home with after my tour in 2007 had been founded on the fact that everywhere we went, no matter how bleak, how devastated, the kids just wanted books and pens, books and pens. I wonder if we're in the wrong game, wasting money on fighting when we should be building schools, but Syed's moved on to family, starts explaining about his sons, how a father can't help loving his most intelligent son too much. About his wife who works all day 'making colours for dresses and textiles. For women's shawls and scarves . . . Her name is Manija. Normally I wouldn't tell someone else because we are hiding our wives and their identities, but I will tell you, her name is Manija.'

I show him a picture of Jen, the girl with her very own village in Helmand. He smiles, but also pauses, confused. She's holding her little baby cousin, who is Japanese.

'The baby, it looks like a Gurkha.'*

* I came across the idea that the Japanese were Gurkhas a number of times and often wondered what the ferocious Gurkhas my great-grandfather had fought with in Burma, gleefully chopping the heads off the hated Japs, would have made of this assumption.

I love this idea, my Gurkha girlfriend, but explain about the half-Japanese thing. Syed is not convinced. 'They are like Hazaras.' I think it was meant as a compliment: I think it should be taken as one.

All the staring at the laptop had attracted a couple of passing warriors. Dirty old Khoja Wakil, of course, who we caught using his camera sneaking around trying to take pictures of pictures of wives and girlfriends. He pointed to the sky.

'Once, Captain Hazrat showed us this star that always points north.'

I found it for them and we all took turns on Syed's binoculars.

'What should we do when we can't see the stars?' asked Khoja Wakil. I shrugged, realized it wasn't a question, was a tee-up, he would tell me. 'We can find north from Afghan people's mosques which always face west.'

To Mecca, that made sense. Probably not a great idea for hulking great ISAF patrols to be orientating themselves on the front of mosques all the time though. Another soldier joined us, I didn't recognize him, but he introduced himself and asked if I was in Gereshk. I nodded. So was he, with Qiam; he had heard I was writing about the *kandak*.

'Do you remember when you told me to fire and I fired thirty-eight RPGs in the operation in Gereshk?' he had asked apropos of nothing. Did I? Syed was one of the only soldiers cool enough not to waste the usually pretty ineffectual rockets. How many times had we crouched low and looked up hopefully as he had knelt bolt upright, exposed and still, and blasted us some breathing space? In these days of courageous restraint it's not so common, but Syed is one of the few Afghan soldiers who approves.

'Yes. This is better than before. I remember when we were fighting in a contact in Gereshk, it was a good memory for me.

Then you gave me a white and golden bracelet and you said, one of my friends gave this to me and I want to give it to you. Take it. Keep it. I think in that time up at Deh Adam Kham village and you fired the mortars, we liked you very much at that time.'

He was laughing, but I was stunned. I had completely forgotten those charity wristbands, the irony that Syed had fought for the next two years for his homeland wearing a crappy rubber band which bored the legend 'Support the Grenadier Guards in Afghanistan'. He had. Far, far more than most.

Syed got a phone-call, brief and business-like but obviously something urgent. He shrugged apologetically and smiled, head slightly to one side in the exact same pose he'd been sat in in the middle of an almighty fire-fight in Kakaran, offering me some of the bread he had taken from the dead Taliban. Like that, he's off on a mission somewhere, won't be back before I head out. I put the Dictaphone under his nose, playing the journalist to great amusement; Syed takes on the part and stands up as if he's being interviewed to camera, puffs his chest out to the amusement of the warriors gathered round as I ask him for a final thought.

'I have been with lots of mentors in the last four years. I want to say to all of them hi. I want a good life for them if they are retired and at home. I want a good life for them if some of them are still in the Army, and we will pray that God will save them. And also, if there is anyone who knows me and you see them, say lots of hi, give them lots of love from all of us in Afghanistan for all English people.'

'Inshallah!' I say.

'Inshallah!' he replies, and is gone.

Omid

As I waited to leave Helmand, the ANA prepared for its biggest operation to date, Op Omid Do, Operation Hope II. Many observers of the ANA were starting to disagree. At the end of 2009 the influential think tank the Royal United Services Institute had published a damning critique of the state of the ANA under the heading 'The Afghan National Army – Unwarranted Hope', identifying the 'hope' in the ANA as 'a product of bureaucratic politics as much as a result of a propaganda effort'.[85]

A little hope was a dangerous thing; Operation Hope felt like tempting fate. Nonetheless there was a real sense of excitement in Shorabak that something significant was underway. Of course, every battlegroup insisted in some way or another that it had done the first this or that with the ANA; we'd done it on Silicon and then again on Tufaan, the first independent ANA sub-unit on a joint op and then the first whole *kandak*-level op. Bully for us. If the Afghans pulled it off, Op Omid might just live up to its name, but it was a big if. Although 3/215 staff was impressive, the planning had been a painful process. On the one hand there was no doubt that the ANA would have been unable to do anything like it only two years earlier, but on the other they still couldn't have done it without our help. I sat in on the formal orders the night before the op and squirmed uncomfortably while the Afghan engineer officer giving the ground brief kept looking anxiously at his mentor; his voice was saying that the IED threat was significant at the chokepoints outside Gereshk, but his eyes were saying: 'Am I doing it right?' Would he have

349

been doing it at all if we hadn't been there? That's what I couldn't work out.

I walked out of the O-group in despair when I actually got a glimpse of the map, saw that the whole thing was a deliberate operation to take back the exact same ground we'd taken on Silicon three years earlier and had then spent months patrolling through, handing out sweets and pencils to smiling kids. Apparently soldiers suffered 'behavioural biases towards optimism' when it came to buying kit. Maybe the problem ran deeper.[86] The narrative gaining traction at home was that our brave boys were victims of their own can-do spirit and enthusiasm who couldn't see the wood for the IEDs. Sceptics said that all over Afghanistan what were billed as brigade-level ANA-led operations were little more than coordinated patrols at *tolay* level in every respect facilitated by the embedded training teams and mentors. Real ANA manning levels were lower than official figures, AWOL rates higher, morale low, illiteracy through the roof, and we marched blithely on, lauding the ANA's fighting spirit and clinging to the growth in the baseline size of the Army as if everything was OK.

I had once thought this was overly pessimistic; now I wasn't so sure. The ANA was getting bigger and bigger and for the first time it wasn't clear to me for what. There was no doubt the *kandaks* looked awesome on the square, unrecognizable as the riotous rabble of three years ago. But the headlines on day one of Op Omid Do could have been the headlines of any journalist embedded jointly with ISAF and the ANA over the past five years: 'Tensions between UK and Afghan troops on patrol in Helmand', accompanied by the obligatory photo of two immaculate kitted, uniformed, helmeted and body-armoured Jocks in firing positions and the young, T-shirt-wearing ANA warrior, beret perched on the top of his head like a French cartoon, gaudy coloured stickers on his rifle butt. 'It's an Afghan thing,' was the quote from a British soldier.[87] I was not leaving Helmand on a high.

I wandered across from the tin huts of Tombstone to the old 1st Kandak lines in the now much expanded Camp Shorabak. With the *kandak* deployed in Nad-e Ali, Shorabak is its rear camp, and in theory the only soldiers there are administrative support staff or those coming back from or going on R&R. The lines are mostly empty, and the bleak sixty-man blocks with their Japanese-donated steel bunk-beds are deserted, the odd malingerers preferring to hide out discreetly in the smaller NCO and officer rooms at the end of each block.

Shorabak was still unloved, even expanded, upgraded, even after five years with the towering red-and-white Roshan* antenna like a mini-Eiffel Tower at its centre. Only the gardens have a hint of home, carefully tended and lovingly watered oases with improvised wooden benches and tables hidden between the featureless concrete huts. Two smiling young warriors were supervising a hose as I approached to ask where we might find someone vaguely responsible. For those looking to be frustrated by the topsy-turvy logic of how the ANA work, these guys were perfect: busily tending gardens in Shorabak while their own fighting companies struggled on the front line. One could question the priorities in the chain of command or one could recall that back in the UK and Germany and in its various home bases the British Army was famous for its fastidious approach to keeping camps clean and orderly – the old joke at Sandhurst had been 'if it moves salute it, if it doesn't move

---

* Afghanistan's main telecommunications company, like Orange but with better signal and customer service.

pick it up and if you can't pick it up, polish it', or something similar. Shorabak may have been 20 kilometres from what passed for the front line down in Helmand, but it was still 'home' to the units that were based there and psychologically more like Aldershot or Catterick than Bastion.

I stood in the sun, waiting patiently while the cool and serious-looking 'terp called David dressed head to toe, far too accurately and smartly, in British Army issue like an Airsoft Walt, chatted to one of the uniformed gardeners and tried to find out who, if anyone, was in charge of the *kandak* 'rear party'. I wasn't in a particular rush; my mind was in that limbo of return, already on the plane, already back in London, wondering about the fun to be had that weekend at some wedding or other. A familiar voice called out from behind one of the windows, lilting up at the end, caught with a frog in the throat, questioning – *Padi* – and then the door swung open and there, smiling in an old, heavy green-and-red ANA T-shirt and a purple pair of Thai fishing trousers, was Mujib.

So unexpected that the only thing for it was to feel completely normal. Distracted by thoughts of home and the pretty gardens and the air of calm before the big op which hung over Shorabak, I hadn't noticed that we were actually stood outside Mujib's office, outside the cool, stone-walled room in which the two of us had spent exasperating, excruciating hours wondering from where and amongst whom we were going to conjure up a *kandak* three long years earlier. No one knew where Mujib was, injured of course, anywhere but actually in his office, in his home camp. My first reaction was to stare incredulously at his T-shirt. Cheap itchy nylon which the warriors had hated when they were issued back in 2007, but which I guess now marked one out as a salty veteran. All armies are the same. Having given up quizzing the youngsters with the hose, David must have missed the astonished look that passed between Mujib and myself and was about to carry on the same line of questioning with the new, T-shirted soldier when I stepped past and grabbed Mujib warmly by the hand as we both started to simply laugh. We were still laughing in disbelief when Sharaf Udin stepped out into the garden and waved, not his hand exactly but his whole arm, stiff in an enormous white plaster cast but unmistakable with his Charles Bronson moustache and, behind him, looking least changed of all the ANA officers I had known and smart as a carrot in full new digicam, Gholam Nabi. The whole gang had been chilling out down in Shorabak all along.

Where to start? Mujib was supposed to be missing in some hospital, Sharaf Udin out of the Army. All my pessimism and curiosity about the preparations on the square vanished in an instant. A young soldier I didn't recognize was sent to get more drinks, and we settled down in the cool room, music playing at low volume from a radio somewhere nearby. I practically had to pinch myself. Where to start? Sharaf Udin wanted to start exactly where we had left off when we'd said goodbye three years earlier, up in Sangin.

'After you left we discovered lots of mines.' That was Sangin all right. Seven in one day on the worst day, apparently. Hazrat had been injured, I discovered. 'He got mortar fragments here,' said Sharaf Udin, pointing at his own, injured shoulder. Gholam Nabi interrupted at the talk of casualties.

'How is Mr Kuku? How was his leg?'

Of course the last any of them had seen of Kuku was bloody and woozy on the back of the Chinook. There was good news there, at least. He was fine, I told them, had been back out to Helmand, was very sad to have missed them.

'And Toran Rob?' Gholam Nabi's mentor, Captain Rob Worthington. Out of the Army, I explained. Heads shook disappointedly. Married, I added, by way of explanation, but it didn't pass, and I felt their silent disapproval at my own, non-military attire. Mujib was playing with my laptop, keen as the guys in Shawqat had been to burn photos on to the new CD-ROMs that the ANA proudly seemed to carry everywhere, not that there was a computer in Shorabak to play them back on. Sharaf Udin snorted at one of us all together up in Sangin.

'You got fat. Fatter than before, in the old pictures to now, there is a very big difference.'

As we talked, the conversation came back to the *kandak*. The memories were good. '*Kandaki awal*,' says Mujib, and heads nod enthusiastically. I reminded Mujib with amusement that we were in the same room where we had our first tentative meetings and grappled ineptly with 3 Company. What he said next surprised me. He remembered that time well; it was a time of great concern for him. Apparently he'd only been in Helmand province five days longer than I had and had never met the soldiers he was nominally commanding. 'What about the first mission in Gereshk?' I asked, incredulously, not realizing that the whole time I'd thought he was the one who knew what we were supposed to be doing, I'd been wrong. He shrugged and smiled apologetically.

'Yes . . . this was also my first time. I had no idea how to control a hundred soldiers. I had never done this job before.'

Poor old Mujib had only been in Shorabak five days when we arrived and started bombarding him with questions about a unit he didn't know and missions he'd never been on. He told me that the day before we arrived he had considered just doing what still too many men in his position were doing: a runner: 'I tried to go back to Kabul, but on the fifth day you arrived with the mentors, and I got courage.' Probably the only positive effect we had in that first week, and I never even knew.

'Do you remember,' Gholam Nabi cut in, 'Qiam used to say

that the 1st Kandak was *kharkus*: proud, brave.' That seemed to be the final word on the matter. The *kandak* was fine; it was the ANA that was a mess.

'We are disappointed because we are always fighting and on the missions, and the more senior officers never support us with the fighting.' Sharaf Udin came straight to the point, Mujib took it up – the lament of the front-line officer.

'The big mistake is that our officers do not recognize talent. They get selected at training and after that are captains, but not talented.'

It felt strange to have someone with all the relevant experience confirm your own suspicions. Part of me was disappointed, wanted to have been wrong in the creeping sense that the momentum of brave *kandaks* was not enough, that the systemic problems were too serious, terminal even, maybe.

'We don't see any result due to the change in Kabul. There has been no result, no difference achieved in Helmand. They have changed the system, they want to make the officers those who are good in class but they should take those who are fighting and send them to Kabul and then send them back after training. After six months we are not seeing any results.'

It was pretty damning stuff. These were the good guys. It was a miracle that they didn't just want out of the Army full stop. Two of them with injured families miles away. Gholam Nabi had his eyes on a cushy posting, 'maybe in the north provinces, like Mazar. Maybe Kabul.' Closer to home seemed to be the main thing, except for Mujib, who had too much to hide just then.

'I always call home to my family, and they say you will get injured. I tell them no, I am fine. They say why won't you come home . . .' He rolled over slightly and indicated the wound to his thigh, and the whole room burst out laughing. 'His arse,' was what Sharaf Udin said. I think the 'terp might have picked that one up from the mentors. In the amusement I couldn't work out whether Mujib couldn't admit to his family he'd been injured because they'd be worried or because he was embarrassed to have been shot in the arse. He bit, snapping back at Sharaf Udin, 'I got injured with mine fragmentation making more than ten holes in my back.' Sharaf Udin carried on smirking. I asked Mujib about how it happened.

'We had a horrible mission in Nad-e Ali. When we were in the north, the British soldiers shot us. One officer was injured and six soldiers and one of the mentors. They were wounded but they all got well again. The mentor had only worked with us for a few days and when he got injured he left so I can't remember his name. This was maybe in April. Maybe March. We were in a compound with our mentors, and the British troops were using the under-slung grenades and grenade machine-gun into the compound. They thought that the Taliban were in the compound when it was us.'

Sharaf Udin cut in, as if suddenly aware of the Dictaphone again, leaning towards it slightly.

'It should be clear to you, all our memories are sorrowful.'

A young sergeant came in bearing dinner. Sharaf Udin chuckled and pushed a plate towards me first, helping himself only to tea. 'You are not fat in your stomach. Only in your face,' he added, reassuringly. They teased me a while about not having any children. Gholam Nabi has two sons, Sharaf Udin two sons also, Mujib counts his sons and daughters in his five. The sergeant who brought in the food looks at me in disbelief; he can't be much older than twenty-five himself.

'When I was trained in Kabul, one of the instructors was from America. I asked him how many children do you have, he said one son, one daughter. I told him I had four, and he said is no good, one of each is quite enough.'

They all laughed afresh at the notion, one of each. It was

Then and now. Above: Gholam Nabi (left) myself and Sharaf Udin (right) enjoy a lull in the fighting up in Inkerman, north of Sangin, September 2007. Below, by 2009 we all cut slightly less impressive figures: Sharaf Udin (left), Mujib (centre) and Gholam Nabi (right).

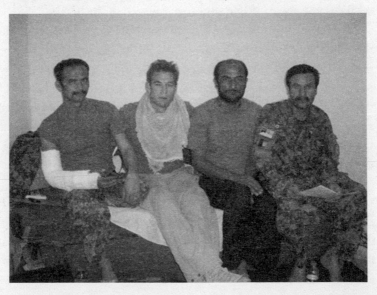

different in England, I explained; the average age of girls getting married was nearly thirty. The sergeant practically dropped his plate; rice tipped over the edge on to the laminated sheet map Mujib had laid down on his bed as a cloth, Sharaf Udin swept it on to the stone floor absent-mindedly, his thoughts turning to something else.

'If the conditions continue like this, if the Taliban continue to fight like this, then the Taliban will win.'

There was quiet. 'Intelligence must play a good role, so we can discover who supports the Taliban, but it is very bad that we patrol, just walk the routes looking for them.'

I tried to work out whether the 3/215 HQ offices are closer to 100 or 200 metres away, pictured the 'higher rankings' and their well-meaning mentors all poring over HIDACZ and IPB, wished they could just come and hear what their officers had to say.

'But we don't have the resources or the ability or the money to change the tactics. We just have a gun, the M16 ANA gun, which is not good. When you fire it five times, it breaks.'

Mujib broke in. 'When we were in school during the war, all the schools were getting damaged, so we had at that time to get guns and fight against our enemy. The big difference between the Mujaeed war and this time was a big difference. When I was with the Mujahideen the lines were clear: this side is the enemy and this side is the Mujahideen. It is very clear where are the enemy, but this time we don't know where the enemy is. The Taliban are using the Mujahideen tactics, the special tactics of Massoud, the irregular fighting which is the best way to beat a big, imperial army.

'There is a big difference between the face-to-face war and the irregular fight because when you get injured, once the mine explodes, then they ambush you. During the Russian war it was also an irregular fight: you always ambush their convoy and in this we could beat them.

'When we were with you, if you see one enemy, then you can fight, even if we were six men, we can all fight at the same time. Now, maybe we see eighteen Taliban. We told the helicopters you must shoot them, and the helicopters said we are not allowed to shoot them.

'You see the Pimon camp in Nad-e Ali. One of the British guys was hit by a special gun, an SPG-9. You took a photograph from the helicopter that this gun was firing towards the Mastiffs at Pimon. I asked why if you can take this photo you can't shoot him. You must always shoot the enemy, you cannot let him walk around amongst the local people. The same thing happened in operation when we were in the south of Nad-e Ali. A lot of Mastiffs would hit a mine and then the Taliban would fire RPG rockets. And our mentors said the helicopter had seen a man with a gun coming towards us, but we don't understand why the helicopter did not shoot him.'

There was quiet in the small room while we ate, Sharaf Udin sipping tea, waiting for the rest of us to finish, Gholam Nabi, the only one of us in uniform, slowly chewing a piece of bread, his head tilted in agreement with Mujib's long, impassioned speech. David took a deserved swig of Pepsi. The only conclusion seemed to be that things were getting worse.

'During four years I think our *kandak* has given sacrifice maybe more than twenty killed and more than fifty or sixty people injured.'

Gholam Nabi corrected him: 'Eighty-five.'

There it was. 'Shall I say that in my book?' I asked.

'You know this better than us,' Mujib laughed, 'you are the writer'.

'The first *kandak* that you fought with before,' said Gholam Nabi, 'now it is not the same. Now they never do the tasks they did before, they don't have the same officers, soldiers, lieutenants.'

'Why do you think that is?' I asked no one in particular, deflated. Mujib smiled, patient, sarcastic, wounded Mujib.

'They have done their three years' tasks in Helmand. It gets boring.'

3/215 and their mentors deployed out that night on Op Omid Do, Hope II. At the time of writing, the *kandak* is deployed on Operation Omid Haft, Hope VII. Hazrat was dead, but Mujib and Gholam Nabi headed back out to the front. There is always hope.

Two Letters

I left Helmand the old-fashioned way, slowly and chaotically through Kandahar and Cyprus, past the annoying side-burns and the lonely, red telephone in Brize Norton, which optimistically invites those with anything to declare to call up customs and wait for them to come down to the terminal and check. I had planned to hitch a lift into London with some TA bods, but someone had ballsed up the transport, so we got a lift with an RLC minibus to Oxford station and took the train. There were three of us on the busy express to Paddington, the two proper soldiers in frayed and sun-bleached combats, myself ridiculous in mercenary trousers and a hoodie, all of us struggling under bulging bergans and stares and points and whispers. Before getting off the train, we had been thanked and offered support and even a pint by a number of complete strangers, only two of us deservingly.

Before leaving Shorabak, I asked Mujib and Sharaf Udin and Gholam Nabi to write down anything they wanted me to mention, anything they might have forgotten to tell me that they thought should be written in a book about the *kandak* for people in London to read on the Tube. Sharaf Udin shook his head and half-smiled. He motioned towards his arm, in its full cast, as if to say, 'No writing for me,' but I think he probably wasn't the type either. Mujib and Gholam Nabi had obliged, though, and I clutched the thin sheets of notepad paper covered in spidery hand tightly with the Dictaphone the whole way back, scanned them into pdf files like precious ancient parchments and sent them off with bated breath to be translated when I got home.

★

'I am Mujib Ullah, son of Muhammad Rasoul, a captain in the Afghanistan Army. I was born in 1971 in Baghlan province, Khost district. I completed twelve years of civil schooling before beginning my military training in the Kabul Military College. I served in the Army for nineteen years during the Mujahideen government, the resistance against the Taliban and after their fall. Since then I have been serving in the Afghan National Army in Gereshk, Sangin, Musa Qala, Lashkar Gah and Nad-e Ali districts in Helmand province.

'I am certainly happy to be serving in the military at the moment because the foreign and domestic Taliban still exist and do not let our compatriots live in a peaceful environment. Unfortunately, every day I witness hundreds of my compatriots being killed and injured as a result of the Taliban's bombs and bullets. I shall carry on serving in the Army, though it is tiresome and dangerous, until a tranquil and peaceful environment is established throughout my homeland.

'In 1999 in Tagab area, a few kilometres from the Sarobi dam, I was hit by a Taliban bullet, which injured my right knee. Six months later, when my wounds healed, I returned to the Army. In 2000, in 31 West in the Char-e-Anjir area of Nad-e Ali, we were on a clearance operation, searching and de-mining on the road. We had been operating for four days and had experienced serious difficulties as a result of the IEDs and enemy ambushes. I was to deal with a concealed mine in our path. Before reaching it, I was struck by another mine. The explosion injured me from my feet to my waist. Another soldier who had been carrying the radio also injured his hands and feet. Fortunately, no other casualties occurred.

'I enjoy my job despite the fact that we are faced with many difficulties, fighting and IEDs every day. As a matter of fact, I enjoy my job because in this way I have the opportunity to serve my people and nation, to protect my homeland and its territorial integrity!

'We conduct our current duties with the help of advisers who have left their beautiful homeland and their fathers, mothers and other family members, and have come here just to help and work with the people of Afghanistan. They provide military training to the National Army and carry out combat tasks so that eventually the ANA can stand on its own two feet and be able to protect national borders against domestic and international terrorism. Hereby, we thank and acknowledge them for helping us and fighting along with us.'

'I am Captain Gholam Nabi, son of Shir Alam. I was born in 1969 to an intellectual family in the Naser Khan Khail village in the Kohistan district in the province of Kapisa, where I completed my elementary and high-school education. The fall of Sardar Muhammad Daoud Khan's regime [on 27 April 1978] and the subsequent Russian invasion of 1979 led to fighting gradually spreading as resistance to the Russians grew. The war had begun and expanded into all the villages, districts and the province of Kapisa. People had to leave their homes and villages. I, along with my father, mother, sister and my younger brother (who had lost one of his legs as a result of a rocket attack) came to Kabul in 1983. The village in which we were living was attacked by Russian tanks three times and was completely destroyed. The regime then set up government security posts there.

'My passion and interest in the Army led me to enrol at the military academy in 1983. I subsequently served several years as an officer in one of the military units. In April 1992, the regime of Dr Najibullah collapsed, and the political power fell into the hands of the Mujahideen. Heavy fighting started in Kabul as well.

'Thereafter, we had to move from place to place in the city. By far the worst and most unpleasant memory that I have to live with is from 1996, when the Taliban marched into Kabul. They forced me to have a long and bushy beard. I lived with dreadful difficulties for five years and had to stay at home with no job at all. I rejoined the National Army after the September 11 attacks, when peacekeeping forces moved into Afghanistan. I served as an officer in the 1st Battalion, 3rd Brigade of 205th Corps, which is currently known as 215th Maiwand Corps. I have taken part in military operations in the Gereshk, Sangin, Musa Qala, Lashkar Gah and Nad-e Ali districts.

'The advisers I have served with were so great that I will never forget their memories: Captain 'Paddy', Captain 'Rob', 'Sister Coco' and Constable 'Gibbs'.★ They were the best possible advisers in 2007 and participated with us in very difficult and challenging missions. We collaborated everywhere and in every action, always working closely together. They provided us with artillery and helicopter fire support whenever we needed it. We engaged the Taliban using rockets, 82 mm mortars and grenades and had many successes. Lastly, I want to say again, the memories of them are unforgettable.'

Gholam Nabi said it better than I could. The warriors I had served alongside were equally great, the memories of them are unforgettable.

★ I'm sure Gholam Nabi named me out of form. The next name was either 'Rob', which would have been Rob Worthington, another Grenadier, or 'Dog' which presumably would have been Doug Beattie. Sister Coco is pretty obviously Mr Kuku. Some of the *kandak* adopted the British Army's habit of calling lieutenants 'Mister'; others stuck with rank and mostly they just promoted us all to captain to keep it simple. I have absolutely no idea who Constable Gibbs is. It may be a mistranslation of Sergeant, it may be that the *kandak* was mentored by an attached policeman – there were quite a few kicking around Afghanistan. Whoever you are, Gibbs, well done.

Epilogue

Even in the time it has taken to write and edit this book, things in Afghanistan have changed for better and for worse. The ANA continues to grow and take nominal responsibility for more and more day-to-day operations. First relatively stable and latterly even volatile districts like Lashkar Gah down in Helmand have been tentatively handed over to Afghan control without descending into complete chaos. Militarily the Taliban are weakened, but they have responded intelligently, and while year on year ISAF and ANA casualties are down for the first time in the conflict, the insurgents kill ever more civilians, target infrastructure and governance in high-profile terrorist attacks and undermine confidence and credibility through the increased incidence of Afghan soldiers and policemen turning their weapons on their mentors. Whether there is progress depends on how you define that difficult concept. In London and Washington all eyes look to arbitrary withdrawal dates with an embarrassing hunger, politically and financially motivated excuses at the ready; there is a sense that Afghanistan has had enough help now, though no one asks whether it was ever being given the help it actually wanted or needed.

I'm struck when I look at photographs of the ANA, read reports of successful ANA-led operations and watch the increasingly slick and credible ANA self-presentation that we have succeeded in creating an army that is in our own image. Like the scene at the end of *Animal Farm*, as I gaze through the internet at Afghan and American and British uniforms and press releases I can no longer tell the difference. Does this mean the ANA are more effective, more capable and sophisticated? Almost certainly. But I wonder how Afghan they are. Wonder how effective the drip-drip propaganda by which the insurgents dismissively label them all as Western puppets will be in the long term.

I wanted to provide a glimpse of men like Qiam, Syed, Hazrat, Mujib and the others because they weren't the inept jokers we had thought we would work with in 2007, neither are they Western puppets, neither are they a lost cause or the complete solution. They are what we all were: ordinary soldiers doing a difficult, sometimes extraordinary, job. Whatever anyone else thinks, and there are many with more strident and better-formed opinions than mine, the warriors of the ANA, wounded, tired and downbeat though they sometimes were, never doubted that what they were doing was worth the cost. Just as I was finishing this book, I got an email from a friend whose mate had just got back from Helmand. The very first patrol base we occupied, the base Qiam and Mujib fought to take and hold, the base from which Syed and Hazrat and I launched patrols and fished with grenades, has recently been rebuilt, refurbished and renamed. Patrol Base Hazrat.

Dotted across Helmand are many, too many, FOBs and patrol bases and camps named after American and British and Canadian and Danish soldiers who gave their lives a long, long way from home. It is right that we remember them, but it is also right that we remember those fighting for their homes, for their country. What else could they do but take up the sword? Those who were born to an Afghan mother.

Acknowledgements

Having traded in my combats for civvies, my trips to Afghanistan were made possible only by the amused tolerance and encouragement of a few senior officers in the Ministry of Defence and the generosity and patience of various units who had to babysit me. In Kabul, Colonels Simon Diggins and Stuart Cowen were impeccable hosts; likewise all the staff at the British Embassy. Lieutenant Colonel Jeremy Pughe-Morgan kindly gave me the run of the Kabul Military Training Centre, and Jonny Bristow, Jamie Hayward and Euan Sandison their spare time to show me round. Down in Helmand I couldn't have got where I needed to go and see who I needed to see without the help of Captains Patrick Jackson and Paul Green and I couldn't have done what I needed to do without Major Mark Suddaby and Delta Company, 1 Scots and Captain Tom Holmes and B Company, 2 Yorks, who generously let a scruffy civilian live and patrol with them. Most of all, I must thank Lieutenant Colonel Roly Walker DSO and all the Grenadiers who welcomed me back into the regimental family when they had far better and more important things to do. Once a Grenadier, always a Grenadier.

Back home, I'm grateful to all those in the Directorate of Media and Communications who have shepherded the book through the MoD and in particular Lieutenant Colonels Kevin Stratford-Wright and Crispin Lockhart. Major Martin David MC and Captain Andrew Tiernan generously took time out of their busy professional schedules to review manuscripts and point out my errors and omissions and Chris Donnelly provided invaluable guidance and expert advice on all things Afghan, and Abdul Malik Niazi was kind enough to check and polish the sometimes rough-and-ready translations from Dari and Pashtun into English.

I'm always amazed at the process by which messy manuscripts become beautiful books. My thanks to David Watson for his skilful copyediting and to Thi, Jenny, Patrick and everyone at Penguin Press who waited patiently and then worked tirelessly to produce, market and publicize this one.

I had thought writing a book while trying to leave the Army was difficult, but it was nothing compared to writing a book while trying to becoming a barrister. I wouldn't have had the stamina or willpower to start let alone finish this book if it hadn't been for the unstinting support, encouragement and general brilliance of Jim Gill at United Agents and Helen Conford at Penguin: to both of you, as ever, my heartfelt thanks.

Thanks to my amazing Jenny Dean for understanding why I had to go away again, and again, and for supporting me throughout (and for saying 'Yes').

And finally, but perhaps most importantly of all, I must mention all the soldiers of the Afghan National Army, young and old, good and bad, friends and strangers. This is our book, and my thanks go to you all.

Glossary of Military Terms

AK47: Soviet semi-automatic rifle (*Avtomat Kalashnikova obraztsa 1947*: Kalashnikov's automatic rifle 1947)

ANA: Afghan National Army

ATO: ammunition technical officer, bomb-disposal guru

BRF: brigade reconnaissance force

COMSEC: communications security

Dragunov: Soviet sniper rifle

DSO: Distinguished Service Order

Dushka: the Soviet DShK, the heavy machine-gun equivalent of our .50 cal.

EF KIA: enemy forces killed in action

FOB: forward operating base

GPMG: general-purpose 7.62 calibre machine-gun, the venerable 'general'

Green Zone: the narrow strip either side of the Helmand River criss-crossed with irrigation ditches and, in comparison to the rest of the province, thick with vegetation

HAB: hardened accomodation block

Hesco: steel cage boxes filled with rubble and hardcore to form defensive fortifications

HIDACZ: high-density airspace control zone

Humvee: HMMWV high-mobility multi-purpose wheeled vehicle, a US troop carrier

IED: improvised explosive device

IPB: intelligence preparation of the battlespace

IRT: instant response team, a medical emergency unit

ISAF: International Security Assistance Force

ISTAR: intelligence surveillance target acquisition and reconnaissance

J2: intelligence

JTAC: joint terminal attack controller(s) (pronounced 'jay tack'), responsible for coordinating air assets and calling in air strikes from the ground

M16: US Army rifle first deployed in Vietnam in the 1960s and still used all over the world.

Mastiff: armoured six-wheel patrol vehicle

Minimi: section-level light machine-gun

M-RAP: mine-resistant ambush-protected

MRE: meal ready to eat, the US equivalent of our ORP

NAAFI: Navy, Army, Air Force Institute cafeteria and shop

OCS: officer candidate school

OPSEC: operational security

OPTAG: Operational Training Advisory Group

ORBAT: order of battle

ORP: operational ration pack

PB: patrol base

PKM: Soviet medium machine-gun

RiP: relief-in-place, one army unit replacing another

RPD: Soviet light machine-gun

RPG: rocket-propelled grenade

RPK: the Kalashnikov variant light machine-gun

SA-80: the standard issue British Army rifle (SA-80 stood for Small Arms for 1980s)

SPG-9: Soviet 73mm recoilless gun designed for anti-tank projectiles

T72: Soviet main battle tank

TESEX: the laser tag system fitted to rifles, helmets and vests which turned exercises into giant games of Quasar Laser

WMIK: a weapons-mounted installation kit: a stripped-down
and up-gunned Land Rover
ZAP: the unique identifier for each soldier (the first two initials
of his surname and the last four digits of his Army number;
mine was HE2167)

Bibliography

There are now scores of excellent (and some not-so-excellent) books on Afghanistan. The following bibliography is mostly limited to the accounts of the British involvement in Afghanistan to which I have referred in the course of this book. For the most complete reading list on Afghanistan and the current conflict I can do no better than refer the reader to the magisterial bibliography prepared by Toby Harnden for his book *Dead Men Risen: The Welsh Guards and the Real Story of Britain's War in Afghanistan.*

Allan, Alexander. *Afghanistan: A Tour of Duty.* Third Millennium, London, 2009.

Beattie MC, Doug. *An Ordinary Soldier: Afghanistan: A Ferocious Enemy. A Bloody Conflict. One Man's Impossible Mission.* Simon and Schuster, London, 2008.

——. *Task Force Helmand: A Soldier's Story of Life, Death and Combat on the Afghan Front Line.* Simon Schuster, London, 2009.

Bishop, Patrick. *3 PARA: Afghanistan, Summer 2006.* Harper Press, London, 2007.

——. *Ground Truth: 3 PARA Return to Afghanistan.* HarperCollins, London, 2009.

Braithwaite, Sir Rodric. *Afgantsy: The Russians in Afghanistan, 1979–89.* Profile, London, 2011.

Burke, Jason. *On the Road to Kandahar: Travels through Conflict in the Islamic World.* Penguin, London, 2006.

Bury, Patrick. *Callsign Hades.* Simon and Schuster, London, 2010.

Collins, Dan, ed. *In Foreign Fields: Heroes of Iraq and Afghanistan in Their Own Words.* Monday Books, London, 2007.

Danziger, Danny. *We Are Soldiers: Our Heroes. Their Stories. Real Life on the Frontline.* Sphere, London, 2010.

Docherty, Leo. *Desert of Death: A Soldier's Journey from Iraq to Afghanistan.* Faber and Faber, London, 2007.

Dorney, Lieutenant Colonel Richard. *The Killing Zone.* Ebury Press, London, 2012.

Fergusson, James. *A Million Bullets: The Real Story of the British Army in Afghanistan.* Bantam Press, London, 2008.

—. *Taliban: The True Story of the World's Most Feared Guerrilla Fighters.* Bantam Press, London, 2010.

Giustozzi, Antonio. *Koran, Kalashnikov and Laptop: The Neo-Taliban Insurgency in Afghanistan 2002–2007.* C. Hurst and Co., London, 2007.

Grey, Stephen. *Operation Snakebite: The Explosive True Story of an Afghan Desert Siege.* Penguin, London, 2010.

Harnden, Toby. *Dead Men Risen: The Welsh Guards and the Real Story of Britain's War in Afghanistan.* Quercus, London, 2011.

Junger, Sebastian. *War.* HarperCollins, London, 2010.

Keeble, Richard Lance, and John Mair. *Afghanistan, War and the Media: Deadlines and Frontlines.* Arima, London, 2010.

Kemp, Colonel Richard, and Chris Hughes. *Attack State Red.* Michael Joseph, London, 2009.

Kiley, Sam. *Desperate Glory: At War in Helmand with Britain's 16 Air Assault Brigade.* Bloomsbury, London, 2009.

McNab, Andy, ed. *Spoken From the Front: Real Voices from the Battlefields of Afghanistan.* Random House, London, 2009.

Southby-Tailyour, Ewen. *3 Commando Brigade.* Ebury Press, London, 2008.

—. *3 Commando: Helmand Assault.* Ebury Press, London, 2010.

Tootal DSO OBE, Colonel Stuart. *Danger Close: Commanding 3 Para in Afghanistan.* John Murray, London, 2009.

Notes

1. Obaid Younossi et al., *The Long March: Building an Afghan National Army*, RAND National Defense Research Institute, 2009, p. 48.
2. George MacDonald Fraser, *Quartered Safe Out Here*, HarperCollins, 1993, p. xiii.
3. Ibid., p. 178.
4. George MacDonald Fraser, 'The Last Testament of Flashman's Creator', *Daily Mail*, 5 January 2008.
5. Declan Walsh, *Guardian*, 4 May 2007.
6. Colonel Richard Kemp and Chris Hughes, *Attack State Red*, Michael Joseph, 2009, p. 63.
7. Andy McNab, ed., *Spoken from the Front*, Random House, 2009, p. 233.
8. Ibid., p. 249.
9. Kemp, *Attack State Red*, pp. 63–4.
10. Stephen Grey, 'A Bloody Risky Way to Beat the Taliban', *The Sunday Times*, 15 June 2008.
11. Patrick Bury, *Callsign Hades*, Simon and Schuster, 2010, p. 136.
12. http://www.bbc.co.uk/news/uk-13420991.
13. *Today*, BBC Radio 4, 9 November 2009.
14. N. Hopkins, 'Inside Camp Bastion', *Guardian*, 15 August 2011.
15. http://www.understandingwar.org/themenode/afghanistan-national-army-ana.
16. Sam Kiley, *Desperate Glory*, Bloomsbury, 2009, pp. 107–8.
17. Annex 1 to 'Rebuilding Afghanistan: Peace and Stability', 2 December 2002.
18. Dr Antonio Giustozzi, 'Auxiliary Force or National Army? Afghan-

istan's "ANA" and the Counter-Insurgency Effort, 2002–2006', *Small Wars and Insurgencies*, vol. 18, no. 1 (March 2007), pp. 45–67, at p. 47.

19. Younossi et al., *The Long March*.
20. http://www.globalsecurity.org/military/world/afghanistan/ana.htm.
21. Ibid.
22. Giustozzi, 'Auxiliary Force or National Army?', p. 53.
23. Summary of the ANA prepared for the US Naval Postgraduate School's Program for Culture and Conflict Studies.
24. Giustozzi, 'Auxiliary Force or National Army?', p. 54.
25. Younossi et al., *The Long March*, p. 16.
26. Ibid., p. 15.
27. Giustozzi, 'Auxiliary Force or National Army?', p. 58.
28. Younossi et al., *The Long March*, p. 15.
29. Summary of the ANA prepared for the US Naval Postgraduate School's Program for Culture and Conflict Studies.
30. James Fergusson, *A Million Bullets*, Bantam Press, 2008, p. 9.
31. http://www.telegraph.co.uk/finance/newsbysector/industry/defence/8668085/Britain-spent-18-billion-on-war-in-Afghanistan-figures-show.html.
32. *Hansard*, 26 January 2006, columns 1528–1532.
33. Colonel Stuart Tootal DSO OBE, *Danger Close*, John Murray, 2009, p. 22.
34. Patrick Bishop, *3 Para*, Harper Press, 2007, p. 83.
35. 'Lieutenant Tim Illingworth CGC', in D. Collins, ed., *In Foreign Fields*, Monday Books, 2007, p. 390.
36. Leo Docherty, *Desert of Death*, Faber and Faber, 2007, p. 80.
37. Collins, ed., 'Illingworth', p. 390.
38. Fergusson, *A Million Bullets*, p. 80.
39. Tootal, *Danger Close*, p. 53.
40. Docherty, *Desert of Death*, p. 123.

41. Fergusson, *A Million Bullets*, p. 80.

42. Bishop, *3 Para*, p. 232.

43. Docherty, *Desert of Death*, p. 100.

44. Fergusson, *A Million Bullets*, p. 79.

45. Collins, ed., 'Illingworth', p. 395.

46. Ibid., p. 402.

47. Ibid., p. 396.

48. Ibid., p. 411.

49. Doug Beattie MC, *An Ordinary Soldier*, Simon and Schuster, 2008, p. 217.

50. Ibid., p. 94.

51. Ibid., p. 210.

52. Collins, ed., 'Illingworth', p. 413.

53. T. E. Lawrence, quoted in Beattie, *An Ordinary Soldier*, p. 69.

54. Docherty, *Desert of Death*, p. 75.

55. Bishop, *3 Para*, p. 211.

56. Tootal, *Danger Close*, p. 226.

57. Fergusson, *A Million Bullets*, p. 81.

58. Docherty, *Desert of Death*, p. 93.

59. Bishop, *3 Para*, p. 93.

60. Docherty, *Desert of Death*, p. 90.

61. Michael Yon, 'Edward Munch in the Marijuana Patch', http://www.michaelyon-online.com, 24 August 2011.

62. Tootal, *Danger Close*, p. 226.

63. Fergusson, *A Million Bullets*, p. 82.

64. Stephen Grey, *Operation Snakebite*, Penguin, 2010, p. 11.

65. Ibid., p. 11.

66. Ibid., p. 183.

67. McNab, ed., *Spoken from the Front*, pp. 347–8.

68. Bury, *Callsign Hades*, p. 120.

69. Doug Beattie MC, *Task Force Helmand*, Simon and Schuster, 2009, p. 41.

70. Ibid. p. 48.

71. Ibid., p. 253.

72. *United States Plan for Sustaining the ANSF*, Report to Congress in accordance with the 2008 National Defence Authorization Act, June 2008, p. 4.

73. Kenneth Katzman, *Afghanistan: Post-War Governance, Security and US Policy*, CRS Report for Congress, 29 September 2008, p. 39.

74. Summary of the ANA prepared for the US Naval Postgraduate School's Program for Culture and Conflict Studies.

75. Younossi et al., *The Long March*, p. 26.

76. Grey, *Operation Snakebite*, p. 340.

77. Toby Harnden, *Dead Men Risen*, Quercus, 2011, p. 123.

78. Ibid., p. 105.

79. Ibid., p. 258.

80. Ibid., p. 484.

81. http://www.mod.uk/DefenceInternet/AboutDefence/History/HistoryOfTheOldWarOffice/ModMainBuilding.htm.

82. NTM-A Briefing, 22 June 2010 (UNCLASS).

83. Grey, *Operation Snakebite*, p. 340.

84. John Julius Norwich, ed., *The Duff Cooper Diaries*, Phoenix, 2005, p. 101.

85. Antonio Giustozzi, *RUSI Journal*, vol. 154, no. 6 (December 2009), pp. 36–42.

86. Bernard Gray, *Review of Acquisition for the Secretary of State for Defence*, October 2009.

87. Kim Sengupta, *Independent*, 15 June 2010.

ALLEN LANE
an imprint of
PENGUIN BOOKS

Recently Published

Jean Drèze and Amartya Sen, *An Uncertain Glory: India and its Contradictions*

Rana Mitter, *China's War with Japan, 1937-1945: The Struggle for Survival*

Tom Burns, *Our Necessary Shadow: The Nature and Meaning of Psychiatry*

Sylvain Tesson, *Consolations of the Forest: Alone in a Cabin in the Middle Taiga*

George Monbiot, *Feral: Searching for Enchantment on the Frontiers of Rewilding*

Ken Robinson and Lou Aronica, *Finding Your Element: How to Discover Your Talents and Passions and Transform Your Life*

David Stuckler and Sanjay Basu, *The Body Economic: Why Austerity Kills*

Suzanne Corkin, *Permanent Present Tense: The Man with No Memory, and What He Taught the World*

Daniel C. Dennett, *Intuition Pumps and Other Tools for Thinking*

Adrian Raine, *The Anatomy of Violence: The Biological Roots of Crime*

Eduardo Galeano, *Children of the Days: A Calendar of Human History*

Lee Smolin, *Time Reborn: From the Crisis of Physics to the Future of the Universe*

Michael Pollan, *Cooked: A Natural History of Transformation*

David Graeber, *The Democracy Project: A History, a Crisis, a Movement*

Brendan Simms, *Europe: The Struggle for Supremacy, 1453 to the Present*

Oliver Bullough, *The Last Man in Russia and the Struggle to Save a Dying Nation*

Diarmaid MacCulloch, *Silence: A Christian History*

Evgeny Morozov, *To Save Everything, Click Here: Technology, Solutionism, and the Urge to Fix Problems that Don't Exist*

David Cannadine, *The Undivided Past: History Beyond Our Differences*

Michael Axworthy, *Revolutionary Iran: A History of the Islamic Republic*

Jaron Lanier, *Who Owns the Future?*

John Gray, *The Silence of Animals: On Progress and Other Modern Myths*

Paul Kildea, *Benjamin Britten: A Life in the Twentieth Century*

Jared Diamond, *The World Until Yesterday: What Can We Learn from Traditional Societies?*

Nassim Nicholas Taleb, *Antifragile: How to Live in a World We Don't Understand*

Alan Ryan, *On Politics: A History of Political Thought from Herodotus to the Present*

Roberto Calasso, *La Folie Baudelaire*

Carolyn Abbate and Roger Parker, *A History of Opera: The Last Four Hundred Years*

Yang Jisheng, *Tombstone: The Untold Story of Mao's Great Famine*

Caleb Scharf, *Gravity's Engines: The Other Side of Black Holes*

Jancis Robinson, Julia Harding and José Vouillamoz, *Wine Grapes: A Complete Guide to 1,368 Vine Varieties, including their Origins and Flavours*

David Bownes, Oliver Green and Sam Mullins, *Underground: How the Tube Shaped London*

Niall Ferguson, *The Great Degeneration: How Institutions Decay and Economies Die*

Chrystia Freeland, *Plutocrats: The Rise of the New Global Super-Rich*

David Thomson, *The Big Screen: The Story of the Movies and What They Did to Us*

Halik Kochanski, *The Eagle Unbowed: Poland and the Poles in the Second World War*

Kofi Annan with Nader Mousavizadeh, *Interventions: A Life in War and Peace*

Mark Mazower, *Governing the World: The History of an Idea*

Anne Applebaum, *Iron Curtain: The Crushing of Eastern Europe 1944-56*

Steven Johnson, *Future Perfect: The Case for Progress in a Networked Age*

Sebastian Seung, *Connectome: How the Brain's Wiring Makes Us Who We Are*

Callum Roberts, *Ocean of Life*

Orlando Figes, *Just Send Me Word: A True Story of Love and Survival in the Gulag*

Leonard Mlodinow, *Subliminal: The Revolution of the New Unconscious and What it Teaches Us about Ourselves*

John Romer, *A History of Ancient Egypt: From the First Farmers to the Great Pyramid*

Ruchir Sharma, *Breakout Nations: In Pursuit of the Next Economic Miracle*

Michael J. Sandel, *What Money Can't Buy: The Moral Limits of Markets*

Dominic Sandbrook, *Seasons in the Sun: The Battle for Britain, 1974-1979*

Tariq Ramadan, *The Arab Awakening: Islam and the New Middle East*

Jonathan Haidt, *The Righteous Mind: Why Good People are Divided by Politics and Religion*

Ahmed Rashid, *Pakistan on the Brink: The Future of Pakistan, Afghanistan and the West*

Tim Weiner, *Enemies: A History of the FBI*

Mark Pagel, *Wired for Culture: The Natural History of Human Cooperation*

George Dyson, *Turing's Cathedral: The Origins of the Digital Universe*

Cullen Murphy, *God's Jury: The Inquisition and the Making of the Modern World*

Richard Sennett, *Together: The Rituals, Pleasures and Politics of Co-operation*

Faramerz Dabhoiwala, *The Origins of Sex: A History of the First Sexual Revolution*

Roy F. Baumeister and John Tierney, *Willpower: Rediscovering Our Greatest Strength*

Jesse J. Prinz, *Beyond Human Nature: How Culture and Experience Shape Our Lives*

Robert Holland, *Blue-Water Empire: The British in the Mediterranean since 1800*

Jodi Kantor, *The Obamas: A Mission, A Marriage*

Philip Coggan, *Paper Promises: Money, Debt and the New World Order*

Charles Nicholl, *Traces Remain: Essays and Explorations*

Daniel Kahneman, *Thinking, Fast and Slow*

Hunter S. Thompson, *Fear and Loathing at Rolling Stone: The Essential Writing of Hunter S. Thompson*

Duncan Campbell-Smith, *Masters of the Post: The Authorized History of the Royal Mail*

Colin McEvedy, *Cities of the Classical World: An Atlas and Gazetteer of 120 Centres of Ancient Civilization*

Heike B. Görtemaker, *Eva Braun: Life with Hitler*

Brian Cox and Jeff Forshaw, *The Quantum Universe: Everything that Can Happen Does Happen*

Nathan D. Wolfe, *The Viral Storm: The Dawn of a New Pandemic Age*

Norman Davies, *Vanished Kingdoms: The History of Half-Forgotten Europe*

Michael Lewis, *Boomerang: The Meltdown Tour*

Steven Pinker, *The Better Angels of Our Nature: The Decline of Violence in History and Its Causes*

Robert Trivers, *Deceit and Self-Deception: Fooling Yourself the Better to Fool Others*

Thomas Penn, *Winter King: The Dawn of Tudor England*

Daniel Yergin, *The Quest: Energy, Security and the Remaking of the Modern World*

Michael Moore, *Here Comes Trouble: Stories from My Life*

Ali Soufan, *The Black Banners: Inside the Hunt for Al Qaeda*

Jason Burke, *The 9/11 Wars*

Timothy D. Wilson, *Redirect: The Surprising New Science of Psychological Change*

Ian Kershaw, *The End: Hitler's Germany, 1944-45*

T M Devine, *To the Ends of the Earth: Scotland's Global Diaspora, 1750-2010*

Catherine Hakim, *Honey Money: The Power of Erotic Capital*

Douglas Edwards, *I'm Feeling Lucky: The Confessions of Google Employee Number 59*

John Bradshaw, *In Defence of Dogs*

Chris Stringer, *The Origin of Our Species*

Lila Azam Zanganeh, *The Enchanter: Nabokov and Happiness*

David Stevenson, *With Our Backs to the Wall: Victory and Defeat in 1918*

Evelyn Juers, *House of Exile: War, Love and Literature, from Berlin to Los Angeles*

Henry Kissinger, *On China*

Michio Kaku, *Physics of the Future: How Science Will Shape Human Destiny and Our Daily Lives by the Year 2100*

David Abulafia, *The Great Sea: A Human History of the Mediterranean*

John Gribbin, *The Reason Why: The Miracle of Life on Earth*

Anatol Lieven, *Pakistan: A Hard Country*

William Cohen, *Money and Power: How Goldman Sachs Came to Rule the World*

Joshua Foer, *Moonwalking with Einstein: The Art and Science of Remembering Everything*

Simon Baron-Cohen, *Zero Degrees of Empathy: A New Theory of Human Cruelty*

Manning Marable, *Malcolm X: A Life of Reinvention*

David Deutsch, *The Beginning of Infinity: Explanations that Transform the World*

David Edgerton, *Britain's War Machine: Weapons, Resources and Experts in the Second World War*

John Kasarda and Greg Lindsay, *Aerotropolis: The Way We'll Live Next*

David Gilmour, *The Pursuit of Italy: A History of a Land, Its Regions and Their Peoples*

Niall Ferguson, *Civilization: The West and the Rest*

Tim Flannery, *Here on Earth: A New Beginning*

Robert Bickers, *The Scramble for China: Foreign Devils in the Qing Empire, 1832-1914*

Mark Malloch-Brown, *The Unfinished Global Revolution: The Limits of Nations and the Pursuit of a New Politics*

King Abdullah of Jordan, *Our Last Best Chance: The Pursuit of Peace in a Time of Peril*

Eliza Griswold, *The Tenth Parallel: Dispatches from the Faultline between Christianity and Islam*

Brian Greene, *The Hidden Reality: Parallel Universes and the Deep Laws of the Cosmos*

John Gray, *The Immortalization Commission: The Strange Quest to Cheat Death*

Patrick French, *India: A Portrait*

Lizzie Collingham, *The Taste of War: World War Two and the Battle for Food*

Hooman Majd, *The Ayatollahs' Democracy: An Iranian Challenge*

Dambisa Moyo, *How The West Was Lost: Fifty Years of Economic Folly - and the Stark Choices Ahead*

Evgeny Morozov, *The Net Delusion: How Not to Liberate the World*

Ron Chernow, *Washington: A Life*

Nassim Nicholas Taleb, *The Bed of Procrustes: Philosophical and Practical Aphorisms*

Hugh Thomas, *The Golden Age: The Spanish Empire of Charles V*

Amanda Foreman, *A World on Fire: An Epic History of Two Nations Divided*

Nicholas Ostler, *The Last Lingua Franca: English until the Return of Babel*

Richard Miles, *Ancient Worlds: The Search for the Origins of Western Civilization*

Neil MacGregor, *A History of the World in 100 Objects*

Steven Johnson, *Where Good Ideas Come From: The Natural History of Innovation*

Dominic Sandbrook, *State of Emergency: The Way We Were: Britain, 1970-1974*

Jim Al-Khalili, *Pathfinders: The Golden Age of Arabic Science*

Ha-Joon Chang, *23 Things They Don't Tell You About Capitalism*

Robin Fleming, *Britain After Rome: The Fall and Rise, 400 to 1070*

Tariq Ramadan, *The Quest for Meaning: Developing a Philosophy of Pluralism*

Joyce Tyldesley, *The Penguin Book of Myths and Legends of Ancient Egypt*

Nicholas Phillipson, *Adam Smith: An Enlightened Life*

Paul Greenberg, *Four Fish: A Journey from the Ocean to Your Plate*

Clay Shirky, *Cognitive Surplus: Creativity and Generosity in a Connected Age*

Andrew Graham-Dixon, *Caravaggio: A Life Sacred and Profane*

Niall Ferguson, *High Financier: The Lives and Time of Siegmund Warburg*

Sean McMeekin, *The Berlin-Baghdad Express: The Ottoman Empire and Germany's Bid for World Power, 1898-1918*

Richard McGregor, *The Party: The Secret World of China's Communist Rulers*

Spencer Wells, *Pandora's Seed: The Unforeseen Cost of Civilization*